Ethnoterritorial Politics, Policy, and the Western World

Ethnoterritorial Politics, Policy, and the Western World

edited by
Joseph R. Rudolph, Jr.
and Robert J. Thompson

Lynne Rienner Publishers   •   Boulder and London

Published in the United States of America in 1989 by
Lynne Rienner Publishers, Inc.
1800 30th Street, Boulder, Colorado 80301

and in the United Kingdom by
Lynne Rienner Publishers, Inc.
3 Henrietta Street, Covent Garden, London WC2E 8LU

Library of Congress Cataloging-in-Publication Data
Ethnoterritorial politics, policy, and the western world / edited by
  Joseph R. Rudolph and Robert J. Thompson.
     p . c m .
  Bibliography: p.
  Includes index.
  ISBN 1-55587-095-3 (alk. paper)
  1. Ethnic groups—Political activity. 2. Ethnic relations.
I. Rudolph, Joseph R. (Joseph Russell), 1942- . II. Thompson,
Robert J. (Robert Joseph), 1949-
JF1061.E87   1989
323.1—dc19   89-30268
                                                             CIP

British Cataloguing in Publication Data
A Cataloguing in Publication record for this book
is available from the British Library.

Printed and bound in the United States of America

The paper used in this publication meets the requirements of
the American National Standard for Permanence of Paper for
Printed Library Materials Z39.48-1984.

Contents

Tables and Figures _____

TABLES

FIGURES

The Contributors

Robert P. Clark is professor of government and politics at George Mason University, where he has taught since 1977. In addition to numerous articles on Basque politics and regionalism, he is author of *The Basques: The Franco Years and Beyond* and *The Basque Insurgents: ETA, 1952–1980*. He is currently writing a book on the emergence of the Basque autonomous government during the decade-long Spanish transition to democracy.

Michael Keating is professor of political science at the University of Western Ontario. He has written or coauthored ten books focusing on regional government and politics in the United Kingdom and Western Europe, Scottish politics and government, and Labour Party affairs, and is now working on a book on ethnoterritorial politics in Western Europe.

Peter M. Leslie is assistant secretary to the Cabinet for the office of Federal/Provincial Relations in Ottawa. For more than twenty years, he taught political studies at Queens University, Kingston, where he was until recently director of the Institute of Intergovernmental Relations. He is editor of *Canada: The State of the Federation* and author of *Federal, State, and National Economy*.

Joseph R. Rudolph, Jr., is associate professor of political science at Towson State University, where he has taught since 1986. He has written many articles on ethnicity and state policy.

William Safran is professor of political science at the University of Colorado at Boulder. He has written or coauthored four books on French politics, including *The French Policy*, a widely used text.

Robert J. Thompson is associate professor of political science and chair of the Department of Political Science at East Carolina University, Greenville, North Carolina. He is author and coauthor of many articles on both political leadership and ethnoterritorial politics.

CHAPTER 1

The Ebb and Flow of Ethnoterritorial Politics in the Western World

ROBERT J. THOMPSON
JOSEPH R. RUDOLPH, JR.

One of the more significant developments for Western political systems twenty years ago was the emergence of regionalized nationalist movements in developed countries long believed to have successfully integrated, accommodated, or repressed their national minorities. In Celtic Britain and Franco's Spain, in Quebec and provincial France, political movements emerged to challenge the centralized nature of the states in which they found themselves. In doing so, they also challenged some of the basic assumptions of politics in the Western world; for example, that national integration is a one-way street (i.e., that once integrated, regional groups stay integrated) and that in the modern developed world, class and status have replaced such older bases of political association as ethnicity and region.

Not surprisingly, this emergence of very strong ethnoterritorial movements in the developed democratic world attracted considerable attention at the time. To date, however, no work has systematically examined these movements since their emergence in terms of their interaction with the policy processes in the states housing them. The question of how these movements interacted with policymaking institutions, placed demands upon them and, in turn, were responded to, has not been thoroughly examined. Indeed, the initial academic works in this field focused on the historical and socioeconomic contexts within which these movements became politically salient. The policy dimension was specifically underemphasized as primarily a contemporary response with little significant impact on the basic causes or nature of these movements.

In recent years, the importance of political factors and policy responses has been given greater credence in the conceptual literature on ethnoterritorial politics. That literature, however, suffers from dealing with the political and policy aspects in only a sporadic and inconsistent manner. This book was

1

created out of the frustration felt by its contributors to this state of affairs. Each of the contributors individually believes that greater attention needs to be given to the role of politics in the Western world today. The purpose of this book, therefore, is fairly simple and straightforward. It is to explore, both theoretically and through a series of country studies and comparative analyses, the link between public policy and the most recent round of ethnoterritorial politics in the developed world. A primary objective of the book is to establish the conceptual and political significance of policy responses as an independent and a dependent variable affecting the development, accommodation, and persistence of ethnoterritorial political movements.

THE ROLE OF POLITICS AND POLICY IN THE ETHNOTERRITORIAL LITERATURE: THE CONCEPTUAL DILEMMA

The term "ethnoterritorial" is used in this volume as an overarching concept for various political movements and conflicts that are derived from a group of people, *ethnos* in the Greek sense, having some identifiable geographic base within the boundaries of an existing political system. In some instances the conflicts might be seen as having a heavy regional component. Others might be seen as being a nationalistic movement in the usual historical sense. Whatever term is used, the people must identify themselves or be identifiable as a group distinct in such characteristics as their culture, language, history, religion, traditions and/or political past. They do not need to have been a separate political system in any recent sense, but they do need to perceive themselves as being distinct from the broader population of the overall political system, such as in Wales or Languedoc.

One of the problems in this area of research is the complex of terms used to describe the various conflicts within and between the different academic disciplines that focus on them. This is an old problem and not one we can resolve entirely. Our use of the term ethnoterritorial, though, is derived from a previous work in which we discussed the various types of ethnic conflicts and their overlapping nature with other types of political issues.[1] The most common term that is close in its meaning to ethnoterritorial is "ethnonational." The structure of the conflict under discussion may make the two concepts almost synonymous. The term ethnonational, though, tends to omit groups with a regional base, but whose political demands are not quite as developed and perhaps not as intense. It is not our purpose to quarrel over those distinctions at length. Often what is involved are perceptual differences over such matters as the group's ultimate goals, its historic legitimacy, or its cultural distinctiveness by varying analysts. The editors recognize, for example, as Leslie's chapter on Canada brings out, that a government may respond to the ethnonational aspects of a group's demands, but not to the ethnoterritorial ones. In other words, the government may respond to some policy demand, such as an affirmative action program being put forward by a group in the name of a broader national or linguistic population, but not to some institutional demands based on the population's predominance in a specific territory. For this book's purposes, the editors assume a substantial degree of comparability in the policy problems that these different conflicts present a central government. Likewise, we believe the groups as a whole behave politically in comparable ways. Their demands and tactics are remarkably similar. The term "ethnoterritorial" is, then, a broad one and the variations within its coverage are a central point of the book.

After the political emergence of these ethnoterritorial groups and issues in the mid-1960s, the research literature went in two primary directions. The first direction was largely one of keeping pace with the rapidly changing situations. As the Scots, Welsh, French Canadians, Flemish, Basques, and other groups came on the political scene, a great deal of effort went into describing the groups, discussing the development of their political movements, and analyzing the electoral consequences of their actions. To a large extent, this work was historically oriented political journalism. Because the groups had long been ignored in a political sense, much attention had to be given to filling in the gaps in our descriptive knowledge of current events. This was an important task, but an incomplete one by itself.

The second direction in which the research literature went was in search of the conditions or factors that now gave rise to these movements. There was an implicit assumption that, since these groups had existed historically for long periods, something had changed in the society, political system, or even in the world that now made their identity politically salient. For most analysts, the political emergence of these groups was simply the most recent manifestation of a historical sense of distinctiveness. There was also a tendency to look for macrolevel explanations. In part, such explanations were sought because the social sciences were in a phase in which broad theoretical explanations were in vogue. In part, they were sought to provide a linkage between the historical roots of identity that the groups exemplified and their current manifestation. But, mostly, they were utilized to counter the excessive attention that the emphasis on current events placed on parties, leaders, and other contemporary features of the political process. The emphasis on the particular characteristics of each case to which the focus on current events led tended to overlook the fact that a number of these movements became politically significant almost simultaneously and that they shared many comparable features. The macrolevel concepts that were developed were thus an attempt to bridge the specifics of individual cases in order to understand multiple cases comparatively.

When one looks at these various macrolevel concepts of the "causes" of the emergence of the ethnoterritorial conflicts, one sees them largely as attempts to specify various conditions, which in the appropriate mix would or would not lead an ethnic group to exert itself politically. All of these "causal" conditions assume an ethnic identity that may be more or less latent, but that must be present. The identity is thus a necessary, but not sufficient, cause for the emergence of ethnoterritorial political movements. Ostensibly, these conditions would give rise to dissatisfaction with and resentment of the current pattern of politics and policy, thereby leading to political demands to rectify the situation. These conditions are reflected in such concepts as: uneven economic development,[2] perceptions of relative deprivation,[3] internal colonialism,[4] differential modernization,[5] a failure to assimilate ethnic elites into the dominant culture, postindustrialism,[6] and the demonstration effect of one movement on others.

These concepts have been discussed at length in multiple works.[7] What is of concern here is the role to which politics and policy are assigned in the explanations of those concepts; consequently, a fair degree of generalization will be utilized. Most of the "causal" conditions concern the economic standing of the ethnoterritorial groups and regions in comparison to the dominant population groups and their central regions. The concepts are based on the fact that many of the regions that have active ethnoterritorial movements have experienced varying rates and patterns of economic growth and integration as compared to the core regions of the political system. This has also generally meant that the region's population has historically had differential standards of living, lower social status, a smaller share of high-status political and economic positions, and a denigration of their cultural distinctiveness. They are from a peripheral region in the eyes and priorities of the dominant population group controlling the political and economic institutions of the society. However, not all of the regions have suffered economically. Some, like the Basque region and Cataluña, have faired better than other regions economically, but have experienced deprivation politically and culturally. For the most part, though, it is fair to characterize the concepts as hypothesizing that the historic economic and social conditions have created a context that generates the political saliency of the ethnoterritorial identity (see Figure 1.1).

A basic problem with these "causal" conditions is their level of abstraction. They attempt to explain contemporary phenomena in long-range, macrolevel terms. They specify important environmental conditions, long-term characteristics important to the analyst, without being able to demonstrate their linkage to the contemporary political behavior that is the supposed empirical manifestation of those conditions. They implicitly or explicitly rely on the concept of the perception of relative deprivation to provide the linkage. The ethnoterritorial population and its elites begin to

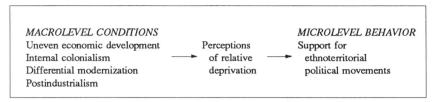

Figure 1.1 Hypothesized Relationship of Macrolevel Conditions to Microlevel Political Behavior

perceive the empirical reality of their situation, which generates discontent and serves as a basis for political mobilization around the ethnoterritorial identity rather than such forms of identity as social class.

Most of the concepts also rely on variables and relationships that operate on the ethnoterritorial population over time. There is thus a delayed facet to their effects and perception. This helps, in their proponents' views, to account for fluctuations in the political saliency of the ethnoterritorial identity over time. We argue, instead, that these concepts highlight important environmental conditions of logical significance and then assume that there is, in fact, a relationship between them and political behavior. That assumption may or may not be warranted, but at any rate it creates a gap between the macrolevel conditions of the region as a whole and microlevel political behavior. We agree with Peter Gourevitch's point, "Regions are not actors; their inhabitants are. If a particular territory becomes nationalistic, we must explain why some of its residents find nationalism attractive, and, if the nationalism is new or suddenly much stronger politically, why they have abandoned old appeals for new ones."[8]

If theorists are going to posit that the current political behavior of individuals and groups is due to their perceptions of the macrolevel conditions affecting the region, then they ought to be able to document such motivations. That, however, has not been the case. Only a few studies have actually attempted to establish empirically such relationships, and their findings have been only weakly supportive of their theses.[9] This is not surprising, given the fluid nature of the conflicts and the variety of issues that might serve as motivating factors for behavior. Moreover, the various cases are seldom amenable situations for conducting the kind of research that would be necessary to assess adequately individual perceptions on a representative scale. As a consequence, we are left with a theoretical gap between the level of explanation and the level of the events to be explained. It means that a substantial amount of variation both within and between individual cases of ethnoterritorial conflict therefore goes unaccounted.

In our view, even if one could conduct the kind of empirical research necessary to test the perceptions of the ethnoterritorial population, an important theoretical component would be missing from the relationships the macrolevel concepts hypothesize—that is, the role given to politics and policy. For the most part, politics and policy are seen only as dependent variables. The proponents of these concepts tend to accept the line of reasoning adopted by Philip Rawkins in a criticism of Michael Hechter's internal colonialism model. He criticized Hechter for his preoccupation with the state (really state actions) as a key variable in his analysis.

> What is deficient in such an interpretation is the preoccupation with sovereignty rather than the social bases of authority. This results in the divorce of government from society, which in turn produces a tendency to reify the state. It is not the state which brings about integration in society, but rather the relationships of interdependence among the members and groups of society which provide the foundation for the state. It is the state, Marx observed, which is "held together by civil society." As civil society undergoes changes, so must the character of the state.[10]

This perspective ignores several significant aspects of the question at hand. First of all, it criticizes Hechter on an unjust point. Hechter's focus was considerably broader than the actions of the state alone and, we would argue, it inadequately conceptualizes the role of political elements. Second, and more important, it does not take into consideration the changed role of the modern state. Apparently socioeconomic conditions may change, but not the extent of the state's involvement in them. This is not an argument that the state determines social conditions or that it alone brings about societal integration, but rather that its actions influence those conditions and the degree of integration attained in the society. The impacts may be positive or negative, but the fact is that modern political institutions have become so involved in the various sectors of society that their impacts cannot be disregarded. To do so is to divorce society from government. Political institutions should therefore be conceptualized as simultaneously being a dependent and an independent variable in the development of ethnoterritorial movements. Figure 1.2 illustrates this relationship.

Obviously, some of the conceptualizations of ethnoterritorial politics have considered politics and policy to a degree. For example, Hechter and others associated with the internal colonialism model have responded, in part, to criticisms. Their application of the rational choice model of political behavior to ethnic conflicts recognizes a greater role for the political dimension than did their initial efforts.[11] Scholars like Studlar and McAllister have taken steps to link the changes in demographics, standards of living, and political attitudes associated with postindustrialism to support for the Scottish National party and the Welsh party, *Plaid Cymru*.[12] Similarly, others have brought in the necessity of incorporating the breakdown of traditional partisan allegiances and party organizations.[13] Such occurrences create opportunities for individuals and groups interested in using the

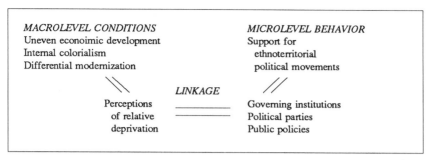

Figure 1.2 Linkage Role of Politics and Policy

political process to further their causes to do so outside the traditional electoral mechanisms.

A wide variety of analysts have written on individual cases and the policy decisions made in these cases; however, the comparative literature on ethnoterritorial conflicts in the Western world is rather short on such pieces.[14] Much more work has been done concerning this facet of the topic in reference to ethnic conflicts in Asia and Africa.[15] It may be that those scholars more widely perceive governmental and political institutions as major actors than have many of the scholars focusing on Western cases. It is interesting, for example, that Milton Esman's work on ethnic politics began with the Malayasian case and was extended to Scotland and Quebec.[16] The one area of research on Western political systems directly relevant to the matter of policy responses, consociationalism, initially drew the interest of analysts, but declined as their focus shifted to broader gauge concepts and as they interpreted the emergence of ethnoterritorial political issues as a denial of the continued efficacy of consociational devices.[17]

Our problem with these considerations of the relationship of politics and policy to ethnoterritorial conflicts is that they deal with these dimensions in only a sporadic and inconsistent manner. What has been neglected in the literature is a full consideration of what makes people think political action is a possible avenue for resolving their problems. Thus, due consideration needs to be given to the consequences of politics and policy in the creation of theoretical explanations of the emergence and significance of ethnoterritorial movements.

Our conception of the role of politics and policy in ethnoterritorial conflicts is one of linkage between the macrolevel conditions and microlevel political behavior. Politics is a multidimensional phenomenon involving conflict, representation, and dialogue. It is the process through which different groups articulate their demands and compete for public resources. It is a process of give and take with winners and losers. It concerns perceptions about the rights and privileges of various groups. It also involves issues of the equity of public and private patterns of activity. It is through the political process that activists and leaders are recruited and followers mobilized. Finally, politics is ongoing. Today one may achieve one's objectives, or perhaps not, but tomorrow presents both new opportunities and risks, which is why groups seek to institutionalize their agreements on issues through laws, policies, and the methods of decisionmaking.

It is odd that political activity has not been given a more prominent theoretical role since it is principally through political action that all of the ethnoterritorial movements have sought to change the governmental and socioeconomic conditions to which they object, and it is through policy responses that the decisionmaking institutions act. The puzzling nature of this situation is compounded by the increased impact of state policies on society as a whole. Contemporary governments are expected to deal with virtually every dimension of their societies. They all have some formal policies on the economy, education, health care, housing, civil rights, civil liberties, social security, transportation, and other matters. The breadth of these policy commitments makes it much easier for ethnoterritorial groups to see political action as a viable, if not the only viable, means for rectifying their problems.

Political actions and policies have both short-term and long-term effects. The same applies to the strategies and tactics used by ethnoterritorial movements and governments. It also extends to the organizational talents of the ethnoterritorial activists. Contemporary political actions and policies have a cumulative impact. They create a contextual legacy within which future activists (even in the immediate future) must operate. The legacy also becomes a mechanism for transmitting a collective political memory. That is one of the most important political consequences of policy decisions that institutionalize aspects of ethnoterritorial identity. In a sense, even if one accepts the validity of the macrolevel concepts, one needs to recognize that it is through politics that the ethnoterritorial movements manifest their perceptions of past problems and future possibilities. But that process of manifestation and the policy responses it generates from the central decision-making institutions inherently transform the situation for the next set of ethnoterritorial actors and central decisionmakers. The transformation may be relatively minor or it may be major, but it occurs. Thus, our conceptualizations need to take this into account.

By recognizing politics and policy in this capacity as an intervening variable, we can achieve more balanced explanations. Furthermore, thinking of the emergence of ethnoterritorial issues in these terms will permit the theories relying upon macrolevel conditions analytical latitude. As matters stand now, these theories are hard pressed to explain the patterns of development for individual cases, let alone multiple cases. That does not mean, however, that they are heuristically or analytically insignificant—only incomplete. If political institutions are conceptualized as being the linkage agents employed in these cases, then this set of factors may explain much of the fluctuation that occurs in the fortunes of each of these cases. They may also help account for important differences existing between contrasting cases of ethnoterritorial conflict. Lastly, this modification will force analysts to be more aware of the interactive nature of the relationships existing between these variables. There is nothing preordained in these relationships, only those outcomes that are likely to occur given a certain set of circumstances.

RESOLVING THE CONCEPTUAL DILEMMA

This book is intended as a step toward the resolution of the conceptual dilemma described above. We do not promise to achieve it fully. There are too many areas of research yet to be done before we can develop the necessary conceptual interconnections. We have thus consciously chosen not to advance a theory in the broad sense that is commonly applied to that term. The preceding section made the conceptual argument for giving more credence to the impact of politics and policy in theories about ethnoterritorial conflict. Each of the chapters that follows seeks to document the significance of politics and policy for a particular case. Each chapter is an original piece of work written for this book. The authors, however, have been active in researching and writing in this field for longer than most of us care to remember. All are specialists in the countries or cases on which they wrote.

In order that these chapters blend both substantively and theoretically, each of the authors agreed to address a common set of core questions. They have done so, although obviously each not in precisely the same order. Additionally, we chose to have fewer cases so that each of the authors would have sufficient space to develop their arguments fully. Too often edited volumes and journal articles severely limit the space available for the meat of the argument to be expressed as completely as we would like. The core questions included topics such as these. To what extent do the ethnoterritorial conflicts within your political system overlap or reinforce one another? Do they contradict or conflict one another in any ways? To what extent do the ethnoterritorial groups pursue joint strategies and tactics, or otherwise communicate with one another? What are the basic issues, demands, and policy conflicts? What have been the ranges of demands for policy responses that have been made or are being made of public decisionmakers? What is the range of demands that enjoy the support of the movements' activists and general supporters? Are there differences between the demands of activists and those supported by the members of the various organizations? What are the different types of spokespersons in each ethnoterritorial community? Do multiple spokespersons strengthen or weaken the success of the community in the political process? To whom do the policymakers respond and why? Relatedly, how representative or comprehensive are the groups or individuals to whom the policymakers respond? What has been the basic pattern of policy decisions for your case(s)? How long-standing is this pattern? Why did it develop? When deviations have occurred, why did they occur? What have been the direct consequences of these decisions? Were they essentially foreseen or unforeseen consequences? What have been the secondary or spin-off consequences of the policy responses? What changes have occurred in the ethnoterritorial movements in structure, goals, etc.—and to what extent have these changes reflected policy outputs? What differences exist in terms of policy response preferences among the major policy actors (the major parties, their leadership, the bureaucracy, etc.) and why? What has been the continuity of policymakers and has this had any effect? To what extent have other factors or developments influenced the priority given to ethnoterritorial conflict on the government's agenda.

Clearly, this was a tall research order and not all of the cases would involve all of the points. The central thrust, though, was for each analyst to elaborate upon and evaluate the impact of the political and policy processes of their respective political systems on their particular ethnoterritorial conflicts. The chapters are not intended to be historical or socioeconomic reviews of the development of these cases. They were to focus on politics and policy in order to illustrate their significance. The chapter on referendums and the concluding chapter were responsible for pulling together aspects of multiple cases and making comparative comments.

Each of the chapters makes a contribution to the research literature on their respective cases as well as to the policy literature. For example, Clark's chapter on Spain, "Spanish Democracy and Regional Autonomy: The Autonomous Community System and Self-Government for the Ethnic Homelands," deals with one of the most complex sets of ethnoterritorial conflicts in the Western world. He thoroughly discusses the development of the autonomy process with particular attention to the Basque region and Cataluña. In doing that, he gives extensive coverage to such issues as residual sovereignty, education, linguistic rights, and regional government financing, which have complicated the implementation process for autonomy. He illustrates how the regional governments and the central government in Madrid have very differing perceptions of the meaning of autonomy and the range of authority that needs to be delegated to the regions to give their separate interpretations substance. His contention that "the Spanish case reveals the limitations of the territorial devolution model (especially when applied to the entire territory of the state) to resolve conflicts that are ethnically based and to accommodate demands that have autonomy (broadly defined) and even independence as their ultimate goal" is well supported by his research.

Similarly, Leslie's chapter on Canada, "Ethnonationalism in a Federal State: The Case of Canada," clearly illustrates how past political actions and policies influence future options. His analysis of the situation in Canada created by the rise of French Canadian ethnonationalism brings out the complexities of that case very well. The *Parti Québécois* has been the primary vehicle for the political manifestation of French Canadian ethnonationalism, but not the exclusive one, especially as it is a provincial party operating within a federal system. Thus, not all French Canadians accept the party as representative of their political views. It is a case in which for institutional and bargaining purposes an ethnoterritorial party seeks to be identified as the ethnonational representative of a population group, while the central government and other provincial parties seek to deny it that role. Moreover, the issues raised by the *Parti Québécois* are complicated by various other constitutional and regional issues of intense concern to the other provinces and to Ottawa. It provides a clear pathway through the multiple bargaining arenas that have been associated with this case. Leslie's discussion forces the reader to recognize that there are not simple relationships between policy decisions and their consequences.

Rudolph's chapter, "Belgium: Variations on the Theme of Territorial Accommodation," describes in detail the various institutional mechanisms the Belgians have adopted to deal with the conflict between the Flemish and Walloons. It also thoroughly considers the impacts this conflict and these attempts to resolve it have had on the governing structures and political parties. In the process, it documents how the delicate balance sometimes struck in this case can be upset by relatively low-level issues and personages, such as a village mayor who refuses to use the legally appropriate language even though he can speak the language quite well. The Belgian case clearly shows the significance of politics and policy to ethnoterritorial conflicts, even if it does not demonstrate a clear capacity to resolve them.

Safran's chapter, "The French State and Ethnic Minority Cultures: Policy Dimensions and Problems," deals with a variety of French examples of ethnoterritorial movements, almost all of which are small in size and political impact. What makes the French case of particular interest is the shift in the approach of the central government to the demands and issues presented by these population groups. Historically, French governments with the concurrence of political parties on the right and left, although for differing reasons, have been extremely hostile to any exhibition of ethnoterritorial sentiments. This policy pattern has undergone substantial change during the Mitterrand years. The government is now more accommodating, at least in symbols towards the linguistic and cultural demands of such groups, although it remains to be seen how extensive the commitment will be in fact.

Keating explores the Scottish and Welsh cases in his chapter, "Territorial Management and the British State." He focuses particularly well on the topic of territorial management, how the central government in London has dealt with territorially based issues within a commitment to a unitary state structure. He points out how the British constitutional arrangements have permitted a good deal of flexibility in how the central government has been able to address ethnoterritorial issues. The chapter also discusses in detail the shifts in positions that have taken place within political parties and the policy approaches that have been adopted since the failure of the Scottish and Welsh devolution proposals in 1979.

The chapter by Thompson, "Referendums and Ethnoterritorial Movements: The Policy Consequences and Political Ramifications," takes a different approach from the country-based chapters. It takes a comparative look at the different ethnoterritorial referendums held in Quebec, Scotland, Wales, the Jura, the Basque region (Euskadi), Cataluña, Andalucía, and Galicia. It is particularly concerned with developing the policy consequences that result from a decision to hold referendums in such cases and the political ramifications for the ethnoterritorial movements and the central decision-making institutions. The chapter concludes by arguing that neither the proponents nor the opponents of referendums are likely to find the results entirely to their satisfaction. The political and policy costs and benefits tend to be greatly exaggerated in the process leading up to the referendum and in the election campaign itself. Whatever the outcome, though, the subsequent results were an important factor in the next set of bargaining over ethnoterritorial issues.

The comparative approach is continued in the concluding chapter, "Pathways to Accommodation and the Persistence of the Ethnoterritorial Challenge in Western Democracies." There the editors draw upon the case study chapters and other works to assess how it is that Western democratic regimes have attempted to cope with their ethnoterritorial movements. We summarize the diversity existing between the various ethnoterritorial groups and the responses that governments have adopted. Despite the variety of devices utilized, we conclude that these groups have achieved their basic goal of gaining more recognition of their movements and some policy concessions from their central governments. Central governments and political parties, though, have not been without their own resources and strategies. Active ethnoterritorial movements within a contemporary Western political system may imply substantial change in the conducting of politics, but it need not imply the breakdown of governing or the breakup of political parties. Moreover, no matter what policy responses are adopted, these ethnoterritorial movements and the issues they articulate are not going to disappear completely from the policy agenda of the Western world.

We would be remiss if we did not conclude this introduction without noting some areas of research that still need to be conducted on the relationship of politics and policy to ethnoterritorial politics. A great deal remains to be done. For example, the degree of comparison between the ways in which ethnoterritorial movements articulate their demands and mobilize their supporters and the ways in which conventional interest groups and single issue groups do likewise needs to be established. Similarly, the degree of comparability in the response patterns of central governments and political parties between the various types of groups needs more exploration. That would further develop our understanding of the distinctiveness of these groups. We also need more analysis of the bureaucratic dimension of the policy responses of the central governments. Very little work has been done on traditions and norms of behavior within the central bureaucracies of the Western political systems and how those may have affected the patterns of policy responses adopted by the governments. Additionally, more detailed work needs to be done on the motivations of the leaders, activists, and followers of the ethnoterritorial movements. We still know too little about what prompts them to engage in this kind of political activity. More comparisons are also needed between the policy responses and the decision-making processes used in these cases and those utilized in the more conventional areas of policy making. And finally, more comparisons are needed between the Western cases of ethnoterritorial politics and policy and those found in other regions of the world. The distinctiveness of this area of research and policy will need to be continually assessed as will all of our generalizations.

NOTES

1. Robert J. Thompson and Joseph R. Rudolph, "Ethnic Politics and Public Policy in Western Societies: A Framework for Comparative Analysis," in Dennis L. Thompson and Dov Ronen, eds., *Ethnicity, Politics, and Development* (Boulder, Colo.: Lynne Rienner Publishers, 1986), 25–64.

2. Tom Nairn, *The Break-Up of Britain* (London: NLB, 1977).

3. William Beer, *The Unexpected Rebellion: Ethnic Activism in Contemporary France* (New York: New York University Press, 1980): John E. Schwarz, "The Scottish National Party: Nonviolent Separatism and Theories of Violence," *World Politics* 22 (July 1970): 496–517; and Roger Allan Brooks, "Scottish Nationalism: Relative Deprivation and Social Mobility," Ph. D. dissertation, Michigan State University, 1973.

4. Michael Hechter, *Internal Colonialism: The Celtic Fringe in British National Development, 1536–1966* (Berkeley: University of California Press, 1975).

5. Peter Alexis Gourevitch, "The Emergence of 'Peripheral Nationalisms': Some Comparative Speculations on the Spatial Distribution of Political Leadership and Economic Growth," *The Comparative Study of Society and History* 21 (July 1979): 303–322.

6. Donley T. Studlar and Ian McAllister, "Nationalism in Scotland and Wales: A Post-Industrial Phenomenon?," *Ethnic and Racial Studies* 11 (January 1988): 48–62.

7. See Michael Keating, *State and Regional Nationalism: Territorial Politics and the European State* (Hemel, Hempstead: Harvester 1988) and Raphael Zariski, "Ethnic Extremism Among Ethnoterritorial Minorities in Western Europe: Dimensions, Causes, and Institutional Responses," *Comparative Politics* 21 (forthcoming 1989).

8. Gourevitch, "Emergence of 'Peripheral Nationalism'," 304.

9. Expecially see Schwarz, "Scottish National Party," and Brooks, "Scottish Nationalism."

10. Philip Rawkins, "Outsiders as Insiders: The Implications of Minority Nationalism in Scotland and Wales," *Comparative Politics* 10 (July 1978): 521.

11. For example, see Margaret Levi and Michael Hechter, "A Rational Choice Approach to the Rise and Decline of Ethnoregional Political Parties," in Edward A. Tiryakian and Ronald Rogowski, eds., *New Nationalisms of the Developed West* (Boston: Allen & Unwin, 1985), 128–146.

12. Studlar and McAllister, "Nationalism in Scotland and Wales."

13. Jack Brand, "Political Parties and the Referendum on National Sovereignty: The 1979 Scottish Referendum on Devolution," *Canadian Review of Studies in Nationalism* 13 (1986): 31–48.

14. Joseph R. Rudolph and Robert J. Thompson, "Ethnoterritorial Movements and the Policy Process: Accommodating Nationalist Demands in the Developed World," *Comparative Politics* 17 (April 1985): 291–311. Also see Zariski's forthcoming *Comparative Politics* article and Keating, *Nations and Regions*.

15. See Neil Nevitte and Charles H. Kennedy, eds., *Ethnic Preference and Public Policy in Developing States* (Boulder, Colo.: Lynne Rienner Publishers, 1986; Crawford Young, *The Politics of Cultural Pluralism* (Madison: University of Wisconsin Press, 1976); Joseph Rothchild, *Ethnopolitics* (New York: Columbia University Press, 1981); and Cynthia Enloe, *Ethnic Conflict and Political Development* (Boston: Little, Brown, 1973).

16. Milton Esman, "The Management of Communal Conflict," *Public Policy* 21 (Winter 1973): 49–78; "The Politics of Official Bilingualism in Canada," *Political Science Quarterly* 97 (Summer 1982): 233–253, and "Scottish Nationalism, North Sea Oil, and the British Response," in Milton J. Esman, ed., *Ethnic Conflict in the Western World* (Ithaca: Cornell University Press, 1977), 251–86.

17. Kenneth McRae. ed., *Consociational Democracy: Political Accommodation in Segmented Societies* (Toronto: McClelland & Stewart, 1974).

CHAPTER 2

Spanish Democracy and Regional Autonomy: The Autonomous Community System and Self-Government for the Ethnic Homelands

———————————————————— ROBERT P. CLARK

As the democracies of North America and Western Europe reach an advanced stage of industrialization some characterize as "postindustrial," their political elites are confronted by two separate but closely related public policy problems. First, they are trying to decentralize political structures and to disaggregate political power to bring government closer to the people. At the same time, they are trying to accommodate the needs of newly resurgent (and, at times, insurgent) ethnonationalist minorities without jeopardizing the unity of the more inclusive state. These developments span the entire industrialized world, from Canada and the United States to Great Britain and the European continent. Where the two issues intersect, the result frequently is some variation of the policy instrument known as devolution, or as in the Spanish case, regional autonomies based in several instances on ethnonationalist as well as geographical criteria.

The transformation of the Spanish state that spanned the decade from 1976 to 1986 rested on the twin pillars of parliamentary democracy and regional autonomy. The successful transformation of the Spanish state from a dictatorship to a parliamentary democracy headed by a constitutional monarch is well known and admired, and properly so. However, a second change, equally significant, has passed almost unnoticed—the transformation of a unitary state into one based on seventeen regional governments called Autonomous Communities. One of the central features of post-Franco reforms was the devolution of increased power, resources, and responsibility to Spain's "historic regions" (those whose autonomous status antedated the Spanish Civil War), as well as other regions that gained autonomous status after 1978. Many would argue that the gains for the autonomous regions during the late 1970s were of monumental importance for

Spanish politics. After the abortive coup attempt in 1981, however, there was a steady deterioration in the relations between Madrid and the autonomous governments serving the Basque and Catalan peoples. Indeed, between the 1982 electoral triumph of the Spanish Socialist Workers Party (PSOE) and 1985, no additional powers and resources were transferred to these governments; and as the decade of the 1980s drew to a close, many salient issues in this area had still not been resolved. With the political transformation of Spain consolidated, one can question how much genuine ethnic autonomy has been achieved and how much more Spanish elites will be inclined to accommodate the demands of ethnic nationalist leaders.

Even under the best of circumstances, the transformation of a unitary state into a more decentralized regime based on either regional autonomy or federalism is one of the most challenging tasks facing any political elite. When the central state in question has been grounded on the unitary principle for the past hundred years or so (as has that of Spain), and when the regions in question are either fiercely ethnonationalist (in particular, the Basque provinces and Cataluña) or have next to no tradition of regional self-governance (as in most of the rest of the country), the task becomes doubly difficult. Nevertheless, at least initially, many Spanish political leaders identified political decentralization as one of their key objectives in the dismantling of the Franco legacy. They quickly found themselves caught in the midst of a severe conflict between ethnonationalist groups seeking to extend the concept of regional autonomy as far as possible, and more conservative forces that saw in regional autonomy the first stage in the disintegration of the Spanish state. Not surprisingly, then, the regional autonomy movement soon found itself stalled far short of its goal of full self-governance for the country's ethnic homelands.

From many different perspectives, the Spanish democratic transition is seen as fundamentally positive and, at least as far as institutions are concerned, basically completed. Virtually all major political groups in Spain accept the legitimacy of what has taken place since 1976. Rightists accept the legitimacy of a Socialist government; Communists accept the legitimate role of the monarchy. The church accepts lay education; the armed forces accept (for the most part) their reduced role in policy making; unions accept a far-from-perfect welfare state, a brutal policy of "industrial reconversion," and a high unemployment rate. Following their bloody civil war and forty years of Franco's dictatorship, most Spaniards appear to have mastered *convivencia*, or what de Tocqueville called "the art of associating together."

Given the central role of the Autonomous Community system, especially after the promulgation of the new constitution in 1978, it is noteworthy, then, that the one place where the democratic transition does not enjoy legitimacy is in Spain's ethnic homelands. Spaniards may accept as legitimate what has transpired in their country during the last decade; but Basques and Catalans still regard the democratization process as a long way from being completed.

One of the chief reasons for this ethnic discontent lies in the inherent contradictions and conflicts built into regional autonomy as a policy option. The autonomy system and process, as embodied in Title VIII of the 1978 constitution, contain a number of fundamental and inherent contradictions that virtually ensure that there will be misunderstandings between Spanish political elites and ethnic nationalists about the meaning of regional autonomy. These contradictions had their origins in the drafting of the constitution in the late 1970s; but in the immediate context of the drafting and approval of the basic law, these contradictions were covered over by ambiguities that allowed people with fundamentally different visions of the future to cooperate with one another, or at least to tolerate one another's point of view. When it came time, however, to turn the constitutional provisions into legislative and political realities, these contradictions surfaced, and what was originally thought to be some minimum consensus about autonomy for the ethnic homelands was revealed instead to be fundamental disagreement. In short, ethnic nationalist leaders expected one thing from regional autonomy; Madrid expected something quite different. Thus, center-periphery conflicts became aggravated through the first half of the 1980s, as the contending elites sought to flesh out the constitutional skeleton of Title VIII. For this reason, the Spanish case reveals the limitations of the territorial devolution model (especially when applied to the entire territory of the state) to resolve conflicts that are ethnically based and to accommodate demands that have autonomy (broadly defined) and even independence as their ultimate goal.

There is much more at stake here than simply the constitutional design of the Spanish state. As Spain enters the ranks of advanced industrial states, and assumes at the same time the responsibilities of membership in the European Community (EC), the success of its democratic experiment will rest to a large degree on the emergence of vigorous and competent governments at the municipal, provincial, and regional levels, for which the ethnic homelands can provide the models. The dependency relationship cuts both ways, however, because the extent to which Basques and Catalans achieve their historic ethnonationalist claims also depends on the nature of the regime that governs from Madrid. Thus, Spain's ethnic homelands and core-state elites confronted one another in the 1980s, needing to cooperate to achieve their objectives, yet inhibited from cooperation by complex historical and political contradictions and conflicts.

SPAIN'S AUTONOMOUS COMMUNITIES: AN OVERVIEW

The land area of Spain, about 491,000 square kilometers, is organized into forty-seven provinces on the Iberian Peninsula, three provinces composed of island chains (Balearics and Canaries), and two city enclaves in North Africa (Ceuta and Melilla).[1] The mainland provinces account for more than 97 percent of Spain's total land area and contain more than 94 percent of the country's population. Spain is a complex country, divided into a number of sharply contrasting regions with widely varying economic and social structures as well as different historical, political, and cultural traditions. To accommodate such complexity in public policies or institutions would be a challenge to any regional autonomy arrangement; and the Spanish polity contains pressures and problems that may yet prove too intense for a system based on devolution.

For example, Spain is one of the most populous officially multilingual countries in the world. People whose mother tongue is other than Castilian constitute about one-quarter of the population.[2] So, in addition to Castilian, which the 1978 constitution designates as the official language in all parts of the country, Autonomous Communities have the authority to designate their respective languages as "co-official" with Castilian, which has been done in the cases of Catalan, Euskera (the Basque language), Galician, Valencian, and Majorcan.[3]

The 1978 Spanish constitution provides for Autonomous Communities as a new level of government between Madrid and the provinces. As such, they are an example of what Victor Pérez Díaz and others refer to as "meso-governments," or government units that stand midway between the large-scale, inclusive sovereign state and small-scale entities such as provinces or cities.[4] There are two ways for an Autonomous Community to come into existence. The easier of the two, via the constitution's Article 151, was established for those regions that had enjoyed autonomous status under Spain's Second Republic: the Basque country, Cataluña, and Galicia. The more arduous route, via Article 143, was reserved for other provinces or groups of provinces that wished to become autonomous communities. During the constitutional drafting and approval process, most Spanish leaders felt that only the three "historic regions" would want, and would qualify for, autonomous status. Nevertheless, less than five years after the constitution entered into force, essentially all Spanish territory had been reorganized into Autonomous Communities by one route or another.

The Spanish Autonomous Community system hinges on the devolution of authority and resources from the center to the regions on a negotiated basis, in contrast to a federal system in which powers are shared on the basis of the inherent rights of both levels of government. Whether through Article

151 or 143, the processes of achieving autonomous community status had these features in common:

1. Submission of a proposed draft autonomy statute by the region to the Spanish government and Congress of Deputies for approval. The draft statute contains a proposed parliamentary structure as well as a list of powers to be transferred to the region by Madrid;

2. Approval of the statute in Madrid through a process involving the president of the government, the ruling party in Parliament, the Constitutional Committees of the two chambers of Parliament, the Parliament in plenary session, and relevant cabinet ministries;

3. Approval by the citizens of the region voting in a referendum, either before or after approval of the draft statute, depending on the route followed to autonomy;

4. Promulgation of the appropriate decree by the king;

5. Election of the Parliament of the Autonomous Community, which then selects the president of the Autonomous Government, who in turn selects his or her cabinet;

6. Negotiation on a case-by-case basis of the transfer of specific powers, responsibilities, and resources (primarily money, fixed and movable property, and personnel) to the Autonomous Community. Negotiations involve the Autonomous Government, a joint commission made up of representatives of both Madrid and the Autonomous Government, the Spanish Ministry of Territorial Administration, other affected Spanish government ministries, the Spanish Council of Ministers and the president of the Spanish government, who must ratify each transfer of power. These negotiations, especially in the Basque and Catalan cases, were protracted and frequently contentious, at least in part because the affected Spanish ministry or ministries were extremely reluctant to lose important powers and resources.

By May 1983, when the regional reorganization of the Spanish state was completed, there were seventeen Autonomous Communities, each composed of one or more previously existing provinces.[5] Seven of these communities are based on a single province the Balearic Islands, and, on the mainland, Asturias (Oviedo), Cantabria (Santander), Madrid, Murcia, Navarra, and Rioja (Logroño). The remaining communities are made up of several provinces, with Andalucía (eight provinces) and Castilla-León (nine) having the greatest number of constituent units.

The Autonomous Communities differ widely in size, population, and economic and political weight. Andalucía (nearly the size of Portugal) is clearly the dominant region in terms of population and land area, with more than 17 percent of the Spanish total in both categories, and 16.9 percent of the members of Spain's Congress of Deputies. Cataluña (larger than Belgium), Madrid, and Valencia are also significant in terms of population, but less so in terms of area, a fact that reflects their densely populated cities. The provinces that make up Cataluña account for about 13 percent of the members of Parliament, while Madrid alone sends slightly more than 9 percent. In contrast, the two communities carved out of sparsely populated Castilla, Castilla-La Mancha (larger than Ireland) and Castilla-León (about the same size as Austria), account for more than a third of Spain's land area but only about one-tenth of its population. In terms of economic weight, Cataluña and Madrid combined account for about 35 percent of Spain's income, while relatively poor but large Andalucía accounts for another 12 percent.

Simple numbers like these are not always reflective of political weight, however. Statistically, the Autonomous Community of the País Vasco (CAPV), consisting of the three provinces of Alava, Guipúzcoa, and Vizcaya, but excluding the largest Basque province, Navarra, does not loom large, with only 5.6 percent of the population, 1.5 percent of the land area, and 8.2 percent of the income of Spain, and only 6 percent of the members of the Congress of Deputies. Few observers of the Spanish political scene would deny, however, the significance of the Basque provinces in the overall effort to decentralize the Spanish state. This significance stems not from the size of the Basque provinces, but from the importance of Basque heavy industry, the stern (some would say intransigent) dedication of their people to the principle of ethnic self-governance, and the ability of the Basque insurgent organization ETA (*Euzkadi ta Askatasuna*) to destabilize Spanish politics with its armed assaults.

THE AUTONOMY PROCESS: 1975 TO 1981

The history of the autonomy process can be divided into three phases. From 1975 to 1978 most Spanish leaders were concerned primarily with completing the opening steps of the transition from the Francoist dictatorship to a parliamentary democracy. At that time, the only political elites much interested in regional or ethnic autonomy were the leaders of the Basque and Catalan nationalist parties. During the second phase, from late 1978 to early 1981, autonomy for the ethnic homelands as well as for other regions of Spain was a major political and constitutional issue that attracted the attention of all Spanish political forces. During these months, the three "historic regions"—País Vasco, Cataluña, and Galicia—all made important strides toward regional self-governance. Other regions with less historical claim on autonomy, such as Andalucía, also gained similar rights. However, this phase came to a close with the abortive Guardia Civil and military coup attempt of February 1981. From that date on, progress in devolution slowed to a crawl, and in a few instances stalled completely. A fourth phase may have begun in January 1985, with the *pacto de legislatura* between the Basque government and the Basque Socialist party, but the true historical significance of this introduction of centralist-regionalist coalitions into regional politics was difficult to discern even two and a half years later.

From General Franco's death in November 1975 until December 1977, regional autonomy had a low priority on Spain's political agenda. In these early days of the transformation, there were simply too many other competing objectives. Throughout this transition process, Basque and Catalan deputies to the Cortes worked to ensure that the new constitution would contain provisions favorable to the granting of autonomy to their regions, and to a degree they succeeded. By the time the new constitution emerged from the parliamentary drafting and amending process, its treatment of regional autonomy was fairly positive, although many ethnic nationalists would have preferred an arrangement for devolving power to the regions that was less cumbersome and that left less veto power in Madrid.

In December 1977, as the constitution was being drafted, the Spanish Ministry of Interior created "pre-autonomy regimes" in Cataluña and in the Basque provinces of Alava, Vizcaya, and Guipúzcoa. Many Basque leaders were angered by the exclusion of Navarra from the arrangement; but conservative Navarrese leaders were strongly opposed to being grouped together with the other Basque provinces and thereby losing the special privileges that Navarra had enjoyed for many years. The work of these pre-autonomy regimes lasted about two years, until the election of the autonomous parliaments in the spring of 1980. In some respects, their work was a success, especially in the preparation of the draft statutes of autonomy that eventually became the fundamental law of the two regional governments. However, in other important ways these pre-autonomy regimes were disappointments. Relatively few actual administrative powers or other resources were transferred; and in the absence of any real transfer of power from Madrid to the regions, the pre-autonomy regimes became the symbolic focal points for complaints and public protest rather than the agents for a smooth transition to regional self-governance. Nevertheless, by the time of the promulgation of the new constitution in December 1978, thanks to the preparatory work of the pre-autonomy regimes, both the Basques and the Catalans were ready to begin work on the long process of proposing and ratifying the exact details of the autonomous regimes that the constitution envisioned.

Many Basque and Catalan leaders now look back on the two-year period from December 1978 to February 1981 as the "Golden Age" in the autonomy movement, a period of euphoric "nation building" and achievement. This is not to suggest that they were entirely satisfied with the regional autonomy promises implicit in the 1978 constitution, for even in 1979 and 1980 there were disturbing signs of difficulties still to come for Spain's ethnic homelands. Yet in the context of the immediate post-Franco period, the gains registered by the Basque and Catalan nationalist leaders were impressive.

The Autonomous Community concept became law in Spain with the adoption of the new constitution in 1978.[6] In December, both Basques and Catalans submitted their draft autonomy statutes for approval in Madrid. Following the second parliamentary elections, in March 1979, and the election of municipal councils and provincial assemblies in April, constitutional review of the Basque and Catalan statutes began in late spring, and went on into the summer. On the political side, negotiations between Spanish President Adolfo Suárez and Basque nationalist leader Carlos Garaikoetxea almost broke down over a number of key unresolved issues in the Basque statute, including the maintenance of public order, the administration of justice, and the financing of the new autonomous government and its operations. These deadlocks were finally resolved through tough negotiations between Suárez and Garaikoetxea in July, and by early autumn the two statutes had been approved by the Cortes.[7]

According to the provisions of the constitution, the draft statutes now had to be submitted to the voters in the affected regions for their approval in referendums. In these referendums, which took place on October 25, 1979,[8] Catalan voters approved their statute, with 59.5 percent of the eligible voters voting, and 87.9 percent voting yes. In the Basque provinces, about 57 percent of the eligible voters went to the polls, and 94.6 percent of them voted in favor of the proposed statute.[9]

The next major step toward regional autonomy for Spain's ethnic minorities came in March 1980 with the elections of the Basque and Catalan autonomous parliaments. On March 9, Basque voters elected the sixty members of the Basque Parliament, with Basque nationalist candidates scoring a major victory over candidates of Spanish parties. The center-right Basque Nationalist party (*Partido Nacionalista Vasco*, or PNV) elected twenty-five members, while the more radical parties, Popular Unity (*Herri Batasuna*, or HB) and Basque Left (*Euzkadiko Exkerra*, or EE), elected eleven and six members respectively. Since the *Herri Batasuna* deputies never occupied their seats, the PNV was able to exercise effective one-party control over the legislative assembly.[10] The strength of ethnic nationalists was demonstrated once again on March 20, when the moderate Catalan nationalist party, Convergence and Union (CiU), won forty-three of the 135 seats in the Catalan autonomous parliament, followed by the Catalan Socialist party with thirty-three and the Catalan Communist party with twenty-five. The weakness of the governing Spanish party, Union of the Democratic Center (UCD) was clearly in evidence as their candidates won only 6 seats in the Basque election and only 18 in the Catalan vote.[11]

Through the remainder of 1980, the two governments devoted themselves energetically to the formation of their administrative bureaucracies and to the development of their operating procedures. It soon became apparent that the issue of financing would be a major stumbling block to full autonomy in the Basque case. Although the autonomy statute had specified that the Basque government would have its own taxing authority, this proved to be somewhat problematical for historical reasons. After the end of the second Carlist war in 1876, Madrid had agreed to what were referred to as *conciertos económicos*, or economic accords, with each of the four Basque provinces. According to these accords, each province was responsible for the levying and collection of its own taxes, a certain agreed-upon percentage of which would be remitted to the Spanish Treasury Ministry each year. Following the Civil War in 1939, the economic accords with Vizcaya and Guipúzcoa were abolished because these two provinces had sided with the Republic. The accords for Alava and Navarra, on the other hand, were retained as rewards to those two provinces for their role in supporting the rebellion. Thus, for the Basques, the *conciertos económicos* were charged with special symbolic significance as well as essential to the running of their government.

For most of 1980 the Basque government financed its operations with funds made available to it by the central government in Madrid and with "in-kind" resources contributed by the provincial governments. The Basques argued that in the long run this arrangement was untenable, for it nullified any pretense of autonomy for the region. On the other hand, Madrid negotiators were reluctant to turn over to any Autonomous Government their own independent financial resources. Negotiations over this point went on until late December 1980, when Basque and Spanish leaders agreed on a new *concierto económico* to cover the three provinces of the País Vasco Autonomous Community as a single entity.[12] This agreement permitted the Basque government to remit certain negotiated sums to Madrid in lieu of payment of personal or corporate taxes directly to the Spanish government. There were problems with this formula, primarily because it would be the *provinces* rather than the Basque government that would do the actual collection of the taxes; but at the time, the *concierto económico* appeared to be a breakthrough of historic proportions. Not only did it give the Basques their own independent source of funds, but it also appeared to heal a major source of friction with Madrid. Thus, as 1980 came to close, hopes were high throughout Spain that at long last the painful issue of Basque and Catalan autonomy was finally headed toward resolution.

THE AUTONOMY PROCESS: 1981 TO 1987

The hopes of the late 1970s, unfortunately, were not to be realized. As a consequence of a number of dramatic challenges to the stability of the Spanish state from both left and right, Spain's political elites decided to halt the progress being made toward decentralization of the country's political structure.

There were, of course, some significant steps taken toward devolution in the rest of Spain during 1981 and 1982, but apart from Galicia, most of these involved the mainly symbolic approval and implementation of regional autonomy statutes in the rest of the country.[13] In the third "historic region", the autonomy statute was approved by the Galician people in a referendum on December 21, 1980. Despite a huge abstention rate (nearly three-fourths of the voters failed to turn out), the statute carried by an affirmative vote of about 73 percent. The statute was approved in Madrid in late April 1981; and on October 20, the Galician Autonomous Parliament was elected. For the first time, control of an autonomous parliament was won by Spanish parties. The conservative Spanish party, *Alianza Popular*, won 34 percent of the votes and twenty-six seats in the seventy-one-seat legislature; the center-right UCD won 32 percent of the votes and twenty-four seats; and the Spanish Socialists, the PSOE, won 22 percent and sixteen seats. Galician nationalist parties won only 13 percent and 4 seats. The Galician Parliament held its initial meeting and began operations on December 19.

It has been suggested that the inventors of the Autonomous Community concept originally envisioned that there would be only three such communities, the three "historic regions", roughly analogous to Wales, Scotland, and Northern Ireland in the United Kingdom, with the rest of the country still governed directly from Madrid, and with the role of the existing provinces left unaltered.[14] Whatever these original views might have been, they were quickly rendered irrelevant by the granting of autonomy to Andalucía.

Despite the fact that Andalucía was not one of the original "historic regions," its leaders still sought its autonomy status through the constitution's Article 151. Since the region had never had its own autonomy statute under the Republic, its people were asked to vote in referendum twice, once merely to ratify their popular approval of gaining autonomy, and the second time for the specific statute that had been drafted and negotiated with Madrid. In the first referendum, on February 28, 1980, about 56 percent of the voters voted for autonomy; but since the yes vote dropped below half in two of the eight provinces (Almería and Jaén), special legislation was necessary to continue the process via Article 151. After much delay, the second referendum was held on October 20, 1981, with 53 percent of the voters participating, and 80 percent voting their approval of the new statute. The statute received final approval in Madrid in January 1982, and Andalucía's first Parliament was chosen in May. Again Spanish parties carried the bulk of the votes, with the socialist PSOE winning 53 percent and 66 of the assembly's 109 seats; *Alianza Popular*, 17 percent and 17 seats; and UCD 13 percent and 15 seats.[15]

Once that step had been taken, all the other regions clamored for their statutes, as if to suggest that anything less would denote second-class status.

"Café para todos," as the popular saying put it. In any case, other regions pressed ahead with the approval of their autonomy statutes. Asturias and Cantabria were given final approval in December 1981; Rioja and Murcia in June 1982; Valencia in July; Aragón, Castilla-La Mancha, Canarias and Navarra in August; and Extremadura, Baleares, Madrid, and Castilla-León in February 1983. Thus, by early 1983, statutes had been approved in all the regions except the North African city enclaves of Ceuta and Melilla. On May 8, 1983, when Spanish voters went to the polls to elect municipal councils and provincial assemblies, they also selected members of thirteen of the new regional parliaments, excepting only the four original assemblies elected earlier in the Basque country, Cataluña, Galicia, and Andalucía. As of that moment, then, one could say that the formal or *constitutional* decentralization of Spain's political system was complete.

At another level, however, where politics and ordinary legislation prevail over constitutional provisions and symbolism, the regional autonomy process was reversed in 1981 and 1982. At the time, the cause of this reversal seemed clear: the dramatic and violent assaults on the stability and legitimacy of the Spanish state. In February 1981, the regime narrowly averted being overthrown by a coup mounted by rightist elements within the army and the Guardia Civil. In March, violent attacks attributed to ETA rose to such a level that Madrid deployed regular Spanish army and navy units to the Basque provinces, the first time that regular military force had been used in a counterinsurgency role. In May, a small group of Spanish rightists seized a major bank in Barcelona and held its customers hostage in an unsuccessful attempt to force the government to release a number of officers arrested for their role in the coup attempt the preceding February. In sum, the period of late winter to spring of 1981 saw a series of blows to the Spanish body politic that weakened the resolve of the country's democratic elite to carry through on the more ambitious aspects of the decentralization effort. Since regional autonomy, especially for the ethnic minorities, was considered by rightists to be the first step leading to the dismemberment of Spain, the leadership in Madrid concluded that brakes would have to be applied to the regional autonomy movement to avoid further attacks on the state itself.[16]

In April 1981, the two major Spanish political parties, the center-right governing party, UCD, and the PSOE initiated a series of meetings and special studies aimed at "harmonizing" the autonomy process. These meetings led to a summit meeting of Spain's political leaders to discuss regional autonomy, to which Basque and Catalan leaders were not invited. The outcome of this meeting was a *Pacto Autonómico*, or autonomy pact, between the two parties whose purpose was to stop further devolution of power to the regions. In July, UCD and PSOE leaders unveiled the Organic Law on the Harmonization of the Autonomy Process, referred to by its Spanish acronym, LOAPA. Spanish leaders insisted that they were still committed to regional autonomy, and the LOAPA was nothing more than an effort to restore order and system to what had become a disorderly, even chaotic, process. Basque and Catalan leaders responded with bristling criticism of the draft law, calling it a betrayal of Madrid's commitment to devolving real power to the ethnic minorities.

Basque and Catalan leaders did what they could to block the implementation of the LOAPA. In private meetings with Spanish political leaders, they urged the withdrawal of the draft law. When that failed, they took to the streets in massive demonstrations against the LOAPA: in Bilbao in October 1981, in Barcelona in March 1982, and across the Basque and Catalan provinces in September 1982. During the campaign prior to Spain's parliamentary elections in October 1982, Basque and Catalan leaders formed an "anti-LOAPA front" to mobilize the voters against any candidate who had voted for the LOAPA in the Parliament. During the parliamentary debate over the LOAPA, the ethnic minorities' deputies did succeed in inserting a provision to delay implementation of the LOAPA until Spain's Constitutional Tribunal could decide its constitutionality. After much delay, in August 1983, the court held that certain provisions of the LOAPA violated the constitution and that it therefore could not be implemented.

Notwithstanding the court's findings regarding the LOAPA, the Socialists continued to insist on the homogenization of the autonomous community system. Since most of the regions are uninterested in acquiring, and incapable of using, as much autonomous power as are the Basques and Catalans, the result has been to try to limit those two regimes to some lesser degree of autonomy.

The position of the González government on the autonomy question can be seen in a number of different areas. For one thing, between October 1982 and March 1985, there were no new powers transferred to the Basque Autonomous Community, even though the Joint Basque-Spanish Committee on the Transfer of Powers had agreed to more than a dozen such transfers during this period. Second, even in those areas where powers had been transferred earlier, the PSOE-controlled Congress of Deputies passed legislation that took precedence over, and essentially negated, laws passed by the autonomous parliaments. One such area was education, where, despite a clear understanding that the jurisdiction of the autonomous communities would be paramount, the Spanish Congress intruded by approving the Organic Law for the Development of Education (LODE). Third, the González government resisted attempts to place on the agenda the discussion of new transfers of authority, such as the administration of courts and prisons, an issue of special importance in the violence-wracked Basque region.

Relations between the Basque government and the Socialists seemed to improve in early 1985 following the *pacto de legislatura* between the new Basque president, José Antonio Ardanza, and the Basque Socialist party's members in the Basque Parliament, led by Txiki Benegas. This pact had several important consequences, including the unblocking of the transfer of the fourteen pending powers or authorities, and the passage of the 1985 budget of the Basque government, which had been stalled in the deadlocked Parliament. Nevertheless, in order to get socialist cooperation in governing the Basque Autonomous Community, the PNV had to back away from a number of its more strongly held positions regarding home rule.

In the 1986 Spanish parliamentary elections, the PNV lost two seats, from eight (in 1982) to six, while the more radical *Herri Batasuna* won five seats (up from two in the previous election) and *Euzkadiko Ezkerra* won two (up from one in 1982). Moreover, the vote total for the PNV declined sharply from 450,000 in the 1984 Basque parliamentary elections to 300,000 in 1986. Many reasons could be advanced to explain the decline of the more moderate PNV and the rise of the more intransigent parties, but a close scrutiny of the electoral data suggests that about 30 percent of the lost PNV votes shifted to more radical Basque nationalist parties because of voter restiveness over what appeared to be an excessively conciliatory attitude toward the Socialists by the Ardanza government.[17] Thus, the faction within the PNV that favored cooperation with Madrid was weakened, and the more hard-line faction strengthened, by the election outcome.

Less than three months after the PNV debacle in the 1986 elections, the factional split resulted in the expulsion from the party of former Basque president Carlos Garaikoetxea and a number of his followers, who responded by forming their own party, Basque Solidarity (*Eusko Alkartasuna*, or EA). In addition to their differences over relations with Madrid, there were a number of other important factors that contributed to this division: personal animosity between Garaikoetxea and PNV leader Xabier Arzalluz, regional rivalries within the PNV between Vizcaya and Guipúzcoa, differences of opinion about how to treat ETA's continued insurgency, and the respective roles of the provinces and the Basque Autonomous Government. Regardless of the causes, the effects were disastrous for the cause of Basque home rule. With the PNV's membership in the Basque Parliament split in half by the schism, Ardanza realized he could not continue to govern, so he dissolved Parliament and convoked new elections for November 30. Despite the fact that 69 percent of the voters voted for one of several Basque nationalist options, the parties were so split among themselves that they were unable to form a Basque governing majority. The result was that for the first time a Spanish party—the PSOE—joined in a governing coalition in one of the ethnic homelands. This development obviously ushers in a new phase in the history of the Spanish regional autonomy movement.

Memories now are understandably quite vague as to what motivated the inclusion in the constitution of Title VIII, "On the Territorial Organization of the State." Rightly or wrongly, however, many leading Basque nationalists now believe that Spanish political leaders on both the left and the right permitted the regional autonomy idea to prosper in the late 1970s, not because of a profound conviction that power had to be disaggregated if democracy were to succeed, but for short-term instrumental objectives that in turn were driven by their concern over the shaky status of the democratic experiment. Since Spain's political elites needed the support of Basque and Catalan leaders for the democratic transformation in general and for the new constitution in particular, they adopted a conciliatory policy toward the restive nationalist provinces. After the coup attempt in early 1981, the core elite's concern over the health of democracy turned to fear for its very survival, and their solution was to reverse the flow of power to the autonomous regions. In the longer run, that is, after the PSOE victory in October 1982, ironically, the very success of the transformation seems to have reinforced the slowdown in the autonomy process. With democracy now seemingly firmly entrenched, Spain's elites see no need to continue the transfer of power to the Basque and Catalan Autonomous Communities. We can debate the motivations for the change, but there is little doubt that the reversal in 1981 has yet to run its course.

These changes coincided with a rapid decline in the popularity of the Spanish governing party, the UCD, and its leader, President Suárez. The weak showing of the UCD in elections for the Basque and Catalan Autonomous Parliaments in March 1980 foreshadowed (and perhaps partly caused) Suárez's resignation in early 1981, another even more devastating loss in the autonomous parliament elections in Andalucía in May 1982, and the final disintegration of the UCD in the October 1982 elections. Ironically, after nearly five years of living under Socialist rule, the Basques have begun to revise their assessment of Suárez, and many of them now praise the former president for the strides they made toward autonomy under his presidency. Felipe González has achieved the dubious distinction, then, of making Suárez look good to the Basques.

The impact of two years of euphoric gains in 1979 and 1980 followed by seven years of disappointment and failure has produced in the Basque and Catalan population feelings of betrayal and frustration. Ethnic vote data offer us a vivid indicator of the depth of anti-Madrid sentiment (what I term "rejectionist voting") in the Basque country[18] (see Table 2.1). Excluding referenda, since 1977 Basque voters have gone to the polls ten times: four times for Spanish parliamentary elections, and three times each for the Basque Parliament and for provincial assemblies and municipal councils. On eight of those occasions, a clear majority of them have chosen what I call the "rejectionist" option, that is, the parties that could be interpreted as anti-Madrid. In a ninth case, the rejectionist vote was exactly half the electorate. Most striking, the rejectionist option was the preferred choice of a majority of voters in the Basque provinces in each of the seven elections held since the

Table 2.1 Evolution of "Rejectionist" Voting in Ten Elections in the Basque Autononomous Community, 1977–1987

Year	Type of Election	Total Rejectionist	Rejectionist Vote as Percent of Total Vote
1977	Spanish Parliament	359,284	35.6
1979	Spanish Parliament	506,677	50.0
1979	Municipal/ Provincial	599,663	62.3
1980	Basque Parliament	589,332	63.6
1982	Spanish Parliament	645,418	53.3
1983	Municipal/ Provincial	619,571	60.6
1984	Basque Parliament	693,747	64.0
1986	Spanish Parliament	589,743	55.4
1986	Basque Parliament	773,328	69.0
1987	Municipal/ Provincial	672,295	69.6
Average 10 elections		604,906	58.3

Sources: For 1977 to 1986, see Robert Clark, "'Rejectionist,' Voting as an Indicator of Ethnic Nationalism: The Case of Spain's Basque Provinces, 1976–1986," *Ethnic and Racial Studies* (in press), Table 1. For other years, see *Deia* (Bilbao), December, 1, 1986, and June 11, 1987.

Note: "Rejectionist" votes defined as all votes cast for a Basque nationalist alternative, thereby "rejecting" a Spanish party or candidate option.

Basque Autonomy Statute entered into force. When one considers that some 40 percent of the population of the Basque provinces are not ethnic Basque and therefore can be presumed to vote most of the time for one of the Spanish parties, it is easy to conclude that the rejectionist option is favored by an overwhelming majority of ethnic Basques. Most significant, the share of the vote given to the rejectionist position has risen fairly markedly since the autonomy statute went into effect, despite the general perception outside the Basque country (and especially abroad) that the statute was a generous policy by Madrid that recognized legitimate Basque aspirations for home rule, and one that reasonable Basque nationalists should have welcomed.

Elsewhere outside the Basque and Catalan regions the gradual development of regional autonomy is having the curious effect of stimulating the rise of regional parties and movements where none existed before. Results from the June 1987 elections for thirteen autonomous community parliaments show that regionalist parties had reached significant levels of electoral strength in Valencia, Aragón, Navarra, Majorca, Cantabria, and Canarias. In the city of Valencia, the *Unión Valenciana* has become the second strongest party; in Cantabria, the *Partido Regionalista de Cantabria* won third place in autonomous community voting; and in Aragón, the *Partido Aragonés Regionalista* has reached a position of power where it can now aspire to placing its leader in the office of president of the autonomous government.[19] This completely unforeseen rise of regionalist parties in regions with little if any sense of historical regionalism promises to alter the political as well as the constitutional map of Spain. Together with the entry of the PSOE into a governing coalition in the Basque Parliament, these trends suggest that the decade of the 1990s will be marked by a complex transformation of political forces in Spain. The Autonomous Community system in the twenty-first century will be quite unlike what the framers of the 1978 constitution envisioned; but it is still premature to try to describe in detail what regional autonomy will look like in Spain by the year 2000.

THE BASQUES AND MADRID:
CONFLICTS AND CONTRADICTIONS

The preceding historical account shows that the regional autonomy *system*, as provided for in Title VIII of the 1978 constitution, as well as the *process* by which these constitutional provisions were transformed into working institutions, were plagued almost from the beginning by a number of fundamental misunderstandings or disagreements between Basque nationalist and Spanish political leaders.[20] A review of these conflicts and contradictions helps us appreciate why a policy of regional autonomy based on territorial devolution is an inadequate policy response to minority demands derived from ethnicity, language, and culture.

Many ethnonationalist groups contend that their rights to autonomy stem from some grant of political authority that may predate the existence of the modern nation-state and may even be primordial in its origins, but which in any case does not depend on any contemporary document such as a constitution or fundamental law. In this, Basque nationalists are no different, arguing that their rights derive from their historic status vis à vis the Spanish state before the Carlist wars, and thus do not depend on any specific grant found in the 1978 Spanish constitution.[21] From this perspective, in the Middle Ages, between 1200 and 1512, the several Basque provinces (voluntarily or under compulsion) entered into a special relationship with the Kingdom of Castile that was governed by the foral laws of that era. Changes in that relationship during the nineteenth century were imposed by force and did not invalidate the earlier status of the Basque provinces.

This version of history and of rights that predate the Spanish constitution is, from the Basque viewpoint, validated by two statutory provisions. The first is the *Primera Disposición Adicional* of the 1978 constitution: "The Constitution maintains and respects the historic rights of the foral territories. Said foral regime will be made current within the framework of the Constitution and the Autonomy Statutes." The second is the *Disposición Adicional* of the Basque Autonomy Statute: "Acceptance of the autonomy regime established in this Statute does not imply renunciation by the Basque People of the rights that might have corresponded to them as such by virtue of their history, which can be made current in accord with the provisions of the juridical framework." For the Basques, if Madrid had had some doubt about the so-called *derechos históricos*, then the Spanish government should not have approved the constitution and the statute containing such wording.[22]

Spanish elites, on the other hand, contend that the Basque autonomous community is not entitled to anything not specifically addressed by the constitution in Title VIII, and by their autonomy statute. This position is supported by the conventional legal interpretation of the constitutional rights of minority nations in modern nation-states, where the organic law of the state is the origin of all rights of all citizens, and none predate that document or are derived from any higher source of authority. Modern constitution-based nation-state elites cannot accept the premise that there exist within their jurisdiction certain groups whose rights and privileges derive from some supraconstitutional origin. Such a premise would erode severely the very nature of nation-state sovereignty.

The Spanish position on the two statutory provisions is that the operative wording in both has to do with the paramount authority of the 1978 constitution. In other words, while the *derechos históricos* of the Basques are guaranteed by the constitution, they can only be given form and reality within the framework that the constitution establishes, and then only if all parties recognize the ultimate supremacy of the constitution. This the Basques have been unwilling to do.

The refusal of the Basques to accept the legitimacy of the Spanish constitution has been demonstrated on several occasions. In the 1978 referendum on the constitution, for example, the Basque Nationalist party urged its members to abstain as a show of Basque discontent with the document; and abstentions reached 51 percent in the four provinces as a whole, 57 percent in Guipúzcoa and Vizcaya. In 1984, following his election as president by the Basque Parliament, Carlos Garaikoetxea had himself sworn into office before King Juan Carlos had officially proclaimed him elected, as the Spanish constitution requires, on the grounds that Garaikoetxea owed his status to the popularly elected Basque representatives and not to the provisions of the Spanish constitution. After Garaikoetxea's resignation, the *pacto de legislatura* between his successor José Antonio Ardanza and the Basque Socialist leader Txiki Benegas required that Ardanza proclaim his "respect" (*acatamiento*) for the constitution, a step that brought cries of "betrayal" and "vendepatria" from the PNV rank and file membership.

Basque and Spanish elites differ, as well, over the real meaning of "autonomy," a term not defined precisely in the Spanish constitution. Article 2 of the constitution simply reads: "The Constitution is based on the indisoluable unity of the Spanish Nation, the common and indivisible fatherland of all Spaniards, and it recognizes and guarantees the autonomy of the nationalities and regions that comprise it [the Spanish Nation], and the solidarity among them." From that point on, the word "autonomy" is used in the context of Article 2 whenever it appears. For what it is worth, standard dictionary definitions of the word usually emphasize independence or self-government, while political scientists would probably define the word as meaning "mutual independence," that is, that two autonomous political entities do not depend on one another for their powers, their resources or, of course, their existence. It is evident that this is not the meaning given to autonomy in the Spanish context.

Basque nationalist see autonomy as synonymous with federalism, or devolution at the very least, as an irreversible grant of power, and eventually as sovereignty. As recently as April 1985, the Basque Nationalist party's governing National Council issued a proclamation on the occasion of the Basque national holiday, *Aberri Eguna*, in which it pledged the party to continue to struggle "for the freedom *and sovereignty* of Euzkadi."[23] The various regimes in Madrid, on the other hand, have interpreted autonomy as mainly decentralization for administrative reasons, with no fundamental cession of sovereign authority. Conflicts over management and control of the Basque autonomous police force illustrate well these differing perceptions.

Although the Basque autonomy statute foresees the eventual withdrawal of all Spanish law enforcement authorities, and their replacement with forces under the control of the Basque government, real authority is shared by the two governments in such matters as the protection of Spanish citizens in the region and the maintenance of public order. Through a joint Spanish-Basque security committee, Madrid ensures constant monitoring of the status of public order in the Basque provinces, as well as the ultimate right to reinstate direct control over the provinces from Madrid if a deterioration of public security threatens to undermine the interests of the Spanish state in the region.

In October 1982, the first elements of the Basque autonomous police, called the *Ertzainza*, went into service, the first time in history that the maintenance of law and order had been the responsibility of an ethnic Basque law enforcement agency. However, the relatively small size of the force and of its budget, its restricted powers limited primarily to traffic control and building security, and the continued exercise of authority over the maintenance of public order from Madrid have meant that this force is still some distance away from taking over responsibility for all law enforcement in the Autonomous Community. The Spanish minister of interior, through the Spanish representative on the Joint Security Board, exercises authority over such matters as the budget of the *Ertzainza*, the kinds of weapons its members may carry, the zones where they may operate, the extent to which they can become involved in criminal investigations or in immediate crises such as hostage and barricade situations, and so forth. Thus, despite the creation of a Basque police force, the Basque government is not yet ready to assume responsibility for the maintenance of public order, so the Spanish units—the national police and the Guardia Civil—have not yet been withdrawn, nor are they likely to be any time soon.

There is also fundamental disagreement over whether the autonomy process should be, or was intended to be, automatic or negotiated. The Basques believed that once the Autonomy Statute was approved the government established, all the powers envisioned in the statute would be transferred more or less automatically, along with the resources (people and money) and authority necessary to implement them. In Madrid, the view was that each transfer had to be carefully and painstakingly negotiated between the autonomous government that was to receive the authority, and the Spanish government ministry that was to lose it. The intermediary in all cases was to be the Spanish Ministry of Territorial Administration; in the Basque case, as in most others, the arena of conflict was the Joint Commission on the Transfer of Powers.

Despite the goals and objectives of regional self-governance written into each autonomy statute, the mere approval of a statute and election of a legislative assembly did not in itself transfer any power from Madrid to the regions. In each case, a Joint Commission on the Transfer of Powers was established to negotiate on a case-by-case basis the transfer of each specific power or authority. In the Basque case, this commission has been a major obstacle to regional autonomy. Following the reversal of Spanish policy on regional autonomy in 1981, the commission met only twice in all 1982, and agreement was reached on the transfer of only one set of powers. In January 1983, the Basque representative on the commission charged that the process of transfer of powers had been "paralyzed for quite some time." Even when the joint commission has agreed on the transfer of powers, however, their decisions must still be ratified at the political level of the Spanish government and implemented by means of decree. From the Socialist electoral victory in October 1982 to the spring of 1985, no new powers were transferred. Following the *pacto de legislatura* in January 1985, another fourteen powers were transferred; but very few have been transferred since that time.

Detailed negotiation has also been required in the area of regional government financing. The *conciertos económicos* were thought by Basques to make their government substantially self-financing. There were, however, real and continuing problems connected with the negotiation of each year's *concierto* with Madrid. The quota of payments obligated to the Basque government, called the *cupo*, is negotiated painstakingly point by point by representatives of the Spanish and Basque Treasury ministries. So far, the two sides have agreed substantially on the size of the *cupo*, and the Basque government has made its payments each quarter as prescribed. Since the *concierto económico* is treated as a temporary accord that must be renegotiated at regular intervals, however, there is always the risk of deadlocked negotiations and defaulted payments, which would jeopardize the entire arrangement.

An equally perplexing issue has to do with "residual sovereignty." The Basques contend that once a specific question has been debated and included in the devolved powers in the autonomy statute, the Spanish Parliament and Government have in effect yielded up their control over the issue, and cannot presume to legislate further in the area. Madrid's leaders respond that such an interpretation would negate Spanish sovereignty over its territory, which they would find intolerable. These differences in perceptions have been sharpest in the areas of language, television, and education.

As noted earlier, the País Vasco Autonomous Community is one of five that treats with special status a distinctive regional language. The Basque language, Euskera, is a co-official language of the Autonomous Community, sharing that distinction with Castilian. No citizen will be discriminated against because of an inability to speak either language. Eventually, all public sector agencies, including courts and schools, will be required to conduct their business in both languages. The Basque government is to have the requisite political authority and economic resources to make the País Vasco a bilingual population.

On May 20, 1982, the Basque Parliament approved the historic law creating a public agency to manage the region's first dedicated television transmission facility, *Euskal Telebista*. The station began to transmit its programs in early 1983 on a channel assigned to the Basque Autonomous Community by the Spanish government. Programming has been almost entirely in Euskera. From the beginning, the Spanish Government, through the Spanish national television service, has intruded repeatedly into the operations of the station. *Euskal Telebista* has been denied the right, for example, to transmit live broadcasts of soccer games involving Basque teams. Madrid has also denied Basque television the authority to receive and retransmit television signals from nearby French stations or from international broadcasts transmitted by satellite. If *Euskal Telebista* wishes to rebroadcast a satellite transmission of an event like the U.S. Open tennis matches, they must tape the transmission from the Spanish national television broadcast in Bilbao and carry the tape to the Basque station in Durango, from where the rebroadcast can occur.

Education remains a source of considerable uncertainty as far as the powers of self-governance are concerned. While many Basque nationalists believed that the Autonomy Statute granted to their government the right to manage the region's educational affairs as they wished, developments in local school districts have cast doubt on the degree to which this autonomy can run. On several occasions in 1982, non-Basque-speaking parents who did not want their children to learn Euskera protested local school policies that were aimed at making Euskera instruction compulsory. The Spanish Ministry of Education has intervened on these occasions to protect the rights of these non-Basque-speaking parents, and in so doing has left in question exactly how much latitude Basques have to manage their local school affairs. There were also problems at the university level. After the creation of the Basque government in 1980, the University of the Basque Country opened its three campuses (in Lejona, Vitoria, and San Sebastian) to an enrollment of some 35,000 students. This university was governed by the Education Ministry in Madrid until mid-1985, when the *pacto de legislatura* unblocked the transfer of authority for university-level education to the Basque government. Finally, the Spanish Organic Law for the Development of Education (LODE) clearly stakes out Madrid's continuing authority to oversee education at all levels, provisions to the contrary in the autonomy statutes notwithstanding.

Following the work of Arend Lijphart,[24] students of ethnonationalist politics have identified two competing approaches to institutionalizing the legislative expression of "the will of people." The majoritarian approach is to give the right to rule to any group that can achieve a simple numerical majority in the representative assembly, regardless of the interests held to be at stake by the remaining minority (or minorities). The consensus approach requires that ruling majorities must be larger than a mere "50 percent plus one," that legislative majorities must contain (or at least recognize) representatives of significant minorities (even if the minorities could be outvoted numerically), and that minorities should have the opportunity to influence (and even veto) legislative proposals that affect them directly. The contending positions of Basque and Spanish leaders differ on this issue, depending on where they happen to constitute the majority.

In Madrid, the Basque Nationalist party has sought to establish the principles of consensus democracy, since Basque deputies to the Spanish parliament are a numerically insignificant 6 percent of the total. In fact, however, both the UCD and the PSOE have pursued a simple majoritarian strategy. As the Congress of Deputies has organized itself, the Basque minority has been numerically swallowed up by the larger Catalan minority in a parliamentary grouping of the ethnic parties. Basque deputies were denied any representation on the committee of the Cortes that drafted the constitution; and they are generally unrepresented on important ad hoc committees as well. While Basque deputies may intervene forcefully in open floor debate, their ability to influence policy decisions is restricted to instances where they can negotiate informally behind the scenes, and then only if the issue in question is one in which the governing majority party does not have vital interests at stake.

Basque and Catalan parliamentary influence was strong in Madrid only between the second parliamentary elections in March 1979 and the coup attempt in 1981. In the 1979 vote, the UCD emerged as a one-party government that attempted to govern with a minority in the Congress of Deputies (35.2 percent of the vote; 167 seats, with 176 needed for a majority). To ensure his party the necessary working majority, Suárez was prepared to be supportive of Basque and Catalan proposals and aspirations. The Basques are not ignorant of the fact that this was also the time of greatest advances for their cause. After February 1981, the dynamics of the transformation in Madrid altered fundamentally the significance of the ethnic minorities, since the goal of Leopoldo Calvo Sotelo, unlike that of Suárez, was not so much to maintain a voting majority in the Congress as it was to save democracy itself. Not coincidentally, then, Basque leaders believe that the most favorable environment for their interests in Madrid is when the ruling party lacks an absolute majority in the Congress and must therefore bargain with the minorities for votes, but yet is confident enough of the armed forces that they need not fear the consequences of yielding to minority sentiments. Since the peculiar situation of the 1979–1980 period has not been seen again since 1981, we have no way to know whether this was a unique state of affairs, or a structural feature of Spanish politics on which the Basques could base a long-range strategy.

In the Basque Parliament in Vitoria, the Basque Nationalist party was able to form two governments unaided by other parties, so the positions taken by the two groups were reversed, at least until after the November 30, 1986 Basque elections. After both the 1980 and 1984 elections, the PNV had the largest number of deputies, although not a working majority in either case. In the 1980 elections, the PNV took 25 of the 60 seats; but since *Herri Batasuna* deputies did not occupy their 11 seats, the PNV had a de facto working majority of one seat (25 of 49). In the second Parliament, however, the PNV took 32 of 75 seats. With *Herri Batasuna's* 11 seats empty, the PNV had exactly half of the members: 32 of 64. Despite these narrow margins, the PNV sought in both instances to govern alone; in other words, they followed the path of majoritarian democracy. The opposition parties, principally the Basque branches of Spanish parties, and especially the Basque Socialist party (PSE), advocated a consensus model of democracy for the Basque Parliament. Soon after the 1984 elections, PSE leader Txiki Benegas proposed a quasi-coalition government of PNV and PSE to facilitate the passage of legislation and the governance of the country. The then Basque president, Carlos Garaikoetxea, was not very positive about the idea, but talks were begun with the Socialists through late 1984. As the PNV became embroiled in its own internal struggles, which led to Garaikoetxea's resignation in December 1984, discussions of the *pacto de legislatura* were postponed; but the incoming president, José Antonio Ardanza, made such a pact a top priority objective of his government. The pact was signed in January 1985, and the Basque Autonomous Community was governed de facto by a "grand coalition" of the type Lijphart would associate with the consensus model of democracy from that date to September 1986. At that time, because of the split in the PNV and the formation of Carlos Garaikoetxea's new party, President Ardanza dissolved the Parliament and called elections for November 30. The results have already been noted: a thoroughly fragmented political party system, leading to a formal coalition government composed of the PNV and the Basque Socialists. Ironically, then, while the PNV cannot persuade the Socialists to adopt the consensus model in Madrid, the Basque Nationalists have been forced, by their own internal discord, to resort to this model in the País Vasco Autonomous Community.

Finally, the Basques and Madrid differ over the question of homogeneity versus diversity among the seventeen autonomous communities. As we have already seen, Autonomous Communities had spread to all parts of Spain by May 1983. It is not clear whether the authors of the autonomy community system intended their creation to cover all Spain, or only the ethnic homelands; but by 1983, their intentions were irrelevant. All the regions of Spain clamored for their own regimes, whether or not they were ready for such autonomy, or knew exactly what they were going to do with their new power. The proliferation of autonomous regimes from three to seventeen in the space of three years was more than the Spanish system could handle, and led to a call from the center for the "harmonization" of the regimes to reduce the disorder engendered by an increasingly decentralized system. The harmonization effort, of which the LOAPA was the centerpiece, provided the legislative framework within which the Basque and Catalan regions, which had received large grants of power in 1980, would be trimmed back to the same level as the other Autonomous Communities, none of which had the desire or the need for powers as extensive as those of the ethnic homelands.

The Basques and Catalans argue that there is nothing wrong with some Autonomous Communities enjoying special powers or rights that others do not have; in Madrid, the position is that all communities must enjoy approximately the same powers and resources. One area where these differences cause conflict is Spain's relations with the European Community (EC). Entry of Spain into the EC in January 1986 has already produced pressures for harmonization of the policies of the seventeen autonomous regimes in such areas as taxation, agricultural and dairy production, fishing rights, and labor legislation. How can the Spanish government undertake its commitments in Brussels, Madrid has asked, if it cannot force compliance with these policies throughout its territory? Even before Spain became an EC member, the issue of the value added tax (VAT) had already emerged as a source of conflict between Madrid and the Basque government. Upon joining the EC, Spain had to bring its tax system into line with that of the Community, which meant replacing many of the country's existing business or corporate taxes with the VAT. Since the VAT is a fairly complicated tax to levy and collect from an administrative point of view, Madrid argued that the tax could not be collected at the level of the autonomous communities, but instead had to be collected by Madrid. The Basque government replied that it was perfectly capable of collecting the VAT for businesses domiciled in the Basque provinces, and it proceeded to pass its own VAT legislation even before Spain became an EC member. As Spain's membership in the Community deepens and becomes more involved, Basque nationalist leaders fear the appearance of a number of "mini-LOAPAs" in the guise of deals struck in Brussels.[25]

CENTER-PERIPHERY CONFLICT IN POSTINDUSTRIAL SPAIN

The conflict between center and periphery continues to rage across Spain, and probably will continue to do so for years, if not decades. What we are witnessing is nothing less than an unprecedented transformation of a tightly centralized unitary state into disaggregated structures of institutions whose eventual shape and character cannot be predicted. I have, in this chapter, suggested some areas of conflict between ethnic nationalist and Spanish political leaders that seem inescapable. In conclusion, I shall place these conflicts in a somewhat broader historical perspective, and suggest why this center-periphery struggle may prove to be a serious hindrance to Spanish political and economic development over the long term.

How one evaluates the progress made toward the transformation of the Spanish state since 1975 depends not only on the actual facts in the matter but also on one's relative expectations. The historical record demonstrates a mixed set of achievements and failures. On the positive side, constitutional arrangements have made possible the creation of seventeen Autonomous Communities where none existed before, each with its own popularly elected legislative assembly and executive authority, as well as some autonomy in such matters as urban use, highway construction, and education. On the negative side, there are still real limits on the autonomy of these regimes to tax and spend their own money, to maintain public order, and to administer their own court system. Limits also exist in many other areas of public administration.

Those who were somewhat pessimistic in 1975 and 1976 about the ability of Spain to overcome the Franco legacy must regard these achievements with admiration. There were many, including numerous Basques and Catalans, who believed that Spain would resume its civil war once Franco was gone. Merely to build a new democratic system seemed unlikely to these observers in the mid 1970s; creation of a system of regional autonomies would have appeared to them improbable even as late as 1976. On the other hand, there are many ethnic nationalist leaders who have criticized sharply the inability or unwillingness of Madrid's elites to move faster or farther toward genuine self-governance for the ethnic homelands. To these critics, Spain's political leadership has timidly yielded to the armed forces and the neo-Francoist right and thus has failed to fulfill the promise of ethnic autonomy.

A forward-looking perspective is essential for us to gauge the achievements of Spain's political elites in the regional autonomy movement. How we project future trends depends on where on the curve of change we perceive ourselves. In the long run, what will be the historical importance of Basque television or of the *conciertos económicos*? Is the long-term trend positive, in which case the LOAPA will be seen as little more than a meaningless footnote to history; or is the long-term trend stable or even turning downward, in which case the LOAPA is truly reflective of fundamental political and economic relationships in Spain, and accomplishments like the Basque *conciertos económicos* are insignificant. Simply to cite these contrasting perspectives is to remind us once again how close we are in time to these events, and how perilous it is to attempt a forecast of things to come.

When one looks at the Iberian Peninsula from the vantage point of its peripheral ethnic homelands, it is hard to be very optimistic. On the question of regional autonomy, my brief historical review suggests that Spain's leaders in the late 1970s did not really appreciate the full import of what they were setting in motion. If they had known what lay ahead, they probably would not have supported with any enthusiasm full self-governance for the country's ethnic homelands, and certainly not for the country in its entirety.

If there were major gains for regional autonomy in 1979 and 1980, this was partly because all of the "easy" (i.e., noncontroversial) transfers of power were accomplished during this time, but also because the Suárez government felt itself on shaky ground, and needed to shore up its position in the Basque provinces and Cataluña. After the transition period of eighteen months between the coup attempt and the PSOE electoral victory, these conditions no longer applied. All of the remaining transfers were "hard" (i.e., controversial), and the González government felt itself (and democracy in general) strong enough not to need support from the ethnic nationalists. Thus, after a period of euphoria and heady gains, all the parties concerned have been brought back to the hard reality that what they are about is revolutionary in scope; and further progress will come about, if at all, only after a prolonged period of bargaining—leading, it is hoped, to a resolution of some of the differences in perspective I have noted here.

I believe, however, that the real significance of regional autonomy can be assessed only by viewing it in the context of Spain's industrial development. Sometime during the decade of the 1980s, Spain crossed the threshold into advanced industrial or postindustrial status. Unlike the earlier and much better-known political transformation, this transition cannot be identified and labeled until well after it has happened; but the trends appear to me unmistakable:[26]

1. In 1981, 14 percent of Spain's labor force worked in agriculture, down 20 percentage points from 1965, and now on a par with Italy, Japan, and Finland. If the 10 percent level marks an important threshold for advanced industrial status (a level the United States passed in 1960), then Spain should have crossed this line in the middle of the 1980s. At the other end of the labor force, nearly half of all Spanish workers are employed in the service sector, up from 31 percent in 1965, higher than Ireland and Italy, and approaching the Netherlands and Japan. Nearly one-third of Spain's women are now in the work force, greater than Ireland, on a par with Greece, and a bare percentage point or two behind Luxembourg, Holland, and Italy.

2. Spaniards today have a longer life expectancy than Belgians, Austrians, or Finns; live in urban centers to a greater degree than Italians, Austrians, or Americans; and, if daily per capita caloric intake is any indicator, eat better (or at least, more) than Britons, Swedes, or Norwegians. Most remarkably, Spain's population growth rate has begun to slow. Its birth rate of thirteen per thousand is lower than the average of industrial countries, lower than France, Australia, Canada, and the United States. In 1985, a quarter of a million *fewer* babies were born to Spanish mothers than in Franco's last year, 1975. A society that added 7 million to its numbers in the twenty years from 1962 to 1982 will add only 2 million in the next twenty years.

3. Finally, Spain has begun to enter the world of high technology, of electronics, computer, and biological engineering. Electronics and communications is the third largest sector of stocks traded on the Madrid stock exchange, behind banking and utilities, but well ahead of construction, chemicals, and iron and steel. The Spanish government is moving toward the creation of at least one, and perhaps several, privately owned television broadcasting networks, a sure sign of the proliferation of telecommunications facilities needed by high-tech firms. Multinational high-tech firms are beginning to see in Spain a fertile land for investment, especially after the country's entry into the European Community in 1986. Since 1984, Spain has received major investments by ITT, Sony, Phillips, IBM, Sanyo, Digital Electronics, Olivetti, Hewlett-Packard, Grundig, Bull, Fujitsu, and Siemens. But the biggest step in this regard was the 1985 accord between AT&T and the Spanish Telephone Company to invest jointly some $200 million in a microchip factory near Madrid.

If the experience of other West European and North American countries is repeated in Spain, this transition to advanced industrial status must be accompanied by a loosening of the centralized institutions that had been built up during the preceding periods of industrialization. As advanced industrial societies become more complex, diverse, and pluralistic, they require regimes that are more decentralized, disaggregated, and autonomous. In Spain, where the existing local and provincial units may be too small or too restricted in other ways to assume a vigorous role in the management of the society, the solution lies in the creation of middle-range political entities called "meso-governments," smaller than the nation-state, but larger and more encompassing than cities or provinces. If this analysis is correct, it suggests that Spain must eventually disaggregate power as one of the central imperatives of its phase of development. The Autonomous Community system, invented principally to placate ethnic sentiments during a very difficult moment in the country's transition to democracy, offers the obvious answer to this need. Whether the leaders of Spain and of its ethnic nations will be able to see beyond the conflicting perspectives cited here, and seize this historic opportunity, remains, unfortunately, an open question.

NOTES

1. See Robert P. Clark, "Spain's Autonomous Communities: A Case Study in Ethnic Power Sharing," *The European Studies Journal* 2, no. 1 (1985): 1–16.

2. Jaroslav Krejci and Vitezslav Velimsky, *Ethnic and Political Nations in Europe* (New York: St. Martin's Press, 1981), chap. 14.

3. There is disagreement over the number of distinctive languages in Spain. Many Catalans regard Valencian and Majorcan as merely dialects of

Catalan, so they usually refer simply to the "four co-official languages": Castilian, Catalan, Euskera, and Galacian.

4. The term comes from Victor Pérez Díaz, "Gobernabilidad y mesogobiernos: Autonomías regionales y neocorporatismo en España," *Papeles de Economía Española* 21 (1984): 40–76.

5. For a table showing comparative data on the seventeen autonomous communities (size, population, etc.), see Clark, "Spain's Autonomous Communities."

6. "España ya es diferente," *Cambio 16*, no. 586 (February 21, 1983): 26–28. See also "Hoy queda configurado el estado de las autonomías," *Deia* (Bilbao), May 8, 1983.

7. Kepa Bordegarai and Robert Pastor, *Estatuto vasco* (San Sebastian: Ediciones Vascas, 1979).

8. Robert Pastor, *Autonomía, año cero* (Bilbao: Editorial Iparraguirre, 1980).

9. See Ronald Koven, "Basques, Catalans Approve Statute to Restore Home Rule: Franco Banned," *Washington Post*, October 26, 1979. See also *Deia* (Bilbao), October 26, 1979.

10. *Herri Batasuna* customarily polls between 15 and 20 percent of the vote in Basque elections, yet it has never occupied the seats it has won in either the Spanish or the Basque parliaments. The party contends that, since it was outlawed during the time when these institutions were created, it does not regard them as legitimate and refuses to participate in them.

11. See Tom Burns, "Nationalists Mark Decisive Victory in Basque Voting," and "Catalans Pick Nationalists, Humble Madrid," *Washington Post*, March 11 and March 22, 1980.

12. According to Basque leaders, the taxation issue (along with the question of the Basque autonomous police force) was resolved only after the direct intervention of King Juan Carlos, who wanted to make a formal visit to the Basque country after the autonomous government began to function. The king intervened after he was told that his visit would be met with hostility and even violence if he came before the resolution of several key questions, including the financing issue. Regardless, he visited the region in February 1981 and was received with hostility and demonstrations.

13. For the complete text of each autonomy statute, see Enrique Tierno Galván and Antoni Rovira, *La España autonómica* (Barcelona: Bruguera, 1985). For a lengthy discussion of the development of the autonomy system, with a detailed chronology, see Gabriel Elorriaga, *La batalla de las autonomías* (Madrid: Editorial Azara, 1983).

14. Jaime García Anoveros, "Autonomías, un proceso abierto," a three-part article appearing in *El País* (Madrid), May 29–31, 1984.

15. The Andalusian Autonomous Parliament election proved to be the beginning of the end for the UCD. Three months later, Prime Minister Leopoldo Calvo Sotelo dissolved the UCD-controlled Spanish Parliament and convoked elections for October. In these elections, the PSOE won decisively to begin their near-hegemonic control of Spanish politics through the 1980s and beyond, and the UCD essentially ceased to exist, dropping from a governing party to only twelve seats in the 350-member Congress of Deputies.

16. It would be impossible to know the true causal relationship between the February 1981 coup attempt and the reversal of policy in Madrid regarding regional autonomy; but Basque political leaders generally are convinced that

UCD and PSOE leaders opposed granting substantial autonomy to the ethnic homelands from the beginning, and simply used the coup attempt as the rationale for trimming back on devolution steps.

17. See Robert Clark, "'Rejectionist' Voting as an Indicator of Ethnic Nationalism: The Case of Spain's Basque Provinces, 1976–1986," *Ethnic and Racial Studies*, 10, 4 (October 1987): 427–447.

18 Ibid.

19. *El País* (international edition), June 29, 1987.

20. For reasons of space, this section of the study concentrates on relationships between the Basques and Madrid, but most of these observations have validity for other ethnic homelands of Iberia, including especially the Catalans. Also, because of the focus of this essay, I ignore what is in my opinion an equally serious problem: the conflicts among Basque leaders themselves and within the general Basque population. Elsewhere I have discussed the lack of consensus within contemporary Basque political culture. See my article "Dimensions of Basque Political Culture in Post-Franco Spain," in William A. Douglass, ed., *Basque Politics: A Case Study in Ethnic Nationalism* (Reno, Nevada: Associated Faculty Press and Basque Studies Program, University of Nevada, 1985), pages 217–263.

21. Gregorio Monreal, "Annotations Regarding Basque Traditional Political Thought in the Sixteenth Century," in Douglass, *Basque Politics*, pages 19–49. See also J.A. Ayestarán, et al., *Euskadi v el estatuto de autonomía* (San Sebastian: Erein, 1979), pages 11–40.

22. See the series of articles in *Diario vasco* (San Sebastian) and in *Deia* (Bilbao), July 16–20, 1985, reporting on the various speeches and presentations made during a week-long conference on the *derechos históricos* in San Sebastian.

23. *Deia* (Bilbao), April 5, 1985. Emphasis added.

24. Arend Lijphart, *Democracy in Plural Societies: A Comparative Exploration* (New Haven and London: Yale University Press, 1977). Arend Lijphart, *Democracies: Patterns of Majoritarian and Consensus Government in Twenty-One Countries* (New Haven and London: Yale University Press, 1984).

25. A poll published in *El País*, June 9, 1985, showed that supporters of the Basque Nationalist party are, by far, the most pessimistic group in Spain with regard to the impact of Common Market membership.

26. The following is based on data drawn from various sources, including The World Bank, *World Development Report, 1985*, (New York: Oxford University Press, 1985); "Spain Joins the World," (Special Spain Survey), *The Economist*, March 1, 1986; Sandro Armesto, "En 1985 nacerán 250,000 Españoles menos que en 1975," *El Correo Español - El Pueblo Vasco*, February 14, 1985; and Pedro Cases, "La tarta electrónica española," *El País* (Madrid), May 12, 1985.

CHAPTER 3

Ethnonationalism in a Federal State: The Case of Canada

PETER M. LESLIE

Nationalism is, as the many books on the subject attest, a complex phenomenon; the term itself is rich in its connotations. In some contexts "nationalism" is virtually impossible to distinguish from patriotism, or attachment to country or homeland; in this usage, its meaning has nothing to do with racial origin or ancestry, or with such obvious cultural attributes as language or religion. In other contexts, nationalism is a form of group solidarity or community feeling *based on ethnicity rather than territory*; it refers to subjective attachments that demarcate one particular group from other groups within a total population. Here, common ancestry (even if mythical), shared historical memory, and a shared cultural heritage—"culture" in this context encompasses artistic attainment, means and styles of self-expression, and the entire social/religious value system that defines a community—may all contribute to the formation of a distinct society coexisting with others within the boundaries of a single state. This is ethnonationalism.

Within an ethnic minority, particularly a disadvantaged one, the rise of ethnonational sentiment may be a positive phenomenon, contributing to its members' sense of self-worth and to their personal development, which cannot occur other than within a social context. Thus ethnonationalism may fill a need for the individual, supplying an indispensable collective dimension to personal growth or self-fulfillment.

Not everyone, however, views ethnonationalism positively, particularly if it develops into a political movement in which the group demands self-rule. To those having a stake in the existing order, the political mobilization of an ethnic group may be a threatening phenomenon, in view of its potential for causing disruption or division (disorder, secession), or for infringing upon the rights, status, or privileges of other groups. Thus, opposition to ethnonationalism, or at least nervousness about it, may be found equally among members of a dominant ethnic majority and among other, relatively small minorities having only slight power or prestige. Indeed, antinationalism *in the ethnic sense* may also be found within the ethnic group itself, because ethnonationalism may be associated with intolerance. Also, in its more radical forms it may threaten the privileges and prestige of traditional elites, whose past compromises with a dominant ethnic group easily become a target of attack. Thus, there are many whose interest lies in undermining ethnonational organizations and weakening ethnonational sentiment, and who would like to reduce the salience of ethnicity in political life.

These thoughts on ethnonationalism and attitudes toward it explain the choice of subject matter for this chapter. It addresses a straightforward question: What governmental responses to ethnonationalism appear to weaken ethnonational organizations and ethnonational sentiment? And conversely: What responses tend to stimulate and reinforce them? One ought not to expect a categorical answer, partly because not enough is known about ethnonationalism and the factors giving rise to it, and partly because conditions obviously vary from place to place and from time to time. Conceivably, a policy that dampens ethnonationalism in one context may heighten it in another. Nonetheless, a study of historical experience can be illuminating. Potentially at least, a good case study may offer insight on the question whether, for opponents of ethnonationalism, the best strategy is to fight it or to accommodate it.

Among "soft" or accommodative responses to ethnonationalism one may distinguish

1. A *favorable policies* response, which involves conferral of benefits both economic and cultural (for example, providing public services in a minority language)
2. An *enhanced participation* response, which involves taking measures to strengthen the group's presence and influence within the central government—for example, apportioning offices by ethnicity, and making institutional changes to give the group a veto over potentially damaging decisions, or else a direct input into governmental decisions
3. A *decentralist* response, which involves conceding a measure of autonomy or self-government, usually on a territorial basis; such decentralization runs the gamut from devolution of administrative powers and the transfer of fiscal resources, to far-reaching constitutional reform (e.g., creating a federation, or extending the powers of state/provincial governments within an existing federation)

With respect to the decentralist response, an interesting question arises: If it appears that some degree of decentralization strengthens the polity, reducing tension among ethnic groups, is there nonetheless some point at which decentralization may become excessive, leading eventually to the breakup of the country?

The case examined is Canada 1960 to 1987 (some earlier background material is also provided). After 1960, a Quebec-centered, French-language nationalism grew rapidly in strength, but appeared to subside sharply after the idea of sovereignty was rejected by Quebecers in a referendum (1980). In 1982, over vehement denunciations by Quebec provincial politicians from all political parties, but with all-party support in the Canadian Parliament (including the Quebec members), major changes were made in the Canadian constitution. Five years later (June 1987) the federal government and all ten provincial governments reached agreement on the text of further constitutional amendments making it possible for Quebec to recognize the legitimacy as well as the legal force of the constitution. These amendments must be endorsed by the federal Parliament and by all provincial legislatures before going into effect; and it is quite possible that legislative unanimity will not be achieved. Even if it is, the underlying issues, as raised by ethnonationalism, will not be resolved.

Before proceeding with our case study, however, one further remark of a conceptual character is needed. I would like to caution against the thought that one might appropriately adopt a one-dimensional classification of ethnonational movements, ranking them along a continuum from mild to extreme. I am thinking of a continuum where, at the "mild" end there are demands for favorable policy outputs; in the middle, demands for full integration into decision-making processes ("We want in!"); and at the "extreme" end, demands for autonomy or ultimately for independence ("We want out!"). Such a classification of ethnonational movements does map out the historical evolution of ethnonationalism in some countries, and it corresponds to the three types of response already noted (favorable policies, enhanced participation, and decentralization), so there is probably some temptation to see them as a progression. And if life were like this, it would certainly be convenient for the scholar-observer: one could posit a single dependent variable ("ethnonationalism"), its intensity waxing or waning as factors exogenous to the political system bear upon it, while another set of factors, these ones endogenous ("governmental responses"), reinforce or counteract the direction of movement. This conceptualization is tailor-made to the social scientist who would give policy advice to rulers seeking to counteract the dangers of secession and division. It might be assumed that some degree of accommodation is desirable (not too little, not too late); but the policy problem would be to know how much to concede, and when to stop.[1] Is there a point at which making concessions simply encourages the formulation of more extreme demands?

These questions, less abstractly put, have been prominent in Canadian politics for a quarter of a century. They are less salient now, because the "separatist threat" in Quebec has receded, at least temporarily. But perhaps the questions were, throughout this period, wrongly put. The reason for thinking so is that they ignore qualitative differences in the types of demands advanced by various francophone[2] groups, and disregard corresponding qualitative differences in various types of policy response made by Canadian governments—the federal government, the Quebec government, and the governments of other provinces. As an ethnonational movement matures, or grows more militant, it will not necessarily progress from a stage in which favorable policies are demanded, to a stage of claiming enhanced participation, and eventually on to a further stage in which independence is the goal. On the contrary, at least in the Canadian case, francophone ethnonationalism has taken different forms in different parts of the country, revealing or reflecting quite different (indeed incompatible) strategic interests between "Quebec nationalists" and "French Canadian nationalists," most but not all of whom are found among the francophone minorities outside Quebec.

Much of what follows will elaborate these basic observations. Before getting to the main part of the argument, however, it will be necessary to set out a few facts, and to sketch in some of the historical background.

ETHNICITY AND LANGUAGE IN CANADA

Canada is a federation of ten provinces of unequal size and wealth, distinctive in their mix of manufacturing and resource production, and differing in ethnic and linguistic composition (see Table 3.1). In addition, there are two sparsely populated territories with a measure of self-government but (unlike the provinces) without constitutional protection of legislative powers.

As is revealed in Table 3.1, the francophone community in Canada (those for whom French is the language most frequently spoken in the home) is close to 6 million, or one quarter of the total population; of these, 5.3 million or 89 percent reside in Quebec.[3] Quebec is the only province with a francophone majority (83 percent).

The francophone minorities are spread through every province, but are concentrated in areas bordering on Quebec. To the east lies the province of New Brunswick, in parts of which French is the predominant language; 31 percent of the provincial population is francophone. However, the total population of New Brunswick is less than 700,000; and thus, in absolute numbers, there are fewer francophones in New Brunswick than in Ontario, Canada's largest province (total population 8.5 million). The respective

Table 3.1 Canada: Population, Income, Ethnic Origins, and Language
by Province, 1981

	Population (thousands)	Per Capita Income (Index)	Ethnic Origins (%)			Home Language		
			Brit.	Fren.	Oth.	Engl.	Fren.	Oth.
Atlantic Region								
Newfoundland	564	65.3	92	3	5	99.3	0.3	0.4
P.E.I.[a]	121	68.0	77	12	11	96.6	3.0	0.3
Nova Scotia	840	79.0	72	8	19	96.1	2.9	1.0
New Brunswick	689	71.8	54	36	10	68.0	31.4	0.6
Subtotal	2214	72.5	72	16	12	88.2	11.1	0.7
Central Region								
Quebec	6369	92.5	8	80	12	12.7	82.5	4.8
Ontario	8534	107.5	53	8	40	86.0	3.9	10.1
Subtotal	14903	101.1	33	39	28	54.7	37.5	7.8
Western Region								
Manitoba	1014	93.8	37	7	56	86.0	3.1	10.9
Saskatchewan	956	100.5	38	5	57	92.8	1.1	6.2
Alberta	2214	110.9	43	5	51	91.7	1.3	7.0
British Columbia	2714	108.8	51	3	46	91.7	0.6	7.8
Subtotal	6897	106.1	45	5	51	91.0	1.2	7.7
Territories[b]	68	102.4	30	4	66	74.5	1.2	24.2
CANADA	24083	100.0	40	27	33	68.2	24.6	7.2

Sources: Per capita income: *Statistics Canada: System of National Accounts - National
Income and Expenditures Accounts*, (13-201) - 1967–1981, page 46, table 36.

[a]Prince Edward Island
[b]Northwest and Yukon Territories

francophone minorities number 217,000 in New Brunswick and 330,000 in
Ontario. While some communities in eastern and northern Ontario (the areas
contiguous to Quebec) are mainly French-speaking, francophones make up
only 3.9 percent of the total provincial population—considerably less than
the 10 percent whose home language is neither English nor French
("allophones"). A similar pattern obtains in Manitoba, to the west of
Ontario, where the 31,000 francophones make up 3.1 percent of the
provincial population but are outnumbered about 3 to 1 by the 111,000
allophones. In the remaining six provinces the francophone minorities are
small both in numbers and in percentage terms; in all but Nova Scotia and
Prince Edward Island they are numerically less important than the allophone
groups.

    The snapshot provided in Table 3.1 is worth studying, but of course it
conveys none of the historical background and none of the dynamics of a
fairly rapidly changing linguistic situation. Canada's first European settlers

were French; by the time of the British conquest of New France in 1760, they numbered approximately 60,000.[4] British colonial policy allowed them, more out of prudence than from generosity, to retain their own language, social institutions, and religion. The influx of English and Scots, considerably augmented by "loyalists" fleeing the American Revolution, was rapid enough soon to make English the majority language,[5] as well as (by virtue of conquest) the economically, politically, and socially dominant one. However, the high birth rate among the *Canadiens* ensured that French remained the majority language in Lower Canada, later Quebec. The present-day francophone population of 5,257,000 consists overwhelmingly of the descendants of the 60,000 who remained after the British conquest.

That there are nearly 6 million francophones in Canada today is testimony not only to the fecundity of their ancestors, but to the French Canadians' determination to preserve their traditional culture and religion. However, it should be observed (again from Table 3.1) that those of French origin outnumber those who still speak French, implying a process of assimilation especially outside Quebec. Assimilationist pressures are great enough that it has been seriously questioned whether French is now a viable language anywhere but in Quebec and nearby areas in New Brunswick and Ontario, or indeed anywhere at all, including in Quebec itself.[6] As I shall show later in this chapter, differing judgments on this point have created conflicts within the francophone population of Canada, especially between Quebec nationalists and leaders of the francophone minorities in other provinces.

While many Canadians think of their country in terms of duality—emphasizing the existence of two cultural groupings, two societies, or two nations distinguished primarily by language—others stress instead the importance of Canada's multicultural heritage. According to the latter perspective, those of French origin are only one minority group within a nation in which there is in fact no longer any ethnic majority. This is literally correct. In 1981, the largest ethnic group, those tracing ancestry to the British Isles, constituted only 40 percent of the population. In the four western provinces those who are of neither French nor British origin slightly outnumber the combined population of these two groups. Notwithstanding the establishment of communities with heavy concentrations of immigrants from continental Europe (besides from France), the British group has historically been the dominant one, and English has become the adoptive language of the overwhelming majority of immigrants, even in Quebec. Apart from the francophones there is no nonaboriginal minority large enough, or sufficiently compact territorially, to aspire to political independence or indeed to any substantial degree of autonomy. Nor does any other nonaboriginal group show any desire for separateness, if we except a few small agricultural communities of religious sects that have rejected all forms of modernization and have sought to withdraw, to the extent possible, from the rest of Canadian society, and certainly from its public life. On the other hand, various organizations of aboriginal peoples do seek self-governing status for their respective bands, communities, or ethnic nations. Though these groups comprise scarcely one percent of the Canadian population, their claims have a moral force and in some cases a legal foundation (treaties and land claims) that make their situation unique. The aboriginal peoples are thus the only significant exception to an otherwise accurate generalization, that while some of the non-British, non-French minorities may wish to preserve ancestral languages or other aspects of their cultural heritage at the community level, they have chosen to integrate fully with Canadian society. They tend to see Canada as dominantly anglophone, and mainly they like it that way. When they resist the centralization of the Canadian state, as frequently they do, it is generally for economic reasons: their support for provincial autonomy is rooted in economic regionalism rather than in ethnonationalism.

Canadian history can be interpreted as supporting either conception of Canada: as *dualist* (all language groups tend to assimilate either to English or to French; francophones have special rights, even outside Quebec), or as *multicultural but dominantly anglophone* (even if particular ethnic groups, aboriginal and immigrant, retain ancestral languages for communication within the group).

The dualist conception sees Canada as a country whose political institutions have been shaped by two centuries of accommodation between distinct societies having their origins, respectively, in the French colony along the shores of the St. Lawrence valley, and in the British merchants and settlers who flowed in after the conquest in 1760. The first military governors of the new British colony adopted a conciliatory policy, to some extent contrary to royal edict. Their actions were subsequently given official political sanction by the Quebec Act of 1774, which conceded to the French and Catholic population the right to their own institutions in most matters pertaining to the relationship between the individual and the state. Though commercial law and the criminal law were imported from Britain, the conquest in most respects did not affect the daily life of the *habitants*. The position of the Catholic church was, if anything, strengthened relative to what it had been under the French regime. Although the conciliatory policy was challenged in 1839 by Lord Durham, who proposed the assimilation of the conquered people, and although the union of Lower and Upper Canada (two colonies corresponding to the southern parts of Quebec and Ontario today) was effected in 1840 precisely in order to bring about assimilation—in the united colony, French would be a minority language and Catholicism a minority religion—the civil rights of the French/Catholic population continued to be respected under the union. It operated to some extent under the principle of majorities, those of Canada East (Quebec) and Canada West (Ontario), a principle that eventually made governance of the united colony impossible and helped provide the impetus for Confederation—the creation, in 1867, of a four-province federation out of three British colonies (Canada, now split into Quebec and Ontario; Nova Scotia; and New Brunswick).

Whereas for the two Atlantic colonies Confederation meant partial absorption into a larger unit, for the *Canadiens*, the French/Catholic population of Canada East, it meant a return to a more autonomous status. It marked official abandonment of Durham's recommended policy of assimilation, since it established a province in which the *Canadiens* constituted a strong majority and consequently controlled the government. Exclusive jurisdiction over "property and civil rights" was vested in the provinces. This phrase was drawn from the Quebec Act of 1774, where it was used to cover, in the words of a distinguished present-day commentator, "all the law except English criminal law, and except the English public law that came to Quebec as necessary context for English colonial governmental institutions;" by virtue of this phrase, the Quebec Act had established that most of the preconquest law and custom were to prevail in the colony.[7] With Confederation, almost 100 years later, these rights were confirmed; although a number of enumerated federal powers had the combined effect of conferring a significant array of economic powers on the federal government, these were exceptions to the general rule that the provinces were to control property and civil rights. The significance of the general rule, however, was that the French/Catholic population was assured the means of maintaining its own institutions in all the respects then considered essential to the preservation of a distinct society and culture (or value system).

After Confederation this constitutionally entrenched power was reinforced politically by a succession of Quebec governments which vigilantly protected their autonomy, and by the presence in the federal cabinet of a bloc of francophone ministers who likewise sought to ensure that Quebec's authority to order its internal affairs would not be violated. Under these arrangements, the distinctiveness of Quebec's institutions, and therefore of its culture, were preserved in one corner of an overwhelmingly English-speaking continent. The uniqueness of Quebec was evident not only in matters such as education and marriage laws, but also in arrangements for social security, the legal authority of the father in relation to his children and his wife, land tenure and inheritance, and (later on) labor relations.

For the political leaders of the French/Catholic community, however, Confederation was far more than a device to set up a Quebec enclave in which an ancestral culture and inherited social arrangements could be preserved. Expansion was intended. Good land was already in short supply in Quebec, given the rapid rate of natural increase. Young men were moving to New England in order to take up industrial employment, generally with a view to returning home when they had acquired enough savings to buy a farm; but of course some stayed and were assimilated. Thus, the community was subject to attrition, and its leaders hoped instead to reverse the pattern. Their aim was to redirect the surplus population westward into new French/Catholic prairie settlements. Indeed, the area that was to become the province of Manitoba in 1870 already contained roughly equal proportions of English/Protestant and French/Catholic settlers (many of the latter being Metis, or French-speaking people of mixed Indian/European ancestry). Confederation was to be an instrument for building upon this pattern, creating across the prairies a set of bilingual provinces with dual (Catholic and Protestant) school systems.

This aspiration was reflected in the Manitoba Act of 1870. However, the hoped-for immigration from Quebec did not materialize to any great extent, and the francophone population was quickly overwhelmed by the influx of English/Protestant settlers from Ontario. As the demographic balance changed, the linguistic and religious rights of the minority were extinguished. The powerlessness of the minority and the incapacity or unwillingness of the federal government to provide effective assistance were revealed during the 1890s, with the dismantling of Manitoba's separate (Catholic, but also in practice mainly French) school system. By the time Saskatchewan and Alberta were set up in 1905, it was evident that the hopes for the creation of a prairie west that was, in anything like the Quebec sense, "home" to French Canadians, were vain ones. Even so, an attempt was made to offer constitutional guarantees for a separate school system in the new provinces. The attempt failed, as it had in Manitoba. In Ontario also, in 1912, the use of the French language as a medium of instruction (in distinction to its being a subject of study) was prohibited. Here the attack on "bilingual schools" was led by English-language Catholic bishops, who were concerned that a potential public outcry against instruction in French might be focused indiscriminately against separate (Catholic) schools. Thus constitutional guarantees for Catholic education, which were expected also to protect the French language, turned out to be not only ineffectual in this respect but also arguably harmful toward francophone minorities.

While, then, a deliberate attempt was made to create an institutional structure that would foster the development of Canada as a dualist or bicommunal polity, demographic trends have worked against dualism, disappointing the early aspirations of French/Catholic political leaders. Quebecers did not migrate in large numbers to the west, as it was hoped they would; instead, the prairie region was settled mainly by migrants from Ontario and immigrants from Europe. It was alleged by some French Canadian nationalists that the federal government's aggressive immigration policy (especially around the turn of the century) was deliberately aimed at preventing the creation of a bicommunal west. Be that as it may, many settlements were established in which the largest linguistic minority, or in some cases the majority, was neither English nor French. Immigrant groups often formed communities of their own, or became the principal minority in areas where settlers of British origin predominated. As a result, across much of the West today, indeed perhaps throughout the region, most people probably consider that the only practical language is official unilingualism. There is also strong support for a policy of multiculturalism; for example, local school boards may sanction the teaching of ancestral languages or even employ them selectively as a medium of instruction. In most communities these languages are less likely to be French then they are to be German, Ukrainian, Icelandic, or Cree.

Among "multicultural groups" (a term generally used in Canada to designate the non-British, non-French, nonaboriginal population that is nonetheless conscious of its ethnic distinctiveness), the dualist conception of Canada is broadly rejected. To them, as to many who are either of British origin or have developed strong loyalties to Britain and often to the monarchy, dualism is inaccurate as a description and undesirable—even threatening—as a political model. Many would like to see ethnicity and language become irrelevant to politics and policy, diminishing in salience over time, as religion has done. Others support policies to preserve Canada's multicultural heritage, or ancestral customs and languages. Still others would like government to launch affirmative action programs to promote full economic equality among diverse ethnic groups, in other words, to eliminate all correlation between ethnicity and income, or ethnicity and status/occupation. These sets of attitudes or prescriptions overlap, but all are sharply distinguished from dualism, both as a principle for guiding policy and as a criterion for shaping political institutions and for filling public offices.

FRENCH CANADIAN AND QUEBEC NATIONALISM

The failure of post-Confederation attempts to build a bicommunal West, equally English/Protestant and French/Catholic, gave rise during the 1880s to an enclave-creating French Canadian nationalism. The leaders of this movement, notably Honoré Mercier (premier of Quebec, 1887–1891), took the view that the only effective protection for their religion, language, and culture was constantly to reaffirm the autonomous constitutional status of Quebec, fighting for the respect of "provincial rights" against federal intrusions. Political autonomy offered cultural protection, enabling those French Canadians who lived in Quebec to withdraw to a large extent from the mainstream of North American life, from both the economy and the culture. Smaller enclaves could also be created in other provinces, and could be supported, to the modest extent possible, by the main body of francophones in Quebec.

Within Quebec the French Canadians could and did create a set of institutions that they controlled. Occupying the central position was the Roman Catholic church, which performed many functions that elsewhere lay within the purview of government. Indeed, the church was more pervasive socially and culturally than government, and in key respects was able to shape policy, especially in education, social affairs, and family law. The council of bishops set the curriculum of the public schools and supervised the hiring of teachers. The church also set up a network of "classical colleges" (so named for the emphasis of Latin and Greek, and more generally on humanistic studies), many of which were directly administered and staffed by religious orders. Since the classical colleges were the unique gateway to all leadership positions, the church enjoyed a monopoly on the selection and training of the entire elite of French Canadian society: its priests, lawyers, and doctors (engineers and corporation executives were notably rare among French Canadians). Hospitals, orphanages, and charitable institutions too were run by the church; and, with the advent of the twentieth century, emerging organizations such as savings institutions, mutual insurance companies, and trades unions were established as confessional bodies, the activities of which were influenced if not controlled by a chaplain or religious adviser. The teaching of the church stressed that agriculture was morally superior to industrialism, that French Canada had a "civilizing mission" within a secular and materialistic North America, and that the state was to be mistrusted, especially if democratic (i.e., claiming authority from the people rather than from God). The practice of weekly meetings between the archbishop of Quebec and the premier did not cease until the 1960s.

Obviously, the federal makeup of the country has offered very different opportunities for French Canadian nationalists, according to whether they have lived in Quebec or in other provinces. Quebec could become a far stronger enclave than could be created by francophones in other provinces, where it was not possible to set up a pervasive network of institutions consonant with and supportive of the culture. Nonetheless, the overall character of French Canadian nationalism was the same outside Quebec as within it. Language and religion were regarded as mutually supporting; indeed, to the extent that it is possible to make the distinction, one could probably say that Catholicism was the essence of the culture, and language a strategic supporting instrument—hence the famous declaration of the nationalist Henri Bourassa, 1910, that language was to be cherished as guardian of the faith.[8] The three dominant features of French Canadian thought, as identified by the historian Michel Brunet (1958)— agriculturalism, messianism (the "civilizing mission"), and antistatism[9]— were shared by francophones in Quebec and in other provinces. And perhaps more significant in view of its contrast with the situation that was to develop after 1960, the strategic situation of Quebec and non-Quebec francophones did not diverge. it was a shared tenet of traditional French Canadian nationalism that the existence of a strong and autonomous Quebec was a precondition for upholding, to the extent possible, the rights of French Canadians elsewhere in the country.

It was logical, and to some degree remains so today, to regard the francophone minorities in other provinces as extensions of the main concentration of Canadian francophones, located in Quebec. A politically strong Quebec was in the interest of the smaller minorities, for two quite distinct reasons. First, their leaders, if not actually raised in Quebec, would necessarily be educated there (France was not only distant, but secular and even anticlerical); cultural self-preservation demanded the maintenance of close ties between francophone elites in Quebec and the other provinces. Or to put the matter more simply, the non-Quebec francophones have never been strong enough to constitute self-contained societies, which francophone Quebec largely considered itself to be. Second, secure in their home province, and forming (as they have done almost consistently since 1867) a solid bloc within the ruling party in Ottawa, French Canadians could wield substantial power in federal politics. This was important for Quebecers, but also for the minorities outside Quebec, for without a federal government in which the francophone presence was strong, the latter had no significant institutional or political basis of support, except perhaps in New Brunswick after 1960.

It must be acknowledged that the help given by the federal government to francophone minorities outside Quebec has been,until recently, extremely limited. In particular, the idea that Ottawa could make good on constitutional guarantees for minority schooling has been more of a hope than a reality. The constitution provides for federal remedial legislation if a province infringes established minority educational rights (Catholic or Protestant, rather than English or French). However, this clause has never been used. In 1896, the federal Conservative government of the day promised to invoke it to reestablish the separate school system that the province of Manitoba had disbanded, and fought an election campaign partly on this basis; but the Liberal party (ironically, under its French Canadian leader Wilfrid Laurier) campaigned instead for the respect of provincial autonomy, and won. Laurier argued that a political compromise over the Manitoba schools question was preferable to an imposed solution, which in any case could not be administratively enforced short of establishing a network of federally financed schools for the minority. While this incident suggests that the identity of interest between Quebec and non-Quebec francophones has been less than perfect, it is probably accurate to say that the French Canadian members of Parliament from Quebec have acted to support, to the extent possible,the interests of non-Quebec francophones. Perhaps they made more compromises than they needed to; but for the most part the leaders of both groups worked together in the defense of French Canadian interests.

One feature of traditional French Canadian nationalism was its acceptance of unequal economic status of anglophone and francophone even within Quebec. While a few isolated voices preached the desirability of taking control of industrial development, the dominant theme of the nationalists was the moral superiority of the rural way of life and the special vocation of the French race in North America. This second theme was captured in its most lyrical form in a sermon by Bishop L.-A. Pâquet in 1902:

> As for those of us who believe in God, . . [we know] how, within the hierarchy of societies and empires, He has assigned to each one of these races a distinct role of its own. . . . We have the privilege of being entrusted with this social priesthood granted only to select peoples. . . . Our mission is less to handle capital than to stimulate ideas; less to light the furnaces of factories than to maintain and spread the glowing fires of religion and thought, and to help them cast their light into the distance.[10]

As this statement illustrates, French Canadian nationalism became a vehicle for a particular ideology that not only accepted economic inequality between the "English and French races" but extolled the economic subordination of the francophones as evidence that they had resisted the temptation (as, again, Bishop Pâquet put it) "to step down from the pedestal, where God has placed us, to walk commonly among those generations who thirst for gold and pleasure."[11] With such sentiments being inculcated by the leaders of French Canadian society, it was all the easier for the anglophones, whose economic dominance was established through the Conquest, to maintain a virtual monopoly over the key positions within the Quebec economy. Their economic power also conferred upon them political power and social privilege. Though their direct participation in Quebec provincial politics was extremely limited, anglophones took advantage of their strategic position as investors and employers, controlling the economic policies of the Quebec government and ensuring that they enjoyed rights in Quebec that francophones either never had or quickly lost elsewhere in Canada.

The dominant position of the anglophones had always been obvious insofar as English capital, whether of British, U.S., or Canadian origin, controlled commerce and industry. However, the extent of the economic subordination of French Canadians even with Quebec was not generally realized until it was devastatingly revealed in 1965 in a study written for a federal government inquiry. The findings, later summarized by one of the authors, demonstrated not only that French Canadians had lower incomes than any other listed group except those of Italian origin, but also that no factor other than ethnicity could be found to explain a substantial part of the differential. In other words, the correlation between income and ethnicity did not disappear if one adjusted for factors such as age and schooling; after doing so, the average French Canadian still had an income about 15 percent lower than counterparts of British descent,[12] and francophones were near the bottom of the hierarchy when one correlated income and ethnicity.

The date of this study (1965) helps explain the widespread attention it received (there were banner headlines in the daily press). Quebec was already launched into a so-called "Quiet Revolution," a period of cultural turmoil, institutional change, and political innovation. The values that earlier had been extolled by the clergy and other elements in the traditional elite were case aside; the Catholic trade unions became the "national" trade unions, and other organizations—the cooperatives, the principal farmers' organization, and the credit unions—also deconfessionalized; the public role of the church was reduced and the role of the state expanded enormously. A controversial measure, accepted by the bishops but strongly contested by much of the traditional elite and by some of the clergy, was the creation of a Ministry of Education in 1964, a move that transferred control over curriculum to the state. It also paved the way for the building of a public secondary and postsecondary system of education emphasizing student choice and offering a wide variety of technical and vocational courses. Equally significant were reforms in the field of income support and social services. Quebec became (and remains) the province of Canada having the most highly developed welfare state, where previously it had probably ranked at or near the bottom (comparisons on this are difficult to make, because the welfare system was run by the church, not the state).

These changes were accompanied, and to a significant degree were guided, by a new form of ethnonationalism. During the late 1950s or early 1960s, French Canadian nationalism was largely supplanted, within Quebec, by a new Quebec-centered nationalism. This new social movement emphasized the importance of equipping the francophone majority to fully enter the modern world. The complaint arose that francophones had obtained limited political rights, in the form of provincial autonomy in social and cultural affairs, at the price of ethnic stratification. Traditionally, as a community they could control those matters that the economically dominant anglophones conceded were internal to their own group, but could not overstep this boundary. The new Quebec nationalists began to assert that francophones, though numerically a strong majority, had accepted *minority status* within their own province. It was also said that French Canada was an "incomplete" or "decapitated" society that functionally could exist only in symbiosis with anglophones, upon whose entrepreneurship francophones necessarily relied to create the material basis for the existence (and certainly for the standard of living) of French Canada.

A potent factor in bringing about this new perception of reality in Quebec was the realization that the old ideology and the behavior that was both justified and shaped by the ideology constituted a dead-end street. Observers complained that the ideology pretended Quebec was something other than it was, a rural society; government had encouraged, through deals made with anglophone capitalists, the industrialization of the province. Indeed it was essential to do so, because without industrialization Quebec could not sustain its existing population, let alone experience demographic expansion. On the other hand, government had done nothing to equip the population to take their place in an industrial economy and society. The education system, in particular, was woefully outmoded. A sharp disjunction had arisen between how Quebecers lived and, on the other hand, the ideology that prescribed how they *should* live; and the institutional structure was adopted to the ideology rather than to reality. A Quebec commission of inquiry, 1956, analyzed the situation in this way:

> Thanks to [provincial] autonomy, the French-Canadians have . . . as a majority group, the political initiative of their cultural and social life and partly of their economic life. . . . [However], the advent of large-scale capitalism and the rapid expansion of industry brought them into the embrace of an economy whose control does not belong to them. . . .
>
> If the industrial revolution, in progress for half a century, has corrected certain consequences of the preceding century's economic and social policy—as, for example, emigration—it has, on the other hand, generalized the disharmony which that policy had already created between the French Canadian and his social structures. . . . The whole institutional system which, up to now, has been the broadest and most synthetic expression of French Canada's special culture, must be completely re-made along new lines. It was not a current of ideas . . . drawn from abroad which modified the milieu of French Canadian culture. . . . Primarily it was the practice of economic and political institutions of British origin which resulted in the creation of an individualistic and liberal mentality among a people whose religious, intellectual and social traditions had within them nothing either individualistic or liberal. . . . Men think along certain lines, but they are induced to live along certain other lines, and they end up thinking as they lie. It is not otherwise that assimilation proceeds.[13]

In short, the creation of an enclave or a policy of withdrawal, though intended to prevent assimilation, was not only incapable of preventing assimilation but in the long run was actually bringing it about. The idea caught hold that the whole institutional system, including and perhaps especially the schools, must be remade along new lines. When the reactionary Premier Duplessis died in 1959, the floodgates opened and Quebec entered upon its Quiet Revolution. Traditional French Canadian nationalism, emphasizing cultural protection, was transformed into a more positive "social nationalism"[14] or a "nationalism of growth"[15] that demanded the extension of Quebec's policy responsibilities and fiscal resources. The new Quebec nationalism created turmoil within francophone Quebec society, but also had other profound effects: new tensions arose between anglophones and francophones, both within Quebec and across Canada, and the structure of the Canadian federal system was called into question.

The essence of the new Quebec nationalism, distinguishing it from French Canadian nationalism, was and is its desire to vest in the francophone community of Quebec, as fully as is possible for any people, full control of its own destiny. That is something very different from securing the extension of, and respect for, minority rights, permitting the building of an enclave within the larger society. The change in the definition of the situation was captured by the federal Royal Commission on Bilingualism and Biculturalism in 1965, when the commissioners wrote:

> What is at stake [in this conflict between ethnic groups] is the very fact of Canada. . . . The chief protagonists, whether they are entirely conscious of it or not, are French-speaking Quebec and English-speaking Canada. And it seems to us to be no longer the traditional conflict between a majority and a minority. It is rather a conflict between two majorities: that which is a majority in all Canada, and that which is a majority in the entity of Quebec.[16]

Perceptive as this statement was, it should not be taken to mean that French Canadian nationalism had disappeared. It continues to exist in parallel with Quebec nationalism; indeed, while Quebec nationalism does have its sympathizers among francophones in other provinces, for the most part these minorities are wary about the expansion of Quebec's powers. They want dualism—of anglophone and francophone across Canada, not of Quebec and the other nine provinces. This point must be made at once, and it will be developed in the next part of the chapter; but for now it will be useful to focus on the burgeoning of the nationalist movement within Quebec.

The new Quebec nationalism defined the political goals of the Quiet Revolution, a cultural phenomenon of the early- to mid-1960s that saw the infusion among Quebecers of a new spirit of self-reliance and self-confidence, the opening of mind toward outside currents of thought, a rejection of traditional authority (especially the authority of the church), the flaunting acceptance of newly permissive sexual mores, the taking of giant strides toward the liberation of women, and the intense politicization of a society committed to building its own future by grasping the levers of political power. There was a complete inversion of the old attitude towards the state as an alien force, controlled by self-seeking politicians who made too many compromises with *les Anglais* or *les Américains*: René Lévesque, then minister of natural resources in the Liberal government of Jean Lesage (1960–1966) captured the new spirit when he declared: "The state is one of us, the best among us"—a silly statement in any other context, but redolent with meaning when seen against the backdrop of antistatism that characterized traditional French Canadian thought.

With the Quiet Revolution, Quebec was launched upon a nation-building enterprise in which the existing federal structure appeared, to many, an unwelcome constraint. The government of Jean Lesage, which upon taking office in 1960 was at best ambivalent towards the forces of change (for it contained some of the most reactionary elements in Quebec, as well as the most progressive), eventually put together and launched a vast program of reforms. Those in the educational field have already been mentioned; others included the reshaping of social assistance, the initiation of a scheme of public contributory old-age pensions (which incidentally gave the provincial government control over investment funds so vast that the agency responsible for managing them could operate, Lesage boasted, something like a central bank for Quebec), the implementation of a new labor code, the reshaping of municipal government, sweeping changes in administrative practices, and a new and active role for the provincial government in economic development. The last-mentioned aspect of government activity involved a huge program of road construction, the nationalization of private electric utilities, and the creation of a cluster of public corporations to promote capital formation, resource development, and the restructuring of industrial enterprise.

Inevitably the expanded activities of the Quebec government bumped up against those of the federal government, and also frequently incurred the opposition of private (mainly anglophone) capital. Quebec wanted to do things in its own way, and the coherence of its policy innovations was limited by its having to share the control of legislative and administrative instruments with Ottawa. Quebec wanted to move fast, and in its own direction. However, it is a characteristic of Canadian federalism that most policy fields are shared between the federal government and the provinces. Not surprisingly, then, government leaders constantly expressed frustration at being restrained to a pace of change, or to a type of policy design, that the rest of the country would accept. Also, the suddenly active provincial government, which was engaged in the greatest program of public works in the province's history as well as the very considerable extension of public services, found itself in desperate need of more tax dollars. Both factors brought the provincial government into increasingly bitter conflict with Ottawa, and sometimes with the other provinces.

Meanwhile, outside government, ethnic tensions were mounting. Economic inequality, formerly seen as inevitable or simply not questioned, began to be perceived as resulting from discrimination and was correspondingly resented. Francophones began to question why they had to develop a bilingual capacity while anglophones remained unilingual; francophones began to feel more keenly their minority status within a province in which they constituted the vast numerical majority. They began to aspire to the status of *majoritaire*—the person "who has never been forced to choose between this culture and his career, has never had to earn his living in a second language, and has never learned that to speak his own language means to be reprimanded, ineffectual, or marginalized; a person who requires only his own language to satisfy all his daily needs, and for whom a second language, if he has one, is a hobby."[17] Naturally, it was those who were in greatest daily contact with anglophones, whether in business or in the federal public service, who experienced the greatest resentments and, in some cases, humiliations. Such experiences provided the emotional charge that, in combination with the frustrations of the new elites who found themselves without adequate policy control and/or fiscal resources, eventually led to the formation of a separatist (antifederalist, but in relatively few cases anti-Canadian) movement in the mid-1960s. The movement was sporadically violent, with occasional bombings of mailboxes or of federal government installations such as an armory. In 1970 there were two high-profile kidnappings, one of a British diplomat and one, which ended in murder, of a provincial cabinet minister.

The bombings and kidnappings were the violent fringe of a generally peaceful and democratic movement for the expansion of Quebec's constitutional powers. Some sought to achieve their goals within the federal system (under a "special status" involving the conferral of powers not exercised by other provincial governments), others aimed to establish a form of confederacy (political sovereignty, but in full economic union with the rest of Canada, an arrangement known as "sovereignty-association"); and still others looked toward the creation of a fully independent Quebec state. The debate among Quebec nationalists regarding the extent of the necessary and desirable powers of the Quebec state—whether the goal should be special status, sovereignty-association, or fully separate statehood—took shape after the reforming Lesage government was defeated at the polls in 1966. The leader of the nationalist wing of the provincial Liberal party, René Lévesque, tried unsuccessfully to move the party (which as early as 1964 had dissociated itself organizationally from the federal Liberal party) towards a constitutional program that would significantly reduce federal legislative powers within Quebec territory and transfer additional fiscal resources to the Quebec government. The party rejected Lévesque's proposed constitutional formula. With this rebuff, he walked out of the party's policy convention and founded a movement for sovereignty-association. The small breakaway group became a rallying point for a number of left- and right-wing separatist movements and political parties, and in 1968 constituted itself as the Parti Québécois (PQ) with Lévesque as leader.

The debate within the PQ on appropriate constitutional options continues to this day. The PQ's main problem has been that its active members (the *militants*) tend to be oriented towards a more radical constitutional platform than the Quebec electorate has so far been willing to endorse. Since the mid-1960s support for outright independence has hovered in the 15 to 20 percent range in cross-province samples, never higher. Caught between its own militants and the electorate, the PQ has vacillated between hard- and soft-line positions. The party won in 1976 on the basis of a promise that it would conduct "good government" and would put off any constitutional adventures until, by referendum, the people of Quebec had endorsed the principle of sovereignty-association. This they refused to do; the vote, held in May 1980, rejected the government's request for a mandate by 59.6 to 44.4 percent, on an 85 percent turnout. Since the referendum, the PQ has been notably moderate and even evasive about its constitutional option, although at the close of 1987 its leader Pierre-Marc Johnson, successor to Lévesque, resigned as a result of dissension from hard-liners within the caucus. The most likely successor, former Minister of Finance Jacques Parizeau, endorses an unambiguously *indépendantiste* position, sovereignty without economic association except in the context of generalized North American free trade.

Many people, especially outside Quebec, appear to think that Quebec nationalism is in terminal decline, effectively having been dealt a death-blow by the referendum. The politicization of the society, which was so evident during the 1960s and 70s, gives evidence of having waned considerably. Polls show that Quebec youth today are largely uninterested in politics, federal-provincial relations, and relations between language groups. They are preoccupied by personal goals; they want most of all to feel good about themselves ("*se sentir bien dans sa peau*"). Family relationships, personal friendships, and work matter most of all to them.[18] Thus it comes as a surprise that a poll conducted in November 1987 showed support for sovereignty-association at 44 percent. Another poll, restricted to the Quebec City area, asking respondents "Are you for or against the independence of Quebec?" yielded 28 percent yes, 55 percent no, and 17 percent undecided.[19] Perhaps of equal interest is that these results appear not to have been reported outside the province. But it was ever thus: in English Canada the modal attitude toward nationalist demands emanating from Quebec (to the extent people have been aware of them) has been neglect and complacency, so that each fresh crisis has caught both the politicians and an indignant public by surprise.

RESPONSES TO QUEBEC NATIONALISM

French Canadian nationalism has required some sensitivity and forebearance from anglophone Canada, and has called for forms of accommodation that have not always been forthcoming (especially in the two world wars, with major crises over conscription; but schools issues, language issues, and civil liberties issues also have been important, and remain so). *French Canadian nationalism* has been not a challenge or a threat to the rest of the country. Not so with *Quebec nationalism*, especially in the period 1976–1980 (from the election of the Party Québécois government until the referendum). Although some nationalist leaders, René Lévesque in particular, tried to allay fears, they had little success in doing so. Lévesque presented sovereignty-association as an arrangement that would benefit the rest of the country as much as Quebec (because it would liberate "Canada" from having to put up with Quebec's opposition to policy initiatives favored by "Canadians"); however, non-Quebecers viewed the PQ option as "separatist," rending the country in two. The Quebec anglophones felt particularly threatened, though Lévesque assured them that their rights would be scrupulously respected within a politically sovereign Quebec. And many francophone Quebecers too were hostile, some because they were worried that independence would impose an intolerable economic cost, and some because they regarded ethnic nationalism as inherently illiberal and reactionary.

Federal political parties and politicians have responded to Quebec nationalism with a mixture of *incomprehension* (the Conservative government of John Diefenbaker, 1957–1963), *accommodation* (the Liberal government of Lester Pearson, 1963–1968, and also the Conservative governments of Joe Clark, an eight-month interlude in 1979–80, and Brian Mulroney, 1984 to present), and *rejection* (the Liberal governments of Pierre Trudeau, 1968–1979 and 1980–1984). Of these three types of response, it is the strategic choice between accommodation and rejection that interests us.

The accommodative response, as exhibited by Pearson and by a succession of Conservative party leaders after Diefenbaker (Robert Stanfield, and then Clark and Mulroney), combined all three elements that were noted at the beginning of this chapter: favorable policies, enhanced participation, and decentralization. At the urging of the editor of the influential Montreal daily *Le Devoir*, Pearson committed himself during the 1963 election campaign to create a Royal Commission on Bilingualism and Biculturalism (RCBB). The commission was instructed to "recommend what steps should be taken to develop the Canadian Confederation on the basis of an equal partnership between the founding races [sic], taking into account the contribution made by the other ethnic groups," and to propose ways of "promoting bilingualism, better cultural relations and a more widespread appreciation of the basically bicultural character of our country."[20] The RCBB's multivolume report recommended the recognition of English and French as official languages of Canada. This meant that French and English would be placed on an equal footing as languages of work in the federal public service, and also that citizens should have the right, wherever practicable, to communicate with government (and that meant also receiving written and oral responses) in the official language of their choice. The aim was partly to make all francophones feel that the federal government was equally at their service as at the service of anglophones, and partly to recruit and hold talented francophones to the upper ranks of the federal bureaucracy. (One is reminded of Lévesque's "the state is one of us"—though of course *he* meant the Quebec state.)

The goals and principles enunciated by the RCBB were accepted by the Pearson government, and have since been essential features of federal policy under Trudeau, Clark, Turner (Liberal prime minister briefly in 1984), and Mulroney. They have involved the bilingualization of the upper ranks of the federal public service, a policy supported by the creation of French-language work units for certain specialized functions. The bilingualism objective required extensive French-language training for senior bureaucrats and also favored the hiring of bilingual personnel (often francophones). The shortcomings of the policy as actually implemented are obvious, and are documented each year in the report of a commissioner of official languages, but the achievements have been considerable when measured against past experience. Far less progress has been made in moving toward other goals formulated by the RCBB: those of developing a bilingual capacity among business leaders, and introducing bilingualism in major associations operating on a cross-Canada scale. Nonetheless, it is now widely accepted among anglophone elites in both the public and the private sectors in Canada that acquisition of a working knowledge of French is a considerable career advantage. Upwardly mobile parents across the country send their children to bilingual schools or French-immersion programs.

The language policies initiated under Pearson were an important step toward extending francophone rights both within Quebec and in other provinces, and were a vital support for achieving a high degree of francophone participation in the federal public service.[21] There were other aspects as well to the "favorable policies" and "enhanced participation" types of response to Quebec nationalism. In fact, a qualitative difference in these areas, distinguishing the 1960s from earlier periods of Canadian history, was attention to economic issues of special concern to Quebec. Regional development was one of these. Whereas, during the nineteenth century, Montreal had been Canada's leading city, by the 1950s, it had been surpassed by Toronto as a manufacturing and financial center. South-central Quebec, originally a beneficiary of national economic policies at least on a par with southern Ontario, now began to resent the shift of the economic center of gravity to Toronto, and to interpret this change as a consequence of neglect by Ottawa. Naturally, Quebecers compared their province with wealthy Ontario, not with the far poorer Atlantic provinces. Thus, during the 1960s, a time when regional development began to be a major preoccupation of the federal government, Quebec demanded to gain a substantial share of federal developmental expenditures. Moreover, economic disparities within Quebec, between the Montreal region and the more remote areas of the province, began to receive considerable attention. The provincial government saw itself as having a responsibility for reducing such intraprovincial disparities, but wanted financial and other forms of support from Ottawa. The response was inevitably less generous than hoped for, but was nonetheless far from negligible.

As with language policies, the Quebec-focused economic initiatives of the 1960s have been carried forward to the present day. During the 1960s a pattern was established whereby the Quebec government and the Quebec caucus in the federal Parliament have both lobbied hard for maximum levels of federal expenditure in the province, especially in the areas of business bailouts, public works (transportation facilities, government offices), and subsidies to agriculture. Several interprovincial "balance sheets" have been produced by various governments, showing federal tax dollars collected and monies expended on a province-by--province basis. In each case the intent has been to demonstrate that a particular province either has a valid economic grievance, or that there is not reliable evidence supporting such an allegation. (The figures purport to show that certain provinces are net contributors to interregional redistribution through the agency of the federal government, and others net recipients.) Quebec has been a grievor, but in other provinces the widespread impression is that Quebec has been and continues to be treated with conspicuous favoritism by Ottawa. The data themselves are inconclusive,[22] and attitudes inevitably are formed on high-profile decisions such as the award (1986) of a multiyear, multibillion-dollar maintenance contract for fighter aircraft. A Montreal firm received the contract, although the federal government's own evaluation showed that the bid of a Winnipeg firm was not only cheaper but technically superior. This decision had a major and strongly negative impact on public opinion in the western provinces, where it was interpreted as evidence of two sorts of discrimination against them. On the one hand, it was said that big provinces routinely get favored over smaller ones; on the other hand, resentments were deepened by the conviction that Quebec is selfish and unreasonable, and that the federal government can't or won't stand up to criticism by French Canadians. Obviously, with the concentration of francophones in Quebec, it is impossible consistently to disentangle regional issues from ethnolinguistic ones; Quebecers and non-Quebecers alike tend to see policies that directly or even incidentally touch the special interests of that province as evidence of discrimination either for or against franophones. Although perceptions of what's "fair" often differ, there would certainly be general agreement that Ottawa is attentive to the economic problems of Quebec to a degree not witnessed prior to the 1960s. It is generally thought, probably correctly, that the rise of Quebec nationalism is mainly responsible for the change.

The accommodative response to Quebec nationalism, as originally formulated by the Pearson government, was evidenced in other ways as well. As noted, federal bilingualism was introduced in part to enhance francophone participation in the federal bureaucracy; similarly, at the political (cabinet) level, Pearson made a determined and successful effort to recruit top-flight francophones. When the Quebec leadership with which the Liberals had captured power in 1963 began to crumble (which it did shortly after the new government took office), Pearson turned to Jean Marchand, a prominent Quebec labor leader who was not a Liberal and was not even active in politics, to become his "Quebec lieutenant." Marchand refused to take the plunge unless places were created also for two close associates, Pierre Trudeau and Gérard Pelletier. The three announced their adhesion to the Liberal party at a joint press conference in 1965, and soon formed the francophone core of the party and of the government. They in turn recruited others. Trudeau succeeded Pearson as party leader and prime minister in 1968, and launched the period of "French power" (as some disgruntled anglophones termed it). For example, French Canadians, for the first time, were appointed to senior economic portfolios in the cabinet. It is now unthinkable that a federal government should be formed if it lacks strong, high-prestige francophones occupying some of the key positions.

The final element in the accommodative response to Quebec nationalism, as shaped by Pearson—but totally rejected by Trudeau after 1968—was decentralization. When Quebec sought the extension of its policy control and fiscal resources, Pearson went along. Of course other provinces, too, put forward similar demands, especially for gaining a larger share of the income tax (which in all provinces but Quebec is a single tax administered by the federal government, with a portion of the total yield being transferred to the provincial treasuries). Ottawa responded by handing over more "tax points" to the provinces, a trend that had been going on since the early 1950s and had been accelerated by the Diefenbaker government. At the same time, new federal initiatives were inducing the provinces to expand the role of government in two major ways—by formulating policies to shape the structure of the economy both nationally and regionally, and by setting up a welfare state that is modest by European standards but highly developed or overdeveloped by American ones. The overall thrust of federal policy fitted perfectly with the new statism in Quebec, except that Quebec now wanted, in many areas, to go farther and faster than Ottawa, and in any case to assert its own priorities. In economic and social policy alike Quebec sought to take the lead, looking to Ottawa to play a complementary and supporting role, especially by supplying a large portion of the necessary funds. Other provinces shared some of the Quebec perspective, but on the whole were readier to go along with federal initiative so long as they did not impose an undue burden upon their own treasuries. (For example, all provinces but Saskatchewan initially opposed the introduction of public compulsory medical insurance in 1966, fearing the costs it would entail; Saskatchewan liked it because the federal scheme was modeled on its own program, which would remain in place but with Ottawa now paying about half the cost.) Quebec's concerns were equally financial and, in the most fundamental sense, political; the other provinces' concerns were mainly financial and administrative. Their complaints focused on the existence of shared-cost arrangements that generated irresistible electoral pressures to enter schemes they could ill afford. The Pearson government responded to some of these concerns (1965) by offering fiscal compensation to any province that "opted out" of federal program set up on a shared-cost basis—i.e., established on the basis of an intergovernmental agreement that Ottawa would pay about half the cost of a particular program lying within an area of provincial jurisdiction, so long as that program met certain stipulated features of policy design. The opting-out arrangement would give at least the appearance of greater provincial policy control, on condition that the program remained in place with its main features intact. However, only Quebec took advantage of the opting-out scheme. A careful look at the new arrangement shows that Quebec gained little if anything out of the arrangement in terms of administrative flexibility or policy control, but it did give the appearance of conferring upon Quebec a more autonomous policy role than the other provinces enjoyed, and the symbolic achievement was in itself significant.

Pearson appeared to be not greatly worried that Quebec would acquire, through the opting-out scheme, a special status in the sense that its policy responsibilities might be (or appear to be) more extensive than those exercised by other provinces. He took the view that the federal and the Quebec governments should work together to improve the position and satisfy the aspirations of francophones. To acknowledge Quebec's uniqueness made sense to him, since (as we have noted) almost 90 percent of Canadian francophones live in that province. Thus, the transfer to Quebec of special policy responsibilities, together with the fiscal resources necessary to fulfill them, was considered by Pearson to be an essential feature of an overall accommodative response to the new nationalist mood in Quebec. Decentralization was seen by Pearson as a necessary complement to the "favorable policies" and "enhanced participation" responses. This view of Pearson's has been shared by the post-Diefenbaker leadership of the Conservative party: Robert Stanfield, Joe Clark, Brian Mulroney, and their closest associates.

Pearson's successor as leader of the Liberal party and as prime minister, Pierre Trudeau, carried forward the "favorable policies" and the "enhanced participation" elements in the Pearson program, but made an about-face on decentralization. He set himself up as simultaneously the supporter of francophone rights and the vehement opponent of Quebec nationalism. In 1968 he wrote:

> I fought [the Union Nationale government of Quebec] until its downfall in 1960. During the entire period, while nearly everyone connected with the Left was urging Ottawa to redress the situation in Quebec, I remained a fierce supporter of provincial autonomy. By 1962, however, the Lesage government and public opinion in Quebec had magnified provincial autonomy into an absolute, and were attempting to reduce federal power to nothing; and so, to defend federalism, I entered politics in 1965. . . .
>
> All the various kinds of "special status" which have been discussed until now, whatever their content, lead to the following logical problem: how can a constitution be devised to give Quebec greater powers than other provinces, without reducing Quebec's power in Ottawa? How can citizens of other provinces be made to accept the fact that they would have less power over Quebec at the federal level than Quebec would have over them? . . . How can Quebec be made the National state of French Canadians, with really *special* powers, without abandoning at the same time demands for the parity of French and English in Ottawa and throughout the rest of the country? . . .
>
> [Under special status, Quebec's] electorate would not be entitled to demand complete representation at the federal level; and, more specifically, it would have to accept that the French fact be limited, legally and politically, to the province of Quebec.[23]

With these words, Trudeau sharply distinguished the concept of dualism on a cross-Canada basis from the dualism that many Quebecers had begun to struggle for during the Quiet Revolution, the dualism of Quebec and the rest of Canada. Philosophically (and Trudeau is probably the only Canadian prime minister to whom the word might be applied) Trudeau had long before established a position hostile to ethnonationlism and in favor of the multinational state:

> The history of civilization is a chronicle of the subordination of tribal "nationalism" to wider interests. . . . The tiny portion of history marked by the emergence of nation-states [in which political boundaries supposedly encompass ethnically homogeneous nations] is also the scene of the most devastating wars, the worst atrocities, and the most degrading collective hatred the world has ever seen. . . . The nationalists—even those of the left—are politically reactionary because, in attaching such importance to the idea of nation, they are surely led to a definition of the common good as a function of an ethnic group, rather than of all the people, regardless of characteristics. This is why a nationalistic government is by nature intolerant, discriminatory, and, when all is said and done, totalitarian.[24]

Trudeau's political career, which spanned the two decades from 1965 to 1984, was dedicated to the destruction of Quebec nationalism and the achievement of full political equality for francophones across Canada, without discrimination against French unilinguals (hence demanding bilingualism equally of anglophones and francophones in leadership positions, particularly in federal politics). Where Pearson sought accommodation, Trudeau deliberately polarized public opinion in Quebec on the issue of "separatism." Where Pearson shaped the accommodative response to Quebec, not really distinguishing provincial demands from those of francophones generally, Trudeau vigorously and consistently emphasized precisely this distinction. He became publicly known outside Quebec only in 1968, when he engaged in a verbal duel with the premier of Quebec at a federal-provincial conference. This event occurred only a couple of months before the party convention that was to choose him as Pearson's successor, and since it was broadcast over national television, it enormously helped his establish a reputation in English Canada as the Quebecer who would stand up to Quebec. For sixteen years this remained the most solid and enduring source of his political support in the other provinces. At election time, the more he was able to play on the separatist threat from René Lévesque and the PQ, the more the voters turned to him. Evidently this did not hurt at all in his own province either, where the Liberals were able virtually to freeze out the Conservatives as long as Trudeau remained at the head of the party.

In sum, Trudeau's response to Quebec nationalism (which is also the response of many federal Liberals today) was to reject and disparage it, while simultaneously accommodating and indeed pressing for the demands of French Canadians as an ethnic/linguistic minority. Some of the policies of his government, such as official bilingualism, were highly favorable to francophones across Canada. Other policies, especially in the economic realm (including regional development), were directed more specifically to the province of Quebec. Trudeau also stressed, more than any other leading Canadian politician has done, the importance of "enhanced participation" by francophones in the federal government, both at the political (elective) and bureaucratic levels. But he saw an expansion of Quebec's powers as a threat to this objective, and affirmed the power of the federal government against the demands not only of Quebec but of all other provinces as well. While deliberately playing to Canadian nationalist sentiment and pursuing a set of nationalistic economic policies, he portrayed himself as a strong antinationalist *in the ethnic sense*, and his confrontational style emphasized the "rejection" element in his response to Quebec nationalism. But, obviously, Trudeau did not cater to anglophone dominance, whether in ethnicity-related or in economic issues. His bilingualism policies, his economic nationalism, and the economic favors his government gave to Quebec earned considerable animosity, especially in the West. Critics attributed all three aspects of the Trudeau policies, at least in part, to the strong francophone presence in the cabinet, and they developed a corresponding resentment of the extent of "French power" under his prime ministership.

ETHNONATIONALISM,
SEPARATISM, AND CONSTITUTIONAL REFORM

Quebec nationalism would be inconceivable without ethnic difference, or the fact that a strong majority of the province's population shares a common ancestry, language, culture, and historical memory. But this does not mean that Quebec nationalism is ethnically intolerant or exclusive. Its proponents share the goal of building an "original" society, unique in its characteristics, and not a copy or imitation of any other. Possession of the territory and the exercise of a considerable degree of political control within its boundaries are prerequisites of its *projet de société*: on this all Quebec nationalists are agreed. However, beyond this point, unanimity dissolves. The movement is internally divided on at least two axes: a constitutional axis, and a social axis. In relation to the former, differences exist on the issue of sovereignty, or the powers required to develop autonomously as a distinct society. The clearest point of difference is between those who believe that adequate constitutional powers can be obtained within the Canadian federal regime, or are at least consistent with federalism, and those who regard political independence as indispensable. In relation to the social axis, no obvious dividing line exists between groups, for there are no dichotomous categories (as there are between "federalists" and "independentists"). But nationalists—even those strongly committed to independence—evidently differ among themselves on the extent of cultural, linguistic, and racial diversity that is to be accepted or desired within the Quebec society of the future. This conceptualization is represented in Figure 3.1. Which is equally a schema for classifying groups of nationalists (or for characterizing individual nationalist figures) and a tool for understanding diverse responses to Quebec nationalism.

Controversy exists over the distribution of Quebec nationalists among the four quadrants, specifically, whether significant numbers are to be found in quadrants I and IV. (Quadrant I comprises federalists who are also nationalists in the sense that they strive for a homogeneous society in which the ethnic *Québécois*—nonimmigrant francophones—predominate culturally, politically, and economically; quadrant IV comprises *indépendantistes* who are committed to an ethnically and culturally diverse Quebec, and accept or encourage the use of minority languages on the condition that French be the main language of business and public affairs.) The touchstones of the "homogeneity option" are a preference for French unilingualism and/or a desire to control immigration.[25] Both language policy and immigration are hot issues in contemporary Quebec politics; they are controversial within as well as between the two main parties, the provincial Liberals and the PQ. Thus, there are Liberals who favor a restrictive language policy (and in particular, favor a French-only policy for the posting of public signs); and there are *Péquistes* who are strongly committed to the building of a

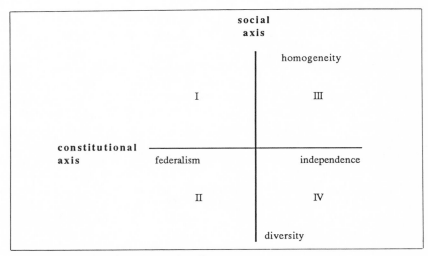

Figure 3.1 Varieties of Quebec Nationalism

multiracial, linguistically tolerant, fully independent Quebec. A particularly dramatic illustration of the strength of feeling within the PQ on this point is provided by an incident in March 1988, where the entire executive of the youth wing of the PQ resigned in protest against the unilingualist polices of the heir apparent to the leadership, Jacques Parizeau (who shortly afterward was indeed acclaimed as leader). The group issued a manifesto that may become a historic document in Quebec politics, and in any case illustrates a fact of fundamental importance: that Quebec nationalism is an admixture of ethnonationalism and a more inclusive form of nationalism *not* based on ethnicity. Some excerpts illustrate this.

> In Quebec, as elsewhere, solidarity is an essential condition of the establishment of a promising future, within which there will be place for all. It behooves francophones to behave as a majority, extending a hand to all those who feel excluded and correspondingly insecure. . . . Our nationalism, the nationalism of tomorrow, a nationalism born of a geopolitical vision of Quebec and its future, is one that encompasses rather than divides. It is obvious that old-style nationalism will find it has less and less appeal, if based on ethnicity or its French Canadian character. Henceforth, our action as Québécois ought to allow everyone, notwithstanding ethnicity or place of birth, to manifest his attachment to the land that has welcomed him, where everything yet remains to be done. . . . The force of consensus around nation-building goals ("un projet de société") will be the cement that constitutes us as a majority. . . . Such a consensus must transcend generations, ethnic groups, political parties, and special

interests, to the greatest extent possible, respecting the attitudes of all ("dans le respect du rythme de tous").[26]

This statement is exceptionally clear as a commitment to a territorially defined rather than to an ethnically defined form of nationalism, but it is far from unique. Some of the leading figures in the PQ, particularly René Lévesque (its founding president; premier 1976–1985; d. 1987), made a real though almost wholly unsuccessful effort to shift the focus of Quebec nationalism from ethnicity to territory. One should not overstate the case, as our subsequent review of language policy will show; but, subject to general acceptance of French as the main working language, the vision of Quebec that has been conveyed by most of the declarations and policies of the PQ is pluralist and certainly nonracial. (In this respect, recent developments within the PQ, involving the resignation of Lévesque's successor Pierre-Marc Johnson, and his succession by Jacques Parizeau, may presage an atavistic twist in its orientation.)

The nuances of Quebec nationalism, indicating a complex and unstable balancing of ethnicity and territory as its defining characteristics, have had little impact, over the years, on political controversies surrounding it. Partly because of the sheer force of the personality and intellect of Pierre Trudeau, and of course because of the politically strategic position he occupied as prime minister for fourteen years, Quebec nationalism has been characterized by most of its opponents as a movement dedicated to ethnic exclusivism and intolerance. The tensions that have arisen as a result of its emergence, and as a result of responses to it (by governments and among the public), have crystallized in intermittent controversies over constitutional reform. These have focused both on the political status and powers of Quebec, and on the protection of individual rights, notably the constitutional entrenchment of language rights claimable by linguistic minorities.

Projects for constitutional change have been a recurring, high-profile item on the Canadian political agenda since the emergence of Quebec nationalism in the mid-1960s. Quebecers have had two main motives for raising the constitutional issue: first, that the existing constitutional framework has been too constraining, (in other words that Quebec has needed a degree of policy control it can obtain only by expanding its constitutional powers); and second, that demographic change has been weakening the province's political weight within confederation. About twenty years ago the province's birth rate, which had been the highest in Canada, dropped to the lowest in the country. In the early twenty-first century, as the population ages, the number of deaths will come to exceed the number of live births. Indeed, the Quebec population has already been declining as a percentage of the total Canadian population: from 28.6 percent in 1951, to 26.4 percent in 1981, and an estimate 25.9 percent in 1987; and this trend is expected to continue or to accelerate. This unfavorable demographic situation threatens to reduce Quebec's political weight in the federal political arena and in federal-provincial relations; and Quebec knows this. Thus it is urgent, from the Quebec perspective, to act quickly to put in place constitutional guarantees of its role and its rights in the federation.

Over the past twenty years the political demands of the province of Quebec have set in motion four major rounds of intergovernmental negotiation on the constitution. Of these, two produced unanimous agreement among the federal government and the ten provinces (1965, 1971), but were not proceeded with because Quebec itself subsequently repudiated them. One ended in an agreement between the federal government and all provinces except Quebec (1981) and was then, as the Constitution Act of 1982, imposed on that province over its vehement objections. The other (1987) resulted in a unanimous intergovernmental agreement, which must be endorsed by all ten provincial legislatures as well as by the Parliament of Canada before taking effect.

Although constitutional matters became prominent on the Canadian political agenda because Quebec succeeded in putting them there, the politics of constitutional change have so far worked to Quebec's serious disadvantage. A factor affecting the treatment of the issue has been that the 1867 constitution, an act of the British Parliament, did not contain an amending formula. Through most of the relevant period it was assumed that unanimity among governments was required to arrive at a formula by which the constitution could be amended in Canada (that is, without having recourse to London). In 1980, as well be related, Prime Minister Trudeau attempted to cut the Gordian knot by proceeding unilaterally, and he partially succeeded. But until that year, all governments acted as if they possessed an absolute veto; and the history of attempts at reform in 1965 and 1971 can only be understood in that context.

The two aborted agreements of 1965 and 1971 elicited a strong negative reaction from Quebec nationalists, in both cases forcing the premier to withdraw the assent he had previously given. The 1965 agreement proposed a rule of unanimity for changes to the division of powers, thus giving Quebec (and of course other provinces as well) an absolute guarantee that its jurisdiction would not be infringed without its consent. In addition, provision was made for the delegation of legislative powers between orders of government, an action that was then and still is unconstitutional. A consequence of the proposed delegation procedure was that over time Quebec could have acquired, if the federal government agreed, a more extensive policy-making role than other provinces. This agreement by Premier Lesage provoked a storm of protest from nationalist forces in the province (which were led in this affair by a constitutional lawyer who later became deputy premier in the PQ government). Their complaint was that the amending formula as negotiated, would have placed Quebec in a "straitjacket" at a time when it was essential not merely to hold onto the powers the province then possessed, but to expand them. Under the agreement, even so small a province as Prince Edward Island, with a population barely greater than 100,000, could veto Quebec's future constitutional development. Lesage decided not to proceed, and the agreement fell to the ground.

In 1971, a more comprehensive agreement was reached by the first ministers at a conference in Victoria, British Columbia. Known as the Victoria Charter, the agreement comprised: (1) an amending formula requiring that changes to the constitutional division of powers be approved by Parliament, the provinces of Ontario and Quebec, at least two Atlantic provinces, and at least two western provinces comprising 50 percent of the population of the West; (2) a charter of human rights giving constitutional status to certain fundamental freedoms; (3) constitutional protection of the rights of linguistic minorities (French and English), giving francophone minorities more extensive guarantees than have ever, before or since, been agreed to;[27] (4) a clarification of federal and provincial powers in matters of income support, determining that in several categories of support federal laws were not to "affect the operation of any law present or future of a Provincial Legislature"; and (5) various other changes mainly restricting federal powers. This package was more favorable to Quebec, and simultaneously to the francophone minorities in other provinces, than any other constitutional proposals on which it has been possible to reach an intergovernmental consensus. But Premier Bourassa, upon his return to Quebec City, let himself be persuaded that it was not enough. Declaring that the income security provisions lacked clarity and gave too much power to the judiciary, Bourassa announced that he would not ask the Quebec National Assembly to ratify the agreement.

The Victoria Charter was the high-water mark of acceptance of official bilingualism and of the principle that there should be constitutional guarantees of minority language rights in Canada. This is not to say that the availability of public services in the minority language (English or French) has diminished since 1971. On the contrary, especially in New Brunswick, Ontario, and Manitoba, significant advances in this respect have subsequently been made. However, except in the case of New Brunswick, the English-speaking provinces have been reluctant to give constitutional effect to their commitments to provide French-language services; and Quebec has moved decisively toward French unilingualism, although it must be emphasized that the anglophone minority there has continued to receive more favorable treatment than the francophone minorities in other provinces, with the possible exception of New Brunswick.

Five years after the collapse of the Victoria Charter, the PQ swept into power, aided by an electoral revolt among the Quebec anglophones. This group had traditionally voted Liberal, and they had every reason to oppose the

PQ, but in 1976 many of them stayed away from the polls. This was apparently in angry reaction to a 1974 language law of the Bourassa government. "Bill 22," as the law was known, declared French the sole official language of the province, though English was recognized also as a "national language." The distinction was in part a symbolic affirmation of French as the primary language of the province, but it also had real effect. French was made the normal language of instruction in the schools, and access to the English-language schools was limited to those who could pass a proficiency test. The intent here, an evident response to the demographic situation described earlier, was to channel immigrants into the French system, in order to counteract their overwhelmingly strong tendency to integrate with the anglophone minority. This policy was a direct reflection of nervousness about the future of the French language even within Quebec. The more pessimistic observers predicted that in the absence of laws constraining individuals' choice of language, Montreal would become a majority-English city within a generation. Other provisions of Bill 22 prescribed the use of French in contracts and on public signs (though English might be used as well), required proficiency in French as a condition of entering professions offering service to the public, established that French was to prevail in "the public administration" (a general phrase that comprised institutions such as municipalities and school boards, which in English-speaking parts of the province had tended to operate uniquely in English), and required businesses that wanted subsidies or contracts from the provincial governments to have an adequate "francophone presence" in management ranks, attested to by an official "francization certificate."[28] To all of this the Quebec anglophones and allophones reacted angrily, staying away from the polls in droves in the 1976 election, thus helping to elect the PQ as a majority government. As noted earlier, the party had promised not to declare independence or a sovereignty-association status without first getting the endorsement of the Quebec electorate by referendum.

The 1977 language law, "Bill 101," was similar in overall thrust to Bill 22, but went further. The minister who introduced it declared: "There will no longer by any question of a bilingual Quebec," a statement reflecting the belief that to have a fully bilingual society in Quebec meant, given demographic realities in North America, the economic and social superiority of English and therefore, for francophones, a situation structured to result in their linguistic assimilation. Another slogan also captured this sentiment: "Quebec must be as French as Ontario is English." Unjust? So indeed it seemed, for many of the Quebec anglophones, who were accustomed—in the case of the older generation but not of most youth—to living within their own unilingual subculture and working in English without economic penalty. This situation was precisely what Bill 101 intended to overturn. The law, also known as "the Charter of the French Language," provided that no employer could require knowledge of any language other than French as a condition of employment, unless it could be established that such knowledge was clearly demanded by the nature of the work. It prescribed fines for firms employing more than fifty people if, by 1983, they had not qualified for francization certificates. It limited access to English-language instruction to the children of those who had, themselves, been educated in English in Quebec, though this rule was to be relaxed for siblings of children already in the English schools, and in the case of those living temporarily in Quebec. (The intent of this clause was to discourage the in-migration of English-speaking people from the rest of Canada and from the United States, and not merely to steer allophone immigrants toward integration with the francophone majority.) Though statues and regulations would be translated into English, only the French version was to be authoritative (this provision was subsequently struck down by the Supreme Court of Canada as unconstitutional). Most public signs and poster could be in French only, not bilingual.

The thrust toward unilingualism in Quebec naturally made it harder to sell the idea of bilingualism elsewhere in the country. This trend, the emotional impact of which was accentuated by the emigration of a substantial number of anglophones from Quebec, was undoubtedly a factor working against the extension of French-language rights in the nine English-majority provinces. Given also the resentment against Quebec for its threat to (as anglophones saw it) "break up Canada," the non-Quebec francophones were placed in a difficult and in some cases ambivalent position. Many of them had considerable sympathy for Quebec *indépendantisme*, but they also realized that the more Quebec went its own way constitutionally and in terms of language policy, the more they themselves were politically isolated. There developed for the first time a real and well-understood community of interest between the anglophone minority in Quebec and the francophone minorities in the other provinces: it was in the interests of both to see the spread of bilingualism and the constitutional protection of minority language rights. It would have been logical had there developed an equally well-cemented coalition—and, given relative numbers, obviously a far more potent one—among pro-unilingualists in all provinces; it was part of the PQ strategy to encourage the formation of such a coalition. However, too many other considerations (including, notably, patriotic ones) got in the way.

Debates over language policy were part of the context of the May 1980 referendum campaign over sovereignty-association. The economic risk involved in any constitutional adventure was also a significant factor, and has generally been regarded by the Quebec nationalists as the decisive one. For whatever reasons, the sovereignty-association project failed by a 60-40 margin, large enough that one may infer it fell short of a majority even among the francophone population. Indeed, this supposition is sustained (subsequent political argument to the contrary notwithstanding) by an analysis of the vote on a constituency basis. Be that as it may, the rejection of sovereignty-association ushered in a period of intense intergovernmental negotiation and constitutional debate on a cross-Canada basis. Where the referendum was intended to strengthen Quebec's hand in subsequent bargaining over the constitution, it had precisely the opposite effect— disastrously so for the nationalists.

The end result of eighteen months' jockeying and sparring over "a renewed federalism" (Trudeau's promise during the referendum campaign) was the Constitution Act, 1982. At first, during the summer of 1980, an attempt was made to reach a comprehensive intergovernmental agreement covering not only the substance of the Victoria Charter but such diverse matters as the reform of some of the central institutions of government and various division-of-powers items. This attempt crashed spectacularly in September 1980 at an acrimonious federal-provincial conference. At that point Trudeau, evoking a fifty-year history of failure to "patriate" the constitution, announced he would proceed unilaterally on a narrower range of items: patriation (necessarily, with an amending formula) and a Canadian Charter of Right and Freedoms. Other matters would be left for a second round. He invited British members of Parliament to "hold their noses" and, notwithstanding opposition from the provincial governments, to pass the required amendments to the British North America Act, 1867,[29] on the basis of a resolution to be passed by the Canadian Parliament. This initiative was supported only by the provinces of Ontario and New Brunswick, and was vehemently opposed by the federal Conservative party. The Opposition's tactics eventually succeeded in forcing a halt to the progress of the resolution in Parliament, pending a decision by the Supreme Court of Canada on the constitutionality of the government's move. When the court ruled (September 1981) that Trudeau's manner of proceeding was constitutional in the legal sense, but unconstitutional in the conventional sense, its decision forced the reopening of talks with the provinces. It was on this occasion, culminating November 5, 1981, that an intergovernmental "consensus"—*actually, excluding Quebec*—was reached. Essentially, the provinces agreed to the Canadian Charter of Rights and Freedoms (about which most were leery, as it stood to crimp their legislative powers), while the federal government agreed to an amending formula put forward by the provinces. Quebec assented to neither. The November 1981 partial accord was the basis of a resolution of the federal Parliament, and that resolution in turn was the basis of the Constitution Act, 1982, enacted on Canada's behalf by the Parliament at Westminster.

The 1982 act goes some distance, but certainly not all the way, toward giving constitutional form to Trudeau's vision of the country. Its outstanding feature is unquestionably the Canadian Charter of Rights and Freedoms.

There is substantial agreement among observers that the charter will transform the politics of the country, by virtue of its emphasis on and support for individual rights, which reinforce the notion that citizenship confers substantially uniform rights or entitlements across the country. Thus, it has been predicted that the charter will have a homogenizing effect on the political community and the expectations of citizens, and indirectly on public policy. French and English are given constitutional recognition as official languages of Canada (i.e., in the federal Parliament and administration, and in courts established by Parliament—though most courts are established by the provincial legislatures). These provisions, as noted above, fall considerably short of what had been agreed to ten years earlier and inscribed in the (aborted) Victoria Charter. In addition, the 1982 charter establishes minority language educational rights, as follows: those whose mother tongue[30] is English or French, or who themselves have received their primary school instruction in French or English *anywhere in Canada*, are entitled to have their children receive instruction in English or French, according to individual choice, within their own province. However, there are two vital restrictions on this right: first, it applies only where numbers warrant (the definition of which the courts will eventually have to rule upon), and second, the stated rights will not come into effect in Quebec until the legislature so provides. Thus, most non-Quebec francophones have more extensive constitutional rights in the matter of language of instruction than is possessed by anglophones in Quebec—although most Quebec anglophones enjoy, in practice, better access to public services in the minority language than is the case with most non-Quebec francophones. This generalization applies both to educational services and to other policy areas, such as health services.

Other features of the Constitution Act, 1982, are also pertinent to our discussion of ethnonationalism in the Canadian federal state. These features of the constitution, by contrast with those just noted, do not so much concern the rights of linguistic minorities as they do the capacity of the Quebec francophones to shape their future development as a collectivity. Whereas Trudeau had entered the referendum debate in 1980 promising a "renewed federalism" if the electorate rejected sovereignty-association, the Constitution Act did nothing to respond to the political aspirations of Quebecers who found the existing constitutional framework too constricting. Moreover, in two major respects the Constitution Act marked, for the Quebec nationalists, a significant reversal. First, the PQ denounced the charter as a general assault on the powers of the National Assembly, as well as a specific infringement of its powers to legislate in relation to language. And it is certainly true that the charter does limit legislative powers equally at the provincial and the federal levels. Second, and perhaps more important, the new formula for amending the constitution was unacceptable to Quebec.

The amending formula was based on, but in one vital respect differs from, a formula agreed to by Premier Lévesque as part of a package of constitutional reforms put forward by eight premiers in April 1981, as a counterweight to the Trudeau initiative. The eight agreeing provinces (all but Ontario and New Brunswick) proposed that almost all clauses of the constitution be amendable by Parliament plus *two-thirds of the provinces containing at least half of the Canadian population, but with an important "opt-out" proviso*. Thus, there was to be a general rule that did not give any province a veto and made no reference to the regions; in both respects this formula contrasted with the formula in the Victoria Charter. While giving weight to provinces on the basis of population, in other respects the new "provincial consensus" was based on the principle of the complete equality of the provinces. To affirm this principle was a major objective of major western leaders such as Alberta's Premier Lougheed; and it was attractive also to the four Atlantic provinces. However, the general rule was qualified by another vitally important clause: that no amendment could infringe upon the legislative powers or the property of a province if that province, by resolution of the legislature, declared that the amendment should not apply. Furthermore, if any amendment transferred policy responsibilities to the federal government, and a given province opted out of the amendment, the province would be entitled to full financial compensation. In other words, an opting-out province would find its treasury enriched to the extent that its residents would, in the absence of the opt-out arrangement, be receiving benefits provided by the federal government. For the resource-rich provinces, Alberta in particular, the opt-out provision was important because they wanted an absolute guarantee that no combination of forces in the rest of Canada could diminish their control over, or revenues from, natural resources. For Quebec, the opt-out provision held out the promise of, potentially, the gradual achievement of special status or even a move toward sovereignty-association. The financial compensation element in the opt-out clause ensured that financial inducements could not lever the province into transferring powers or policy responsibilities it would sooner keep.

The federal government was eventually forced into accepting the main features of the eight provinces' amending formula, but insisted that financial compensation be limited to amendments in the fields of culture and education. This was acceptable to all provinces but Quebec, which at the crucial moment in November 1981, was abandoned by its erstwhile allies. Premier Lévesque denounced them as traitors, and denounced the amending formula, with its more limited financial compensation clause, as a standing threat to the capacity of Quebec to manage its own affairs. The Quebec National Assembly unanimously passed a resolution protesting the Constitution Act. The all-party support for the resolution protesting the Constitution Act. The all-party support for the resolution demonstrated the act's nonacceptability to all major figures in provincial politics.

It is now (March 1988) seven years since these events occurred. In the interval the situation has changed dramatically. In September 1984, a new Conservative government under the leadership of Brian Mulroney came to power in Ottawa, pledged to "national reconciliation" and the amendment of the Constitution Act, 1982, such that Quebec can assent to it "in honour and enthusiasm." In December 1985, the PQ was replaced by the provincial Liberals, once more under the leadership of Robert Bourassa. The party is now unequivocally federalist (whereas in his earlier stint as premier, Bourassa had described himself as merely a "conditional federalist," committed to maintaining the link with Canada only as long as it could be demonstrated to be in Quebec's economic interest). Bourassa and his minister of international affairs, Gil Rémillard, who is also responsible for "Canadian intergovernmental affairs," had both announced their commitment to constitutional reform, and in May 1986 Rémillard set out five conditions for reaching a settlement. They were:

- Explicit recognition of Quebec's character as a distinct society
- Guarantee of extended powers for Quebec in the field of immigration
- Limitation of the federal government's spending power in areas of provincial jurisdiction
- Changes in the formula for amending the Constitution of Canada, in effect giving Quebec a veto power
- Participation by Quebec in the nomination of judges to the Supreme Court of Canada[31]

Three months later the premiers unanimously and publicly agreed to give priority to Quebec's constitutional agenda before raising additional issues of their own. This held out the promise of holding the agenda to manageable proportions, and implicitly acknowledged that Quebec had a well-founded grievance dating back to the 1980–1982 period. Then, through the fall and winter of 1986–1987, in a series of *in camera* bilateral discussions (between Quebec and the other governments, and between the federal government and the provinces), the main features of an agreement were blocked out. The first ministers met, again behind closed doors, at the end of April and, to almost everyone's surprise, reached agreement on a set of amendments responding to the five conditions put forward by Rémillard eleven months previously. This, from the location of the meeting, is known as the Meech Lake Accord, although a final (amended) text was not agreed to until June 3, in Ottawa. The accord requires the approval of Parliament and all ten provincial legislatures. Ratification had been completed by January 1989, except for passage of the required resolutions in the legislatures of Manitoba and New Brunswick, where the governments that signed the accord were replaced following general elections.

Prospects for completion of the ratification process appear negligible to many people, although in the government of Canada and in most provincial governments the commitment to the accord remains strong. In Manitoba and New Brunswick—and indeed outside those two provinces— opposition to the accord has been mounting, partly because old controversies over language policy in Quebec have flared up again. In December 1988 the Supreme Court struck down a provision of the province's language law that prohibited commercial signs in any language but French, on the grounds that this policy infringed freedom of expression as guaranteed in both the Quebec Charter of Rights and the Canadian Charter of Rights and Freedoms. Quebec then enacted a new law reaffirming the French-only policy for storefront signs, but permitting bilingual signs inside. The law invokes a "legislative override" clause contained in both charters, an action that effectively places the new policy beyond the reach of the courts. Quebec's response to the Supreme Court's ruling, in turn, provoked Manitoba to withdraw the Meech Lake resolution from the legislature (where it had been introduced only a few days earlier). In fact, Quebec seems to have played into the hands of anti-Meech forces within the Liberal and New Democratic parties both federally and in several provinces—opposition already strengthened by the poor showing of these two parties in Quebec at the federal election in November. In this combination of circumstances, public opinion in English Canada may encourage Manitoba (and possible also New Brunswick) to insist on Quebec's softening its language policy as a *quid pro quo* of ratifying Meech. If this happens, the accord is almost certainly doomed. In the meanwhile, ethnonationalism in Quebec has received a shot in the arm, and public opinion on language issues has become more polarized.

The debate over the Meech Lake Accord[32] neatly encapsulates the political issues posed by ethnonationalism in Canada today, and highlights other matters of considerable importance to the future development of the Canadian federation. Only two areas of controversy will be touched on here: (1) the recognition of Quebec as a distinct society within Canada, and related provisions on linguistic duality, multiculturalism, and aboriginal peoples; and (2) the alleged aggrandizement of the provinces (not just Quebec) through a set of clauses on the federal spending power, appointments to the Supreme Court and the Senate, and the formula for future constitutional amendments.

Linguistic Duality and Quebec as a Distinct Society

The accord stipulates that the constitution of Canada shall be interpreted consistently with two principles: "that Quebec constitutes within Canada a distinct society," and that "the existence of French-speaking Canadians, centred in Quebec but also present elsewhere in Canada, and English-speaking

Canadians, concentrated outside Quebec but also present in Quebec, constitutes a fundamental characteristic of Canada." However, these principles are qualified by the inclusion of three nonderogation clauses: that this interpretation clause does not alter the division of powers, whether relating to language or other matters; that it does not affect another interpretation clause according to which the Charter of Rights "shall be interpreted in a manner consistent with the preservation and enhancement of the multicultural heritage of Canadians;" and that it does not impair existing rights of aboriginal peoples.

With so many qualifiers, the clause is clearly intended to concede the "distinct society" principle, as demanded by Quebec, without entailing consequences unacceptable to groups other than the francophone majority in Quebec. First, it confers not additional legislative powers upon Quebec and thus apparently respects the principle that Trudeau had fought for, that there should be no special constitutional status for that province. Indeed, a preamble to the accord states unequivocally that it recognizes "the principle of equality of all the provinces," Second, it aims to assure the official-language minorities—both the Quebec anglophones and the francophone communities in other provinces—that their rights will be fully protected. Third, and finally, in case the recognition of Canada's linguistic duality and also Quebec's character as a distinct society could be thought to have negative consequences for multicultural groups and/or aboriginal peoples, the clauses of the constitution referring to these groups are explicitly reaffirmed.

Nonetheless, the "linguistic dualism/distinct society" clause is controversial. Quebec nationalists, while welcoming the "distinct society" principle, consider that with so many qualifiers, and with no attempt being made to state *in what ways* Quebec is distinctive, the clause may be an empty symbolic gesture. They would like to make sure that it really means something, in effect that it *will* end up broadening the authority of the provincial legislature, if only through more generous judicial interpretation of Quebec's existing constitutional powers. Among other groups, exactly the opposite concern is expressed: that the various nonderogation clauses are too narrowly stated to adequately affirm and protect the interests to ethnic minorities and other groups. Some, including New Brunswick premier Frank McKenna, would like a blanket exemption for the Canadian Charter of Rights and Freedoms. The most powerful political force supporting such an amendment is a group of women's organizations—significantly, however, not including women's organizations from Quebec. Also demanding revision of the accord is a set of organizations representing ethnic minorities. The coincidence of interests between the Quebec anglophones and non-Quebec francophones, and the tendency of their organizations to support each other politically, became increasingly evident as the campaign against the accord got under way. These groups want not only ironclad protection of their existing rights but a commitment, constitutionally imposed upon legislatures and administrative bodies, to enhance and extend them. Multicultural organizations and aboriginal organizations also consider their respective groups neglected under the accord. In short, the accord represents a delicate balance between two forces: Quebec's thrust for recognition as a distinct society (and for a constitutional status reflecting that conception of itself), and other groups'—especially women and ethnolinguistic minorities—insistence upon obtaining constitutional protection and support. That delicate balance, as negotiated among first ministers at Meech Lake, is the target of strong opposition in several provinces.

Aggrandizement of the Provinces

As stated, one concern about the Meech Lake Accord has been that Quebec may acquire excessive powers or an expanded policy role, permitting it to accede over time to a special status within Canada, with negative consequences for groups other than the francophone majority in Quebec. However, there is another current of opinion, also hostile to the accord. According to this view, it might have been acceptable for Ottawa to make consessions to Quebec; after all, it does have legitimate and unique concerns. But the nine English-majority provinces insisted upon getting everything Quebec got, and the federal government gave in to them all. The result is a dangerously weakened federation.

Only some of the arguments supporting this view are of interest to use in this chapter, given our present concern with specifically ethnonational issues. We shall take note of only two aspects of the controversy. One concerns the amending formula, and the other the exercise of the federal spending power.

Future constitutional amendments will be made as set out in the 1982 formula, except (1) if a province opts out of any future amendment transferring powers to Ottawa, financial compensation will not be guaranteed in all policy areas, and not in relation only to cultural matters and education, and (2) certain matters hitherto covered by the general amending formula (Parliament plus two-thirds of the legislatures, encompassing half the population of Canada)will henceforth require unanimity. The matters added to the "unanimity list" pertain mainly to the structure of central institutions— Senate, House of Commons, Supreme Court—and offer assurance that basic features of these institutions will not be altered to the detriment of Quebec, or for that matter of any other province, without its consent. The rationale for unanimity in such matters is that here the opt-out provisions (with financial compensation) are irrelevant: Quebec cannot opt out of the House of Commons or Supreme Court.

The "federal spending power" refers to a practice which (by convention, but not hitherto by explicit constitutional provision) has allowed Ottawa to launch new programs in areas of exclusive provincial jurisdiction on a jointly financed basis, that is, through conditional grants or grants-in-aid. The spending power, in this sense, is both affirmed and limited by the Meech Lake Accord. The limitation is that the accord provides, as in the case of constitutional amendments, for provincial opting out with guaranteed financial compensation. However, to qualify for compensation, a province must have mounted a program or taken some other initiative "compatible with the national objectives." There has been considerable argument about what this may mean.

The thrust of English-Canadian criticism of the proposed clauses relating to the amending formula and to the spending power has been that in both respects the accord will inflate the role of the provincial governments and weaken the federal government. And what has this to do with ethnonationalism? Precisely this: that Quebec nationalist have represented, in extreme form, a more widespread tendency to see Canada as a "community of [provincial] communities" associated with each other through a federal state. This concept, articulated by former prime minister Joe Clark, has been vigorously attacked by Pierre Trudeau and the Trudeau wing of the federal Liberal party, whose suppositions are strongly individualistic and, in a pan-Canadian sense, nationalistic. Controversies over the strength (or weakness) of the federal government have become surrogates for opposing views of Canada and alternative conceptions of citizenship and community.

The Meech Lake Accord is a negotiated settlement of several outstanding constitutional issues between Quebec and its Confederation partners, i.e., the federal government and the nine English-majority provinces. To reach agreement, the first ministers resorted to language that included some carefully crafted ambiguities. Opponents on both sides, the Quebec nationalists and *indépendantistes* on the one hand, and a group best (if somewhat narrowly) described as "Trudeau Liberals" on the other, have criticized these ambiguities and sought assurance that their respective interests and goals be more clearly articulated in a revised accord. But it is obvious that whatever might be done to "improve" the accord from the one perspective would make it totally unacceptable from the other. The accord represents a delicate balance that may yet be wrecked by the intransigence of its critics who, as I have shown, lie on both sides of the "ethnonationalism divide." The Quebec legislature has endorsed the accord, so it is at least temporarily safe from the Quebec nationalists. However, if forces outside the province, with the moral support of the Quebec anglophones, insist upon opening up the agreement, it is virtually impossible to imagine that amendments could successfully be negotiated. The Quebec government probably has zero room for maneuvre, even if it were itself willing (as seems unlikely) to backpedal.

CONCLUSION

The character of ethnonationalism in Canada, the strategies of ethnonational organizations, and governmental responses to ethnonationalism all have been conditioned by federalism. Instead of there being (as in some unitary states) a plurality of ethnonational movements focusing their demands upon a single political authority, in Canada there is a single major ethnonational movement, internally divided and expressing incompatible visions of the country, focusing demands upon several loci of political authority. Within the francophone group, there has been tension between those whose primary identification is with Quebec, and the (self-defined) *Canadiens*, whether resident in Quebec or in other provinces.

A Quebec nationalist movement arose during the 1960s, seeking an enhanced constitutional status for that province, either "special status" within the federation, political sovereignty with economic association, or full independence. The new Quebec nationalism, unlike traditional French Canadian nationalism, challenged the economic, social, and political dominance of the anglophones and threatened the political fabric of the country. Among francophone groups in other provinces and antinationalist francophones within the province, as well as among anglophones, it produced a set of reactions ranging from uneasiness to hostility and rejection. One of the least compromising opponents was Prime Minister Pierre Trudeau, who articulated more forcefully than anyone else the fundamental inconsistency of objective between the Quebec nationalists and those who, like himself, sought full political equality for French Canadians on a cross-Canada basis. The more Quebec acquires a special status within Confederation, he argued, the less will Quebecers be able to play a role in federal politics proportionate to their numbers. Moreover, any weakening of the francophone presence in Ottawa cannot but redound to the disadvantage of francophone minorities in provinces other than Quebec.

Policy responses to ethnonationalism include incomprehension, rejection, and accommodation. In a sense the modal response to Quebec nationalism in the rest of Canada has been incomprehension (and, closely related to it, indifference). This explains why crises such as the election of the Parti Québécois in 1976 have apparently caught an overcomplacent country unawares. However, in the context of this chapter such a response, or nonresponse, is less interesting than the more deliberate or *strategic* alternatives: rejection and accommodation. The first Canadian prime minister to face up to Quebec nationalism in a serious way was Lester Pearson, who formulated a three-faceted accommodationist response: favorable policies, enhanced participation by francophones in the federal political arena (electoral politics and the bureaucracy), and decentralization. The three facets appeared to him to be mutually supporting. Under his successor, Pierre Trudeau, the extension of official bilingualism, the constitutional entrenchment of linguistic minority rights, regional economic development with (in part) a Quebec focus, and the promotion of francophones to leading political and bureaucratic positions in Ottawa were all aspects of a response to Quebec nationalism (which by his own declaration goaded him into electoral politics) that combined *favorable policies* and *enhanced participation*. In these respects Trudeau carried forward and intensified Pearson's policy of accommodation; but on the matter of decentralization Trudeau reversed direction. Here he became aggressively rejectionist in relation to provincial pretensions generally but especially vis-à-vis the demands of Quebec for special status or more. On this issue Trudeau deliberately polarized opinion, urging that to endorse sovereignty-association or independence for Quebec would be tantamount to abandoning the official language minorities, both the anglophones in Quebec and the franophones elsewhere. These two groups now increasingly perceive that in language policy matters they can and must make common cause.

It is impossible to say whether the rejectionist response to ethnonationalism is consistently the "right" response, if the aim is to create or strengthen a multinational state. At a critical juncture in Canada's history the implementation of a policy favorable to francophones but confrontational in relation to Quebec-focused ethnonationalism enjoyed a dramatic success. What is at issue now is whether to continue to apply basically the same formula, or, the crisis having subsided, to attempt to patch up the quarrel. That attempt has been made, and the eleven first ministers have reached agreement on a new constitutional formula, which retains the essential features of the settlement forced upon Quebec in 1982 but also modifies it somewhat to make it acceptable at least to the present government of Quebec. It remains to be seen whether opponents outside the province, supported by the Trudeau wing of the federal Liberal party and by Trudeau himself, will sink the deal, and if so with what consequences for the future fortunes of the PQ and Quebec nationalism.

NOTES

I am grateful to Yvan Gagnon and Denis Robert for their insightful comments on an earlier draft of this chapter.

1. In this situation the social scientists would become like a pharmacologist who knows what drug to administer, but has to adapt the dosage to the individual patient (the patient's size, metabolism, etc., are relevant, as is the seriousness of the malady).

2. The terms "francophone" ("French-speaking") and "anglophone" ("English-speaking") are now common political and journalistic usage in Canada. Less common is "allophone," designating persons whose language most commonly used at home is neither English nor French.

3. Canada Census, 1981.

4. The figure 60,000 represents the generally accepted estimate of colonists (*Canadiens*, as they had already begun to call themselves) who remained in the land they had settled after the British conquest of New France (1760). This figure is obviously subject to challenge. The government of Quebec's *Report of the Commission of Inquiry on the Position of the French Language and on Language Rights in Quebec* (Quebec: Editeur officiel, 1972, volume 3, page 38) and Kalback and McVey's *The Demographic Bases of Canadian Society* (Toronto: McGraw-Hill, 1971, page 12) both list the total population of the colony in 1760 as 70,000. The 1871 *Census of Canada*, volume 4, lists the 1754 population of New France as 55,000 and the 1765 population as 69,810. The latter figure would, of course, include some nonfrancophones.

5. Some of the Scots Catholics garrisoned in Canada, however, eventually married francophones and assimilated to French, suggesting that at the time, religion was a more potent factor in acculturation than language.

6. Richard J. Joy, *Languages in Conflict* (Toronto: McClelland & Stewart, 1972).

7. William R. Lederman, "Unity and Diversity in Canadian Federalism: Ideals and Methods of Moderation," *Canadian Bar Review* 53 (1975): 601.

8. The speech is summarized in Mason Wade, *The French Canadians 1760–1945* (Toronto: Macmillan, 1956), 580–582. Cf. Henri Bourassa, "The French Language and the Future of Our Race" [1912]: "We believe that the preservation and development of the language is to us the human element that is most necessary to the preservation of our faith." Bourassa went on, in the same speech, to invoke the significance of the French language as a defense against" the infiltration of Americanism that creeps into all the phases of our [Canada's] national, political, and social life," and on this basis argued that it was in Canada's interest to extend and protect the rights of francophone minorities across the country. The speech is reprinted in Ramsay Cook, ed., *French Canadian Nationalism: An Anthology* (Toronto: Macmillan, 1969), 132–146.

9. Michel Brunet, "Trois dominantes de la pensée canadienne-française: L-agriculturalism, l'anti-étatisme et le messianisme," in his *La présence anglaise et les Canadiens* (Montreal: Beauchemin, 1958), 113–166.

10. [Monseigneur] L.-A. Pâquet: "A Sermon on the Vocation of the French Race in America," [1920], in Cook, *French Canadian Nationalism*, 153–154.

11. Ibid., 158.

12. André Raynauld: "The Quebec Economy: A General Assessment," in Dale C. Thomson, ed., *Quebec Society and Politics: Views from the Inside* (Toronto: McClelland & Stewart, 1973), 147–148.

13. David Kwavnick, eds., *The Tremblay Report*, [Abridgment of the] *Report of the* [Quebec] *Royal Commission of Inquiry on Constitutional Problems* (Toronto: McClelland & Stewart, 1973), 43, 49–50.

14. Jean-Marc Léger, "Aspects of French-Canadian Nationalism," in Douglas Grant, ed., *Quebec Today* (Toronto: University of Toronto Press, 1960), 310–329.

15. Léon Dion, "The Origin and Character of the Nationalism of Growth," *Canadian Forum* (January 1964): 229–233.

16. Canada, Royal Commission on Bilingualism and Biculturalism: *Preliminary Report* (Ottawa: Queen's Printer, 1965), 135.

17. This definition of the *majoritaire* was given by Hubert Guindon at a conference in 1986. See Peter M. Leslie, *Rebuilding the Relationship: Quebec and Its Confederation Partners, A Conference Report* (Kingston, Ont.: Institute of Intergovernmental Relations, 1987), 14.

18. Leslie, *Rebuilding the Relationship*, 11.

19. *Le Soleil* (A Quebec City newspaper), November 30, 1987 and December 4, 1987. The soundings were conducted by independent polling agencies.

20. Canada, Royal Commission on Bilingualism and Biculturalism, *Preliminary Report*, 151.

21. On the other hand, it has been argued that policies to promote bilingualism were not very successful until the passage of the Official Languages Act in 1969, a year after Pearson left office. See Yvan Gagnon, *The Office of the Commissioner of Official Languages and Bilingualism in Canada*, Ph.D. dissertation, University of California at Santa Barbara, 1974.

22. Peter Leslie and Richard Simeon, "The Battle of the Balance Sheets," in Richard Simeon, ed., *Must Canada Fail?* (Montreal: McGill-Queens Press, 1977), 243–258.

23. Pierre Elliott Trudeau, *Federalism and the French Canadians* (Toronto: Macmillan, 1968), xix, xxiv-xxv.

24. Pierre Elliott Trudeau, "New Treason of the Intellectuals," [1962], in his *Federalism and the French Canadians*, 156, 157, 169.

25. To some extent these policy choices are alternatives: a restrictive language policy permits the adoption of a relatively open immigration policy, because immigrants can be constrained to assimilate to the francophone majority; conversely, a restrictive immigration policy may be relied upon to ensure francophone predominance even if language use (in education, public signs, commerce, and municipal politics) is only lightly regulated.

26. "Pour un Québec de son temps," extract from the manifesto of the executive of the youth wing of the Parti Québécois, published in *Le Devoir*, Montreal, March 3, 1988, page 9.

27. D.V. Smiley summarizes the linguistic provisions as follows: "Both English and French might be used in the Parliament of Canada and all the provincial legislatures except those of Saskatchewan, Alberta and British Columbia. Statutes, records and journals of Parliament were to be published in both languages. The statutes of each province were to be published in English and French. Both languages could be used in the courts established by Parliament and in the courts of Quebec, New Brunswick and Newfoundland. An individual had the right to use either language in communicating with the head offices of any agency of the government of Canada or the governments of Ontario, Quebec, New Brunswick, Prince Edward Island and Newfoundland. If any province subsequently extended the rights of the two languages beyond those contained in the constitution such privileges could be revoked only by an amendment to the constitution of Canada." D.V. Smiley, *Canada in Question: Federalism in the Eighties* (Toronto: McGraw-Hill Ryerson, 1980), 76.

28. Alison d'Anglejan, "Language Planning in Quebec: An Historical Overview and Future Trends," in Richard Y. Bourhis, ed., *Conflict and Language Planning in Quebec* (Clevedon, England: multilingual Matters, 1984), 37–40. The ambivalence of the thrust toward unilingualism was illustrated by the vagueness of the term "francophone presence." A reporter asked the official in charge of implementing the program whether a

francophone was a person whose ethnic origin and mother tongue were French. The official stated that fluency in French was the operative criterion. "So the Queen of England is a francophone?" "Yes." And so it was reported, in bright red headlines, the next day.

29. The British North America (BNA) Act as passed in 1867 and subsequently amended, was renamed the Constitution Act, 1867, as part of the 1982 package of reforms. The main part of those reforms is contained in a separate "Constitution Act, 1982"—confusing, but true!

30. The term "mother tongue" does not appear in the charter. The operative phase, found in section 23, is "citizens of Canada whose first language learned and still understood."

31. For the text of Rémillard's speech, see Peter M. Leslie, *Rebuilding the Relationship: Quebec and Its Confederation Partners, Report of a Conference at Mont Gabriel, Quebec, 9–11 May 1986* (Kingston, Ont.: Institute of Intergovernmental Relations, 1987), 39–47; or Peter M. Leslie, ed., *Canada: The State of the Federation 1986* (Kingston, Ont.: Institute of Intergovernmental Relations, 1987), 97–105. Both sources also contain an account of reactions to the speech by participants at the conference where it was delivered.

32. For the text of the accord, see Government of Canada, *A Guide to the Meech Lake Constitutional Accord* (Ottawa: Queen's Printer, 1987). For a full report on the debate as reflected in hearings conducted by a committee of the Canadian Parliament, see Canada, Parliament, *The 1987 Constitutional Accord, The Report of the Special Joint Committee of the Senate and the House of Commons* (Ottawa: Queen's Printer, 1987). (Note, however, that the main concerns of the Quebec nationalists were not represented at these hearings, but rather at hearings earlier held by the Quebec National Assembly.) Commentaries on the accord include the text of papers delivered at a symposium on the Meech Lake Accord held at the University of Toronto, October 30, 1987 (publication forthcoming), and a series of articles by Peter Leslie, John Whyte, Beverley Baines, and Ramsay Cook, in the *Queen's Quarterly* 94:4 (Winter 1987): 771–828.

CHAPTER 4

Belgium: Variations on the Theme of Territorial Accommodation

JOSEPH R. RUDOLPH, JR.

Nowhere in the developed Western world did the postwar wave of ethnoregional politics achieve more prominence than in multiethnic Belgium. Beginning in the late 1950s, structural forces long at work combined with idiosyncratic political events to politicize a regionalized, ethnolinguistic cleavage that Belgian leaders had generally succeeded in containing from the time of the country's birth. Within ten years, ethnopolitical issues came to dominate the public agenda and provided the basis for launching several vigorous ethnoregional movements. Within twenty years, political change had affected almost all of the actors in Belgium's party system, and the country's once firmly established leaders had been forced to revise a 130-year-old constitution in an effort to accommodate the regional movements confronting them.

In this chapter I will examine Belgium's most recent experience with the politics of ethnonationalism, not so much in terms of its origin—an oft-treated topic in its own right[1]—as the effects that the rise of Flemish and francophone organizations have had on Belgium's political system, and the effects that the subsequent policy responses have had on these nationalist actors and the country's political process.

RESURGENT ETHNONATIONALISM: BELGIUM IN THE 1960s AND 1970s

The recent explosion of ethnolinguistic and regional politics in Belgium was scarcely an unforeseeable development. Ethnolinguistic and ethnoregional politics were a distinct possibility from the time of the state's creation (in 1830–1831), given (1) a centuries-old "linguistic frontier" running east-west approximately across the middle of the state; (2) the overlapping cleavages separating the country's Flemish-speaking numerical majority—but political, economic, and cultural minority—north of the line in Flanders from the French-speaking and more economically successful Walloons south of the line; and (3) the presence of the country's French-speaking capital *in Flanders*. This division was somewhat blunted during the nineteenth century by a limited franchise that offset the importance of the numerical majority of the Flemish population in Belgium's democratic system. However, the division was also further widened in the nineteenth century by the industrial revolution, which favored Wallonia at a time of Flanders' economic stagnation and had the side effect of making even more pronounced the differences in religious practice between the two regions. The Flemish, overall, remained much more devout in their Catholicism than the industrializing and already less devout Walloons.[2] Yet, even the gradual enfranchisement and political mobilization of the masses, which began during the last third of the nineteenth century, did not immediately result in intercommunal politics dominating the Belgian state. Rather, as the people were enfranchised they were normally recruited into one of the country's socioeconomic "spiritual families"—Catholic (Social Christian/Christian Democrat), Liberal, or Socialist. Each of these had its own regional base of power—the Catholics in Flanders, the Socialists in the Walloon south, the Liberals in the Brussels area—but each was also organized on a systemwide, bicommunal basis. The parties that emerged from these "families" during the 1800s and collectively dominated Belgian politics for nearly a century thereafter thus had a vested interest in managing the ethnolinguistic cleavage dividing their country. It divided *them* as well.[3]

It was within this framework that the early demands of Flemish nationalists for the right to use their own language in schools, courts, and administration in Flanders were initially accommodated by the essentially French-speaking elites of all three families. These demands could be met by allowing the Flemish the right to use Dutch in local administration (1866), in criminal proceedings (1873), in public secondary schools (1883), and ultimately in university education (1930)—all without the country's francophone leadership losing control of the national political process. Indeed, the techniques these leaders developed to control the country's linguistic cleavage during the nineteenth and early twentieth centuries enabled Belgium to create the type of managerial "government by elite cartel designed to turn a democracy with a fragmented political culture into a stable democracy," which Arend Lijphart has described as "consociational democracy."[4]

It was the combination of postwar changes in the environment of Belgian politics and a sharp increase in the visibility of (ethnoregionally sensitive) trends long in progress that eventually made it impossible for the country's traditional leadership to control the conflicts between the country's Dutch- and French-speaking communities within the existing, issue-management channels of decision making. Indeed, the Second World War itself aggravated communal tensions. Collaboration with the enemy occurred on both sides of the linguistic divide; however, as during World War I, it was more conspicuous in the north, with the result that Walloon Belgians emerged from the war with the sense that Belgium's francophones had been once again betrayed by the Flemish during wartime.

Of even greater importance were demographic and economic changes affecting the relative importance of Flanders and French-speaking Belgium. The 1947 census revealed that Flanders not only still possessed an absolute majority of the country's population (51.3 percent; 55 percent by 1970) but that Wallonia's share of the population had dropped from over 40 percent in 1890 to less than a third in postwar Belgium.[5] The economic arena held even worse news for the Walloons, for while the south's metallurgy-centered economy—once the centerpiece of Belgium's economy—continued to slide throughout the postwar period, Flanders enjoyed a sustained economic boom. This steady shift of economic power from the south to Belgium's more populous north resulted in a strong sense of Flemish self-awareness and dissatisfaction with the comparatively low level of the concessions previously granted to them. In particular, the Flemish resented the fact that, despite their demographic and economic status, they held only a minority of the leadership positions in the country's government, bureaucracy, and military.[6] Meanwhile, in the south a certain amount of alarm began to emerge in response to both the growing *minorization* of the francophone in the country's population and economy, and the growing self-confidence and self-assertiveness of the country's Flemish majority.

Eventually, these changes would have probably produced conflict between Belgium's Flemish north and Walloon south. What accelerated that development in postwar Belgium was a sudden decline in the importance of the cross-communal issues that had previously helped to restrain regional and linguistic rivalries. As late as the mid-1950s Belgium's ethnolinguistic cleavage was still of tertiary importance; the more significant issues challenging the country's consociational system involved economics and religion. Then, in 1958, the leaders of the traditional parties disturbed the hierarchical ordering of cleavages upon which managing the country's linguistic cleavage at least in part depended. The occasion was the negotiation of a political truce (the *pacte scolaire*) in which the three principal parties agreed to table for a dozen years the politically sensitive issue of public versus church-controlled schools. The effect was to depoliticize one of the country's two major cross-communal issues. Three years later, in the Great Strike of winter 1960–1961, the economic cleavage was extensively regionalized when random strikes against the country's post-Congo austerity program escalated into a general political protest much more widely supported in the Walloon south than elsewhere.

With the depoliticization of the religious issue and the regionalization of economic issues, the environment was ripe for the emergence of a strong round of ethnolinguistic politics. An important manifestation of Flemish nationalism emerged almost immediately in Flanders, where the *Volksunie* (VU), a Flemish nationalist party born in the 1950s to replace a handful of smaller Flemish parties and dedicated to advancing the power of Dutch-speaking Belgium in the national government and to halting the spread of French-speaking Brussels into its Flemish environs, acquired a claim on nearly one-fifth of the Flemish electorate by the late 1960s (see Table 4.1). The *Volksunie*'s successful mobilization of the Flemish community and pursuit of its goals, in turn, contributed to the development of defensive ethnoregionalism in francophone Belgium and the emergence of increasingly competitive ethnonational parties there: the *Rassemblement Wallon* (RW), dedicated to arresting, through a federal reorganization of power, Walloon Belgium's economic slide under the alleged neglect of an uncaring central government; and the *Front Démocratique des Francophones* (FDF), a cadre-style party dedicated to protecting the rights of Brussels' French-speaking majority, including their right to take their culture with them into the city's commuter suburbs.

Given the rapidly changing environment of Belgian politics, the emergence of these ethnonational actors was perhaps inevitable. The traditional parties could not articulate ethnoregional sentiment because of their bicommunal, systemwide nature. Yet, the zero-sum nature of many of the ethnoregional demands (e.g., those pertaining to Brussels, as articulated by the *Volksunie* and the FDF) meant that the demands could not be settled solely within the traditional parties. Rather, such demands placed stress on the linguistic wings of the traditional parties—hardly a state of affairs lending itself to accommodation politics. Of equal importance, by the late fifties there were large numbers of well educated, middle-class professionals in both linguistic communites who found themselves frozen out of the decision-making process monopolized by the traditional parties, and who were eager to supply the leadership of new political parties committed explicitly to ethnoregional goals.[7]

For the Belgian political process, these developing, regionalized actors represented both something old and something quite new. They represented something old in the sense that ethnonational demands and even ethnonational parties have historically played roles in the country's political life. The success of nineteenth-century Flemish organizations in achieving the legal right for the citizens of Flanders to use Dutch in official functions in their own region has already been indicated. Other gains of the same ilk were also achieved by these essentially cultural organizations, for example,

Table 4.1 Party Strength in Brabant, Wallonia, and Flanders, Measured in Percent of Votes in Belgian General Elections, 1965–1987

Region: Party	1965	1968	1971	1974	1977	1978	1981	1985	1987
Brabant									
Catholic	27.1	29.2	24.5	27.6	30.9	30.2	21.0	23.9	22.3
Socialist	26.8	22.8	22.3	21.3	19.3	18.5	18.6	22.8	26.5
Liberal	30.0	25.6	18.3	10.4	14.8	14.6	23.5	26.8	27.7
FDF-RW	6.9	13.0	24.1	27.8	21.3	21.2	12.9	5.7	5.7
Volksunie	4.3	6.7	8.8	9.2	9.2	5.8	7.9	6.3	6.5
Wallonia									
Catholic	24.8	21.4	19.3	22.8	25.9	27.0	20.1	23.0	23.6
Socialist	35.8	35.0	35.1	37.4	39.5	37.6	37.1	40.4	45.0
Liberal	23.0	26.2	17.7	15.1	18.9	17.2	21.1	23.3	21.0
RW	3.2	9.8	19.6	17.6	10.6	8.6	6.7	—	0.6
Flanders									
Catholic	44.7	39.5	38.4	40.3	44.2	44.3	32.8	34.6	31.7
Socialist	25.2	26.2	24.7	22.6	23.0	21.3	21.0	24.0	24.3
Liberal	15.5	15.2	15.5	16.7	14.0	16.9	20.8	17.2	18.2
Volksunie	12.5	17.5	19.4	17.0	16.3	11.6	16.1	12.8	13.1

Sources: All returns are based upon figures published after the elections in *Le Soir* (Brussels).

Notes: Until recently, the Catholic, Socialist, and Liberal parties were composed of different linguistic wings in Wallonia and Flanders, with both wings contesting elections respectively in the French- and Flemish-speaking districts of the officially bilingual province of Brabant. Now their candidates essentially run under the labels of different parties, some of which have chosen different names.

The FDF-RW figure for the 1974 elections is for an alliance between these two parties and the francophone wing of the Liberal party in Brussels. The 1974 decline in the Liberal party's share of Brabant's vote also reflects this deviation from past and subsequent elections. FDF and RW returns for 1981 utilize votes garnered by the descendent PW (parti Wallon) outside the city of Brussels, as do the 1985 returns; the 1987 returns incorporate the newly refurbished RW.

the government's decision in 1898 to begin publishing the country's laws in both French and Dutch. Moreover, no sooner had Belgium adopted universal male suffrage than frankly ethnonational parties began to emerge in Flanders to articulate much more "extreme" demands and to achieve considerable electoral success, obtaining approximately 15 percent of the Flemish vote by the time of Belgium's last parliamentary election before the Second World War.[8] Thus, what was occurring in Belgium during the late fifties and early sixties was—properly speaking—a *resurgence* of ethnonational politics, not a birth of such politics. The new round, however, was significantly different from the old in several important ways.

In contrast to earlier regionalist movements, which were almost exclusively Flemish, the most recent (and so far most dramatic) wave of ethnolinguistic politics in Belgium produced ethnonational spokespersons for both of the country's major linguistic communities and all three of its regions (Flanders, Wallonia, and Brussels). Consequently, the linguistic wings and grassroots political organizations of the three traditional parties were simultaneously exposed to previously unknown levels of stress. Second, whereas the Flemish movements of the late nineteenth and early twentieth centuries occurred in a political process preoccupied with important, cross-communal class and religious issues—with the Flemish demands therefore having to compete against powerful issues for a place on the public agenda—the more recent ethnonational groups were able to raise their demands in a setting virtually guaranteeing them a prominent hearing. Third, whereas prior ethnoterritorial demands were generally addressed to the country's French-speaking elite by Flemish organizations essentially seeking specific *outputs* from the political process (the right to use Dutch in courts and in the administration in Flanders, for example) or (later) a share of decision-making power, the most recent movements have focused on demands that involve a redistribution of power within the state (i.e., the issue of whether the Flemish or the francophones are to govern the state) and the restructuring of the state in a federalist direction. And, finally, the most recent round of ethnopolitics in Belgium may be differentiated from previous ones by the far greater consequences it has had for and the nature and institutional arena of policy making in Belgium, for the actors involved.

POLITICAL BARGAINING, CONSTITUTIONAL CHANGE, AND THE CHANGING FACE OF BELGIAN POLITICS

The traditional parties hardly rushed to respond to the demands that the VU, RW, and FDF articulated during the 1960s. Rather, the initial pattern was for all three of the traditional parties to ignore the ethnonationalists or to attack them as a danger to the state (hence the arguments equating regional calls for federalism with separatism and the dismemberment of the country), and to try to placate the regional communities with the minimal concessions. In an effort to defuse the VU's electoral appeal, the traditional leadership thus collaborated between 1961 and 1963 in passing language laws that froze the linguistic frontier (which had been slowly creeping northwards as Flemish parents along it encouraged their children to learn French to get ahead), made Dutch the exclusive language of public education and public affairs in Flanders, and accorded a special status to Brussels. To understate the matter, the effort did not succeed. Demands for power sharing at the center and a regionalization of power in the state continued to be aired in the north, and those concessions that were made to quiet the Flemish infuriated Belgium's francophone community, contributing to the emergence of the RW in 1964 and the formation of the FDF the following year.

Next came the *dédoublement* phase of accommodation of the mid-sixties, when the country's traditional leaders tried to reduce ethnolinguistic sentiment by creating separate administratiye facilities for the two linguistic communities in such sensitive areas as education and cultural affairs. During the same period, the principle of parity was applied in the creation of cabinets (which were to be composed of equal numbers of Dutch- and French-speaking ministers). And the principle of communal proportionality was adopted for such matters as determining the composition of the civil service. Again, the concessions neither defused ethnonational sentiment in the state's lingusitic regions nor arrested the electoral success of those regions' respective ethnonational parties. To the contrary, by the late 1960's, all three ethnonational parties were exhibiting a growing electoral credibility (see Table 4.1), and public opinion polls indicated that the issues they were articulating—including regional home rule—had appeal far beyond the voters supporting the VU, FDF, and RW. Most ominously for Belgium's existing decision-making system, by the late 1960s ethnopolitical issues were beginning to permeate the traditional parties and undermine their working relationship with one another and internal cohesiveness.

The effect of these changes on Belgium's traditional cartel became painfully apparent in 1968 when the Flemish wing of the country's largest party, the Social Christian party, refused to support the government's policy of neutrality on the issue of whether the University of Louvain, located in Flanders, should continue to have a French-speaking section. This issue eventually caused the party's Flemish ministers to resign, brought down the government, forced elections in which francophone nationalist parties scored significant gains, and precluded the formation of a new government until it was finally agreed that the university's French-speaking division would be relocated across the linguistic frontier or reconstituted in officially bilingual Brussels.

Following the Louvain Affair, the issue for the traditional parties was not whether to respond to the specific demands of the ethnonational parties and the challenge posed by them, but how to contain the damage and cut the electoral ground from beneath these competitors. Conversely, for the ethnonational organizations the issue became how best to exploit their growing influence and capitalize on any concessions that might be forthcoming in order to achieve additional gains for their respective regional communities and themselves.[9] The meeting ground for these two sets of actors became constitutional reform, a process that dominated Belgian politics from 1968 until the 1980s.

The constitutional revision process itself unfolded in two distinct phases. During the first, which began with the 1968 election of a Parliament authorized to undertake constitutional reform, the ethnonational parties participated in the deliberations leading to the constitutional revisions enacted in 1970. However, political leadership remained in the hands of the traditional parties and the reforms that were adopted fell far short of the federalist schemes endorsed by the ethnonationalists.[10] Anthony Mughan, among others, has suggested that the steps taken at this time (as well as later) were "placatory rather than remedial."[11] Certainly they left the unitary state, still firmly under the control of the traditional parties, intact, albeit with some interesting and potentially far-reaching modifications.

From the standpoint of the ethnonationalists, the major gain was that the revised constitution *provided a basis* for regionalizing power in the state (especially Article 107-*quatre*, which provided for the creation of autonomous regional assemblies for Wallonia, Flanders, and Brussels); the constitution's major failing was that it stopped far short of doing so. Indeed, the reformers gave at least as much attention to creating decision-making arrangements that would minimize the importance of the regions in policy making as to regionalizing power in the Belgian state. Cultural councils for Dutch- and French-speaking Belgium were thus created *inside* the central Parliament out of its Dutch- and French-speaking members, leaving council members with the mixed mandates of representing their linguistic communities as well as their localities and—to the extent they were committed to the manifestos of political parties controlling the center—their government.

Elsewhere, reforms very clearly bore the stamp of the traditional parties, and were aimed more at making it possible for the country's different communities to live together at the center than at giving the linguistic or regional communities decision-making autonomy. A warning-bell system was thus instituted whereby two-thirds of either language group in Parliament could suspend sensitive proposals from immediate action, and a double-majority system was adopted, which was certain to have the effect of making future constitutional reform in sensitive areas extremely difficult. (To create the regional councils mentioned in the constitution, for example, it would be necessary for proposals to obtain a two-thirds overall majority in Parliament and a majority within the parliamentary representatives of *each* of the country's major linguistic communties.)[12] Even those advisory regional assemblies created in 1974, at the end of this first period of constitutional reform, followed the mixed (or dual) mandate system and were composed of members of the Belgian Parliament. They were also endowed with so little influence that their dissolution three years later scarcely provoked any reaction.

The next series of steps towards implementation of Article 107-*quatre* did not begin in earnest until after Belgium's 1977 parliamentary election and differed from those of the 1970–1974 revision process both in participants and nature. Although "government by elite cartel" remained the modus vivendi for constitutional reform—with the major revisions initially formulated outside of Parliament in ad hoc commissions and meetings involving party leaders rather than government ministers—the composition of these negotiating sessions altered. The Liberals, for example, were absent from the discussions that culminated in the Egmont Accord, the blueprint for further constitutional reform hammered out after the 1977 elections; the party was no longer necessary to achieve the two-thirds majority required to continue the revision process. In its place were representatives for all three of the ethnonational parties, all of which had continued to enjoy good electoral fortunes in the 1968–1977 period. Moreover, because further progress towards regionalization, especially on the issue of Brussels, necessitated a compromise between the FDF and VU, the Egmont discussions were at times led by these parties, and the federalist direction towards which the accord pushed Belgium clearly bore their stamp. Nevertheless, the most substantial difference between the post-1977 efforts to amend Belgium's constitution and those surrounding the 1970 revisions was that after 1977 *each* party's move in the revision process tended to reflect its individual calculation of the electoral advantages of pursuing or opposing further constitutional reform. The party's search for a solution to the demands of the linguistic communites for greater control over communal and/or regional affairs was often of secondary importance.[13]

The Egmont Accord was the first victim of such inter- *and intraparty* calculations. When the accord, produced by party presidents meeting at Egmont Palace in marathon bargaining sessions, appeared to be weighted too heavily in favor of the country's francophone minority,[14] the country's Flemish Catholic party's prime minister permitted members of his party to oppose it despite its prior acceptance by their party's president. As a result the accord lost the support of the two-thirds necessary in Parliament to implement it, the government fell, and new elections had to be held.

Subsequent bargaining reflected similar efforts on the part of all participants to outpoint their opponents. Eventually, all of the ethnonational parties either dropped out of or were dropped from the negotiations, and the VU was badly stung in the 1978 elections when Flemish Catholics successfully attacked it for having betrayed the Flemish cause by accepting the Egmont Accord. However, the return to a negotiation process constructed out of Socialist, Liberal, and Catholic politicians—by this time untraditionally to be found in not three but six separate parties—scarcely proved to be more successful in brokering the regionalization-of-power issue. Indeed, between 1978 and 1980, Prime Minister Martens (Flemish, Catholic, and his party's president at the time of the Egmont Accord) headed four different governments before finally obtaining the requisite majorities for the passage of a revision statute. It is possible that had the government continued to focus exclusively on the constitutional issues, the revision might have been even longer in coming. But, while the political process concerned itself with constitutional reform, other problems—especially the country's growing

economic difficulties—began to acquire prominence on the public's mind and
to demand the attention of government.

As early as the 1978 election, public opinion polls indicated that
economic problems such as inflation and unemployment (particularly severe
in Wallonia) had overtaken constitutional change on the public agenda, and
that half of the electorate was so tired of the "constitutional crisis" that they
thought the 1978 election unnecessary and did not really understand many of
the constitutional issues being argued in it.[15] Yet, responding to the
economy depended upon making progress in revising the constitution; the
parties had too strong a vested interest in completing the next stage of the
revision process to table it. Moreover, just as it had earlier become
impossible to move forward in constitutional reform by relying on the
ethnonationalists—after the 1978 elections neither the VU nor the FDF were
willing to risk confrontation with the militants in their own parties by
compromising on the issue of the future status of Brussels—so cabinets
structured out of Catholics, Socialists, and Liberals in order to muster the
two-thirds majority required for constitutional revision tended to fall apart on
economic matters, given the different economic philosophies of the Liberals
and Socialists.

The impasse was only overcome through a series of bargains in 1980 in
which the Socialists agreed to support an austerity program in return for the
Liberals supporting constitutional revision, and in which the French-
speaking Liberal, Socialist, and Catholic parties agreed to drop their
insistence on settling the Brussels matter in return for their Flemish
counterparts in the government abandoning their opposition to
regionalization per se.[16] The result was the 1980 revision of the Belgian
constitution, in which cultural councils were replaced by (or, rather, became)
community councils, and regional councils were created for Wallonia and
Flanders in such a manner that they would eventually be entitled to have their
own individual executives responsible to them (even though they would
continue to be composed of members of the Belgian Parliament for the
foreseeable future).

In summary, as Covell observes, throughout its twelve-year period,
the 1968-1980 revision of the Belgian constitution "reflects the role of
elites in creating and pursuing conflict as well as resolving it."[17]
Furthermore, as time passed, the arenas for conflict seemed to
steadily increase to include: conflict inside the parties (between
uncompromising purists and practitioners, and between party presidents
and party ministers in the government, all juggling for position against
one another); conflict between the linguistic parties of the same
"family" (i.e., Flemish Socialists and francophone Socialists); conflict
between these successors to the traditional parties and the ethnonational
organizations; conflict between the ethnonational parties; and conflict

between Belgium's traditional partisan rivals (Socialists versus Liberals, for example).

The multiple arenas and opportunities for conflict ensured the delayed and watered-down nature of constitutional revision at the time, and has similarly influenced the subsequent efforts to implement the constitutional design. These results have in part flowed from the double-majority requirement for constitutional amendments, but they have also been a consequence of the manner by which sensitive issues are normally negotiated in Belgium. Three separate hurdles must usually be cleared. Agreement is first sought among the presidents of the parties represented in the government or likely to form the government after an election. Next, the ministers in the government must consider the proposal. Lastly, it is placed before the two houses of the Belgian Parliament for action. At each point different individuals, under different pressures and calculating self-interest from different vantage points, are involved in the process. Thus, the Egmont Accord negotiated and accepted by the profederalism presidents of the *Volksunie* and Catholic parties was torpedoed by a Catholic prime minister and Catholic members of Parliament, and later supported by only 75 percent in the Catholic party's 1978 congress in Flanders and by only 66 percent of those attending the *Volksunie*'s preelection congress in 1978.[18]

Similarly, as Covell also notes, although it is desirable to have as many parties as possible represented in negotiations in order to gain support for any proposal that might emerge (a "settlement" of the Brussels issue negotiated without the FDF's participation would have been nearly impossible to sell to francophones living in Brussels in 1980), the more parties present in the preliminary negotiations the less likely it is that any agreement will result. Such is especially true if the negotiators have memories of their fellow negotiators bargaining in bad faith in the past.[19] It is therefore not especially surprising that Belgian policymakers, preoccupied with ethnopolitical concerns for the better part of the last twenty years, required more than a decade to revise their country's constitution and concluded with some significant issues still unsettled, including the key issue of Brussels' status in a regionalized Belgium. Rather, it is almost surprising that the government, even given the need to clear its deck in order to act on the economic front, *was* eventually able to muster the necessary majorities to create regional assemblies for two of the three regions recognized in the 1970 revision of the constitution and to endow them with an executive of their own.

But what has been the effect of this action on ethnolinguistic politics in Belgium? And what does the effort of Belgian leaders to respond to ethnolinguistic demands tell us about public policy and ethnonationalism in the developed world?

ETHNOLINGUISTIC POLITICS, POLICY MAKING, AND CONTEMPORARY BELGIUM

At the most general level, Belgium's recent experience with ethnonational politics suggests the need to maintain a clear distinction between ethnonational parties on the one hand and ethnonational sentiment and politics on the other. It is convenient for political leaders at the center to equate the former with the latter, but as Belgium's success in containing the political influence of the FDF, RW, and VU during the past decade indicates, the linkage does not necessarily exist. Thus, although these ethnonational parties may only be, at best, minor players in Belgian politics today, the actors, institutions, and environment of contemporary Belgian policy making testify to the difficulty and costliness of containing the communal cleavage in a multinational polity once it has achieved prominence.

The Actors: Belgium's Changed Party System

Measured against the party system of only twenty years ago, partisan politics in contemporary Belgium resembles the last act of *Hamlet*. The landscape is liberally filled with dead, apparently dying, or seriously wounded actors. The ethnonational parties that cut such a wide path in Belgian politics a decade ago are the most obvious casualties. The RW was gone by Belgium's 1985 election; indeed, the ecological parties outpaced it in Walloon Belgium in the 1981 election. The FDF is still around, but its representation in the Belgium Parliament has steadily decreased since 1974 and it is no longer the dominant party it once was in Brussels—its vote in 1985 dropping to half the support it enjoyed four years earlier and to less than a quarter its former strength. Even the *Volksunie*, while it has recovered some of the ground it lost in the 1978 election, has returned only to the level of support it enjoyed in 1965, with about one vote in eight in Flanders.

Then there are the traditional parties. The Catholic, Socialist, and Liberal parties may have won the battle to turn back the ethnonational hordes, but in the process they lost the war, splitting themselves into separate linguistic parties, many of whom now articulate regional/linguistic demands on behalf of their communal groups at least as well as the ethnonationalists did at the peak of their success, and often in just as shrill a manner. Their current form is one consequence of the constitutional debate, during which the linguistic and regional wings of these parties regularly turned on one another. Their rhetoric is the legacy of their wars with the ethnonationalists, in which they often learned to survive in regional campaigns by outbidding the ethnonationalists in asserting fidelity to the regional or ethnolinguistic cause. In short, the status of the traditional parties may be explained in terms of Belgium's recent political history. But what happened to the ethnonationalists? Can their demise be tied to the public-policy course taken by Belgian leaders to disarm them?

Table 4.2 indicates just how fast these parties have lost political ground during the past decade. It is tempting to attribute this loss to the degree to which they were outflanked in the constitutional revision process by the leaders of the traditional parties (for example, the VU by the Flemish Catholics) or lost their appeal in Flanders and Wallonia once these regions received their desired regional assemblies. Such explanations probably do account somewhat for why these parties lost momentum during the past decade. However, it is difficult to explain the magnitude of their losses solely in such terms. Nor does the regionalizing nature of the political environment seem a complete explanation for their decline (the FDF and VU) or demise (RW). Cultural and regional councils *may* have addressed the original cultural and economic dimensions of, respectively, Flemish and Walloon nationalism, but by the 1980s it was clear that such councils were not a sufficient response to the problems facing either region. Nowhere is home rule an answer to the economic misery of a poor region during a global recession, or even to the economic difficulties of a comparatively better-off region for that matter. And the most recent global recession was very hard on Belgium in general, and on Wallonia in particular—so hard, in fact, that strikes by Flemish coal miners in the north had become a part of the Belgian political picture by the mid-eighties, while in the south the problem of servicing municipal debt brought Liège in 1983 to the edge of bankruptcy and forced the city to pay workers with IOUs.[20]

On the other hand, the deteriorating nature of the Belgium economy itself had a significant, if perhaps indirect, effect on the fortunes of the ethnonational parties. By the 1980s Belgium's economic life had become so bad, with one of Europe's highest unemployment figures (13.7 percent, the second highest in Europe at the time of the country's 1985 election) and an austerity program producing the third highest tax rate in Europe, that the overall satisfaction-with-life level of the Belgian population had plunged from one of the highest in Europe to one of the lowest.[21] In this setting, economic considerations significantly reduced the importance of communal issues—the "bread-and-butter" of the FDF, RW, and VU—except where they could be coupled to economic issues (for example, Flanders subsidizing the Walloon economy). As Henri Simonet, former foreign minister in Belgium, summarized at the time of the 1985 parliamentary election, "Circumstances have forced people to care more about their [standard of] living than about the way they live with others. The kind of friction once experienced over linguistic issues was a luxury we could afford when things were going well. But now, with the economy in such poor shape, we cannot."[22] Simonet's conclusion was apparently drawn by the Belgian public as well during the 1980s.

Table 4.2 Seats Held by Regional Parties in Belgian Chamber of Deputies Following Parliamentary Elections, 1974–1987

Party	1974	1977	1978	1981	1985	1987
Volksunie	22	20	14 [a]	20 [a]	16 [a]	16 [a]
Front Démocratique des Francophones	10	10	11	6	3	3
Rassemblement Wallon	13	5	4	2	–	–

Sources: Le Soir (Brussels).

[a] A breakaway faction of the *Volksunie* has won at least one seat in each of the previous four elections. It, the Vlaamsche Blok, was formed following the VU's participation in the government, and its seats are not included in the above figures. The Belgian Chamber of Deputies has 212 seats.

The best explanation for the decline in the strength of the country's ethnonational parties may nevertheless lie in the nature of the parties themselves. They are inherently fragile actors in a developed system for at least two reasons. First, in a developed polity, where voters have already been generally mobilized and usually already identify with an established party, an ethnonationalist party's long-term success depends on a long-term realignment of the electorate—not a frequent occurrence in any democracy. In this area the *Volksunie* enjoyed an advantage over the FDF and RW; Flanders has long had a segment of its electorate oriented towards voting nationalist, though the specific Flemish nationalist organizations have come and gone in the past. The VU could thus begin from an electoral base, which the francophone organizations lacked.

In the short term this weakness in the FDF and RW was not apparent. To the contrary, the parties found their newness and the broadly aggregative nature of the ethnonational umbrella—which could be stretched to accommodate francophone Liberals, Catholics, and Socialists alike—an asset in party building. They could collect protest votes against the established parties; they could harness the voters of that segment of the electorate persistently attaching itself to the fresh and new (the ecologist parties of today?); and they could attract the voters and sometimes the politicians of the established parties who were no longer satisfied with those parties but resisted realignment with one of the traditional opposition parties. In the long term, however, the weakness became apparent. When economic issues resurfaced, voters returned to their traditional political reference points. When electoral setbacks confronted the ethnonationalists, still other supporters (and sometimes party officials) deserted them, accelerating their electoral decline. In 1974, when for the first time the FDF-RW alliance did not substantially improve its performance over its showing in the previous parliamentary election, FDF-RW officials responded, when asked what happened, "We cannot grow indefinitely." Yet, given an electorate already aligned to established parties, new parties need to grow, if not indefinitely then for a very long time. Their ability to attract and retain voters may depend more on their image as bold, new, *growing* forces in politics than on the quality of their message. When Belgium's ethnonational parties ceased to expand their electoral support, they were in trouble.

At the same time—and secondly—electoral success can be a source of weakness to an ethnonational organization. As a growing party with a still-small electoral following, its leadership will have comparatively little trouble in maintaining a united front in articulating the party's case against the traditional leaders of the state. But once the party begins to achieve success at the ballot box, it must face new sets of challenges and its leaders must deal with new sources of stress. Should it, for example, join the government if invited to do so? If it does, it risks looking like the other parties, especially when those other parties' respective regional wings are beginning to sound like it in election campaigns. And what if it joins the government and cannot translate its most important political commitment into public policy (the box in which the FDF found itself on the objective of creating a separate region for Brussels)? Similarly, what if it does not join when given the opportunity? Can it still claim to be its region's strongest defender in the political process? And finally, if it does join the government, will the purists in the party's headquarters support party members in the government when the latter depart from previously uncompromising positions in order to participate in the give-and-take nature of political bargaining in pluralistic democracies everywhere? It is probably not coincidental that intraparty conflicts—often leading to breakaway factions—accompanied the participation of each of Belgium's ethnonational parties in the country's government, and that each suffered an electoral setback in the national election immediately following its participation in the government.

Institutional Change in the Belgian State

Belgium's institutional arena and policy-making process have also experienced profound change during the past quarter century. Constitutional reforms born of intense bargaining sessions have resulted in the creation of a new set of potentially important, communal and regional decision-making arrangements in Brussels. The oldest and most conspicuous of these are the cultural councils, created in the reforms of the early seventies, and renamed community councils and endowed with greater legislative authority in the 1980 revisions. Additionally, there are the regional councils, which possess the ability to form their own executives based on party strength within each assembly. In the case of Belgium's (Dutch-speaking) Flemish community, the executives of the community council and the regional council for

Flanders have been merged into a single body—a reform blocked for francophone Belgium by the central leadership's inability and/or unwillingness to create a regional body for the predominantly French-speaking Brussels-Brabant area and the impolitic nature of any proposal to merge the francophone community council with the regional assembly for Wallonia in the absence of such a body.[23]

Still elsewhere the decisionmaking arena was restructured by the introduction of new rules, such as those requiring communal parity in the cabinet, introducing warning-bell and dual-majority systems for controversial legislation in Parliament as well as for further constitutional reform, and providing for proportional (communal) representation in the civil service. Weaving many of these reforms together was an extended use of a dual mandate system in which members of the national Parliament would also provide the membership of the regional councils and the communal councils.[24] Indeed, until the mid-eighties this dual mandate system, which was designed to apply central brakes on regional and linguistic centrifugal pressures, even extended to the civil service, in the sense that most of the civil servants who were officially transferred to the regions remained in Brussels in their national ministries of origin.[25]

Unfortunately, the changing environment of Belgian partisan politics has worked somewhat against the ability of these institutional arrangements to control centrifugal tendencies in the state. As we have already noted, Belgian government has historically been a negotiational government, with policy the product of negotiations among the spokespersons for the major parties, both inside and outside of Parliament. To an extent, it still is a negotiational government; however, the changes in Belgium's party system during the past twenty years have deeply altered the nature of that policy-making process. Whereas parties once focused on the politics of accommodation and tried to control, within a consociational format, issues likely to divide the general public, the more recent tendency has been to use negotiation processes to outscore partisan rivals.[26] Thus, as Covell notes, the process of revising the country's constitution illustrates clearly "the role of elites in creating and pursuing conflict as well as resolving it." It also exemplifies the different arenas in which conflict can occur (such as intraparty negotiations, interparty negotiations outside of Parliament, and parliamentary negotiation within the government), the different sets of actors who participate in such negotiations (from party presidents to premiers to backbenchers), and the difficulty the group negotiating a settlement can encounter in selling it to a different audience along the gauntlet that proposals have to run in order to become policy in the Belgian state.[27] All of which leads to the broader question of the extent to which the policy process has coped with the ethnopolitical challenge in contemporary Belgium.

The Pervasiveness and Persistence of Ethnolinguistic Politics

By the mid-1980s ethnolinguistic and regional issues seemed to have declined to a lower status on Belgium's political agenda than at any time during the preceding quarter century. The 1985 parliamentary election revolved around such issues as the performance of Belgium's economy, the outbreak of urban terrorism, and the growing number of non-European workers in Belgian cities. The issue of further regionalization did not figure high in the manifestos of any of the successful parties. The ethnoregional parties, whose earlier success had forced the traditional parties to revise the constitution, were no longer serious political forces and hence no longer able to set the agenda. Thus, the major issue confronting the leaders of the state was the economy, not further constitutional reform, and given the state of the Belgian economy—with unemployment about equal in Flanders and Wallonia (at about 14 percent of the work force)—the economy was operating as a significant, cross-communal issue. However, to have concluded that the creation of the formal community councils and regional councils had satisfied ethnoregional desires, or that the primacy of economic considerations reflected an absence of communal issues, would have been a fundamental error. Ethnolinguistic and regional politics were still very much a part of Belgian politics, and within two years they had sprung from a local linguistic issue to the center of the "national" political process—paralyzing government, forcing new parliamentary elections, and blocking the formation of a new government for nearly five months.

The crisis of 1987 grew out of a long-standing trouble spot in Belgian politics: the Fourons (or Voeren in Dutch), a French-speaking region officially left in Flanders by the language laws of the early sixties. The early eighties found its francophones persistently electing as their mayor a man who maintained he could not speak the Dutch required of all public officials in Flanders (even though records indicated that he graduated at the top of his class in Dutch as a boy). A legal conflict resulted, and in 1986 a Belgian court annulled his election over the protest of the Fourons French-speaking majority, who then reelected him to office, to the outrage of the province's Flemish population. Matters quickly escalated, and caught in the middle was the cabinet, which initially intervened to calm the dispute by getting the mayor to agree to take Dutch lessons and later almost fell apart when he did not meet his agreed date to take a language qualifying test. (In the resultant debate in Parliament, Flemish members of the Catholic party threatened to resign from the cabinet if he was reinstated; the French members of the Catholic party said they would do the same if he was not reinstated.) The drama reached crisis proportions in the period between October 1986 and December 1987, when Belgian Prime Minister Martens, unable to solve the crisis or govern effectively as it lingered, twice offered his resignation before finally tendering it and calling for a new round of national elections. Even then the crisis continued for months before a new government (composed of Flemish and francophone Catholics and Socialists, plus the *Volksunie*) could finally be assembled around a compromise formula which—to draw Flemish support—reaffirmed the need for officials in Flanders to demonstrate an ability to speak Flemish and guaranteed the Flemish minority in Brussels' heavily francophone districts a seat on the city's governing council. And—to draw francophone support—the compromise offered assurances to Flanders' French-speaking minorities of an increased voice in regional affairs.

For the Fourons' French-speaking citizens, the "settlement" was seen as a "sellout." However, elsewhere the compromise, coupled with a pledge by the new government to use its two-thirds parliamentary majority to accelerate the devolution process, freed the political process to return yet again to other issues, including the economic ones confronting the state. Still, the enduring lesson of the crisis is that ethnopolitical issues are now an engrained part of the public and governmental agendas in Belgium. Moreover, these issues are likely to retain that status for decades to come as a consequence of both what has occurred in Belgium during the last three decades and what has not happened there.

Belgium remains very much a multinational state whose ethnolinguistic cleavage has been an accepted topic for political debate for more than a generation. Consequently, its political process is not likely to be easily, if ever, cleared of ethnolinguistic topics, no matter how the state might be restructured. Furthermore, the process of reorganizing the state has by no means been concluded; nor have all major, constitutional issues been resolved. The immediate future is therefore likely to see continued, specific debate on such key, and communally loaded, questions as (1) whether the Belgian state is sufficiently federalist (all parties now seem to have vocal prounitary and profederalist wings within them willing to debate this issue), (2) what to do with the Brussels question, and (3) whether the executives of the Walloon regional council and French-speaking community council should be unified if the impasse on the Brussels issue continues?[28]

Unresolved constitutional questions are not the only—or even the most persistent—ethnopolitical issues confronting policymakers. Such matters pervade the entire political process. The regionalization process did not draw election districts sharply enough to spare the system the problem of dealing with a VU candidate elected to the community council for francophone Belgium (he was not seated by the council). Nor, as in the case of Brussels' commuter suburbs as well as in the case of the Fourons, has it prevented local language controversies from escalating into national events. Nor, at a more mundane level, has it altered a way of life that continues to be "business as usual," Belgian style. Flemish locals still delete directions to Brussels from roadmarkers in Flanders; French-speaking construction workers in Brussels are still apt to walk away from their job if the canteen concession is given to a firm owned by a Dutch-speaking Belgian; and Flemish officials in Brussels' commuter suburbs still have been known to appropriate land set aside for a French-speaking school on the grounds that the land is important to "Flemish tourist heritage."[29]

Such matters would be difficult enough for policymakers to treat were it not for a second factor ensuring the continuance of ethnopolitics in contemporary Belgium: the oft-mentioned, altered nature of the country's parties. The opportunities for ethnoregional conflict begin with a revamped party system in which Belgium's traditional parties have restructured themselves along linguistic lines into a party system that frequently pits Socialist against Socialist and Liberal against Liberal in debating issues which themselves have become regionalized, and in which the gap between the parties of the same "family" is often quite wide. For the first five years after the constitutional reforms of 1980, for example, officers of the Walloon wing of the Socialist party did not even attend the annual meetings of the Flemish Socialists, to whom they still refer as their *"amis-ennemis."*[30]

Compounding the tendency of Belgium's parties to regionalize the national political debate is the necessarily coalition nature of the central government, given the number and relative strength of the parties composing the Belgian party system, which now has the distinction of possessing the largest number of parties of any party system in Western Europe. In this setting there is an inevitable and immediate tendency for regional and local issues to penetrate to the core of the government at the center and, frequently, to disrupt the cabinet.[31] The effects of the Fourons issue on the Belgian cabinet is but one case in point. Belgium's 1985 election provides another. The election took place two months earlier than necessary because of a division within the Catholic party in the cabinet over whether financial and political control of education should reside in the central government or—as advocated by the Flemish Catholics—should be shifted to the regional authorities.

Cabinet instability can also result when regional issues unite parties inside a region against their counterparts in the other linguistic community, especially when one of these parties is a member of the central cabinet. Jean-Maurice Denhousse, a former Socialist prime minister of the Walloon regional assembly, probably expressed the outlook of many politicians today when he said that he feels "closer affinity with a Walloon capitalist than a Flemish syndicalist."[32] Such sentiments place constant pressures on coalitions at the center.

In short, Belgian parties may collaborate in central government but they run for office in the regional communities, and must constantly shape themselves to the regional concerns. The practical consequence of this situation, as Covell notes, is that Belgian cabinets are constantly watched by the parliamentary and extraparliamentary components of their member parties, as well as by the opposition, for signs of regional or ideological "sellouts," and that regional and national politics are fused at the center by the nature of partisan politics in Belgium.

Nevertheless, perhaps the most important reason why Belgium's decision-making process is unlikely to return to the days before the politicization of the ethnolinguistic cleavage is the changed nature of its political structure. Even without having adopted a fully developed, conventional form of federalism, today's Belgian state is far removed in structure from the unitary state of twenty years ago, and the newly added institutions and political layers provide new opportunities for ethnopolitical conflict. There is, for example, the opportunity provided by the fact that the regional assemblies for Wallonia and Flanders can have executives composed of different party coalitions—with differing priorities—than the coalition composing the central government—a state of affairs that complicated the formation of a Socialist-Catholic coalition at the center after the 1987 parliamentary elections returned to office a Catholic-Liberal coalition in the Flemish Assembly. Indeed, in the mid-1980's the center's efforts to *avoid* this possibility for institutional conflict became a source of considerable turmoil in Belgian politics when the ruling Catholic-Liberal coalition in the capital sought control of the Walloon Assembly, on which it held fifty-two of the 104 seats, by expelling the Dutch-speaking *Volksunie* senator who had somehow been elected from French-speaking Nivelles. The coalition succeeded by (excluding the VU senator's vote) a 52-51 margin, but only at the cost of creating a situation in which the regional executive's stability depended upon a 100 percent turnout of all Catholic and Liberal members and at the additional expense of increasing tension between the center and the regional body. It was a victory hardly worth the battle, especially given the fact that even under the best of circumstances the membership of these assemblies can be expected to raise issues of concern to the regional and/or linguistic communities that the cabinet might prefer to keep mute.

The bottom line is thus simple to state. The creation of political machinery to represent Belgium's linguistic communities and ethnoterritorial divisions has, in the context of Belgium's present party system, not only guaranteed that linguistic and ethnoregional politics will remain a major part of politics in Belgium; it has provided them with institutional platforms at the heart of government in the contemporary Belgian state.

NOTES

1. For readily available English language treatments of this topic, see Val Lorwin, "Belgium: Religion, Class and Language in National Politics," in

Robert Dahl, ed., *Political Opposition in Western Democracies* (New Haven: Yale University Press, 1966), 147–187; James A. Dunn, Jr., "Consociational Democracy and Language Conflict: A Comparison of the Belgian and Swiss Experience," *Comparative Political Studies*, 5 (1970): 3–40; Martin O. Heisler, "Institutionalizing Societal Cleavages in a Cooptive Polity: The Growing Importance of the Output Side in Belgium," in Martin O. Heisler, ed., *Politics in Europe: Structures and Process in Some Post-Industrial Democracies* (New York: David McKay Company, Inc., 1974), 178–200; and Aristide R. Zolberg, "Transformation of Linguistic Ideologies: The Belgian Case," in Jean-Guy Savard and Richard Vigneault, eds., *Multilingual Political Systems: Problems and Solutions* (Quebec: Lies Presses de l'Université Laval, 1975), 445–572.

2. For a brief but solid discussion of the cultural and economic bases of the north/south division in Belgium, see André P. Frognier, Michel Quevit, and Marie Stenbock, "Regional Imbalances and Centre-Periphery Relationships in Belgium," in Stein Rokkan and Derek W. Urwin, eds., *The Politics of Territorial Identity: Studies in European Regionalism* (Beverly Hills: Sage Publications, 1982), 251–278, esp. 257f. There is also a German-speaking community in Belgium numbering approximately 66,000 in a population of nearly 10 million and located on the German border in eastern Wallonia. It has tended to imitate the other groupings in the political process—articulating its own ethnonational demands and even developing its own ethnonational party during the 1960s—and to date has benefited somewhat from the concessions made to the country's French- and Dutch (Flemish)-speaking communities (receiving its own, albeit lesser, cultural council, for example). On the other hand, because it has essentially piggybacked on political events rather than shaped them, it is deleted from this study. For a detailed treatment of this community, see J. Brassine and Yves Kreins, "La réforme d'état et la communauté germanophone," *Courrier hebdomadaire du entre de recherche et d'information socio-politique (CH du CRISP)*, nos. 1028–1029 (1984).

3. See Joseph R. Rudolph, "Belgium: Controlling Separatist Tendencies in a Multinational State," in Colin Williams, ed., *National Separatism* (Cardiff: University Press, 1982), 263–298, esp. 267f.

4. Arend Lijphart, "Consociational Democracy," *World Politics* 21 (1969): 207–225, especially 216.

5. Frognier, et al., in *Politics of Territorial Identity*, 257. By 1985 the figures had become 57.5 percent for Flanders to only 32.5 percent of the Belgian population in Wallonia. The balance—approximately 10 percent of the country's population—lives in Brussels, which is 80 percent French-speaking. Overall, the linguistic division of the country is thus about 60:40, with the francophones in the minority.

6. See Rudolph, in *National Separatism*, 269–270.

7. Joseph R. Rudolph, Jr., "Ethnonational Parties and Political Change: The Belgian and British Experience," *Polity* 9 (1977): 401–426, esp. 406–416.

8. François Nielsen, "The Flemish Movement in Belgium After World War II: A Dynamic Analysis," *American Sociological Review* 55 (1980): 76–94, especially 80.

9. Rudolph, "Ethnonational Parties," 405–406.

10. See Rudolph, in *National Separatism*, 284–285, and Anthony Mughan, "Belgium: All Periphery and No Centre?", in Yves Meny and Vincent

Wright eds., *Centre-Periphery Relations in Western Europe* (London: George Allen & Unwin, 1985): 273–299, esp. 276f, 284–286.

11. Mughan, in *Centre-Periphery Relations*, 288. See also the same author's "Accommodation or Defusion in the Management of Lingusitic Conflict in Belgium," *Political Studies* 31 (1983): 434–451, esp. 439f.

12. On the general subject of Belgium's 1970 constitutional revisions, and the intent of the various actors, see Mughan, in *Centre-Periphery Relations*; Maurice Boeynaems, "Les années 1970 et 1971 sur le plan communautaire et linguistique," *Res Publica* 15 (1973): 881–914; and James A. Dunn, Jr., "The Revision of the Constitution in Belgium: A Study in the Institutionalization of Ethnic Conflict," *Western Political Quarterly* 27 (1974): 143–164.

13. See especially, in this context, Mughan, "Accommodation or Defusion," and Maureen Covell, "Agreeing to Disagree: Elite Bargaining and the Revision of the Belgian Constitution," *Canadian Journal of Political Science* 15 (1982): 451–469.

14. The accord seemed to the Flemish to be especially biased against them because of its acceptance of a three-region formula for Belgium, which would have led to the division of the state into two francophone-majority regions (Brussels, with its large Flemish minority as well as Wallonia) but only one Flemish region, despite Dutch-speaking Belgium's majority in the population.

15. In Wallonia and Brussels, 70 percent of the voters ranked unemployment as the country's number one problem at the time. See Andrew MacMullen, "The Belgian Election of December 1978: The Limits of Language-Community Politics?," *Parliamentary Affairs* 32 (1979): 331–338, especially 334, 336.

16. These concessions were also encouraged by the fact that polls showed that all of the parties of the traditional "families" would be hurt if new elections had to be held in 1980. See Covell, "Agreeing to Disagree," and MacMullen, "Belgian Election 1978." On the subject of Martens's difficulty in forming a stable coalition in the context of nine-party politics in Belgium, see also "Belgian Roulette," *The Economist* 277 (October 18, 1980): 17–18.

17. Covell, "Agreeing to Disagree," 452.

18. MacMullen, "Belgian Election 1978," 383.

19. Covell, "Agreeing to Disagree," 452.

20. "Debt Ridden Belgian City Pays Workers with IOU," *Wall Street Journal*, April 4, 1983.

21. Ronald Inglehart and Jacques-René Rabier, "If You're Unhappy, This Must Be Belgium: Well-Being Around the World," *Public Opinion* (April–May 1985): 10–15.

22. "Belgian Voters Go to the Polls with the Economy on Their Minds," *Christian Science Monitor*, October 10, 1985.

23. For details of the specific powers of these councils and assemblies, see John Fitzmaurice, "Belgium: Reluctant Federalism," *Parliamentary Affairs* 37 (Autumn 1984): 418–433. Subsequent reforms have devolved still additional decision-making authority to these bodies, perhaps most significantly in August of 1988 when communal authorities obtained authority over, among other things, education, scientific research, and roads, ports, and other public works. Altogether, items accounting for approximately 30 percent of the central budget were transferred at that time;

however, the legal status of the Brussels-Brabant area was once again left in limbo.

24. In fact, it is more of a triple-mandate system. Belgium has long accepted the common practice on the continent of allowing local mayors to retain their posts when elected to Parliament.

25. Maureen Covell, "Regionalization and Economic Crisis in Belgium: The Variable Origins of Centrifugal and Centripetal Forces," *Canadian Journal of Political Science* 19 (June 1986): 261–269.

26. See Rudolph, "Ethnonational Parties," 423–426, and Mughan, "Accommodation or Defusion," 21–37, on the difficulty of returning to the earlier consociational form of politics once a state's ethnoterritorial or linguistic cleavages have been thoroughly politicized.

27. Covell, "Agreeing to Disagree," 454–461. On this point see also David M. Rayside, "The Impact of the Linguistic Cleavage on the "Governing" Parties of Belgium and Canada," *Canadian Journal of Political Science* 11 (March 1978), 61–97, esp. 91–96.

28. See, for example, "Que deviendrait Bruxelles si l'on fusionnait les exécutifs communautaire et wallon," *Le Soir* (Brussels), January 1, 1986.

29. Alan Osborn, "Linguistic Divide Key to Belgian Nation," *Europe* (March–April 1984): 34–35.

30. "Après le discours de Gand," *Le Soir* (Brussels), February 22, 1986.

31. See Covell "Agreeing to Disagree," 274.

32. Cited in "Economics Is New Basis of Belgian Divisions," *Wall Street Journal*, October 16, 1985.

CHAPTER 5

The French State and Ethnic Minority Cultures: Policy Dimensions and Problems

WILLIAM SAFRAN

The development of a public policy of accommodation to the cultural-linguistic strivings of France's ethnic minorities constitutes one of the significant achievements of the period of Socialist rule under the presidency of François Mitterrand. That is not to say that the measures adopted between 1981 and 1986 were entirely novel. Indeed, in some particulars they were continuations of hesitant steps taken by preceding regimes, and they have been roughly parallel to the policies chosen in other industrialized democracies. However, in its "ethnic" policies France has been faced with greater obstacles than have some of its neighbors in Western Europe. Unlike Belgium or Spain, France had no recent experience of local or regional ethnic autonomy; unlike in Britain, Switzerland, Canada, or the United States, there has been in France a deeply rooted ideological hostility to any distinction between membership in the political community—i.e., the state—and membership in an ethnocultural one—i.e., the nation. And in contrast to Belgium, Canada, West Germany, and Sweden, ethnic accommodation policies in France have had to concern themselves not merely with one or two clearly identifiable ethnic communities but with a large, fluid, and highly differentiated number of subcommunities.

A preliminary ethnic "inventory" suggests the following taxonomy for the minority populations of France:

1. Old indigenous and territorially based ethnics—such as Bretons, Occitans, Basques, and Gallicans;

2. Ethnics based in regions incorporated into the Hexagon during the more modern period who are considered almost as "native" as the majority—such as the Alsatians, Catalans, Corsicans, and Flemings;

3. Geographically scattered, and highly assimilated, descendants of older

immigrant stock—such as Provençal, Spanish-Portuguese, and perhaps Alsatian Jews;

4. Nonterritorially based, and partially assimilated, descendants of more recent (i.e., nineteenth and early twentieth century) immigrants—such as Armenians, Gypsies, and East European Jews;

5. Repatriates—North African settlers of French stock or citizenship, including Algerian and Moroccan Jews;

6. Descendants of naturalized immigrants of non-European and non-Christian origin—such as the children of French army veterans of North African provenance (*harkis*);

7. Natives of former French colonies or French Overseas Territories who settled in France before or since decolonization—such as black West Africans, Martiniquais, and New Caledonians;

8. More recent immigrants from European countries with cultures reasonably similar to that of France—such as Portuguese and Spaniards;

9. More recent immigrants from non-European, and non-Christian, countries—Maghrebis (North African Arabs), Indochinese, and Chinese.

This list is not exhaustive, nor are the distinctions precise, for there is a continuum of ethnic consciousness within all these communities and there are phases of selective assimilation and "re-ethnicization." Moreover, there is considerable ethnic mixing between Gallicans and Bretons, between European and North African Jews, and among East Asians, such that within many individuals several ethnic strains and consciousnesses converge. To complicate matters even further, there are within ethnic regions several clusters of subethnic communities, differing from one another in language, dress, and folkways. Thus, the Occitan region comprises such cultural-linguistic subgroups as the Gascon, Languedocien, and Provençal. If one adds the populations of ethnic minority origins, native and immigrant, residing in France, one easily arrives at a figure of over 20 million, i.e., nearly 40 percent of the country's total population. This statistic is, however, a maximal one, for many of the people included in it would identify as simply French men or French women and attach little or no cultural significance to their origins.

BACKGROUND:
THE BUILDING OF A "NATION-STATE" AND THE FATE OF THE ETHNOREGIONAL COMMUNITIES

The construction of a politically strong French kingdom required a welding of the diverse ethnic communities into a unified nation—that is, the gradual imposition of a common language, culture, and ideology emanating from Paris and its growing bourgeoisie. Efforts in this direction were begun early:

in 1539, the French royal government issued the Ordinance of Villiers-Cotterets, which stipulated the exclusive use of the French language in official acts and legal documents. Later, between 1792 and 1804, followed the reforms of the French Revolution—thereafter continued by Napoleon—which aimed at the abolition of all geographic, socioeconomic, and ethnic "intermediaries" between the citizen (viewed as a more or less atomistic unit) and the state (viewed as a manifestation of the "general will"). Those reforms also proclaimed French the "language of liberty" and transformed France into "a republic, one and indivisible" by means of a strongly centralized administrative system.

The principal ideological expression of these developments was Jacobinism, which defined democracy, rationalism, and progress in terms of an idealized universal state. Such a state must be achieved in stages; one of its stages (or means) was the nation-state, which results from the gradual integration of particularistic units—local governments, provinces, tribes, religious communities, and ethnic groups—into an enlarged and more efficient unit possessing common political and cultural symbols. To the extent that regional or ethnocultural orientations survived, they were viewed as relics of a dangerously reactionary particularism or, at best, as symptoms of an irrelevant primordialism. The pattern of cultural centralization that was associated with such attitudes led to a denigration of peripheral languages and cultures and to their demotion to "dialects" and "folklores," and concretized the status of the provinces as "internal colonies" by making them psychologically and culturally dependent on Paris and hostage to the elitist pretensions of its bourgeoisie. In conformity with such pretensions, Brittany was viewed as a colony much like overseas colonies in its exoticism. Its culture was considered capable of producing folk dances, not science,[1] and its people were to be "civilized" as they were more firmly assimilated to the French way of life.[2]

By the time the Third Republic was inaugurated (between 1870 and 1875), French governments had not yet succeeded in "civilizing" Bretons, Corsicans, and other peripheral communities. Well over half of the population of the Hexagon and probably 80 percent of the inhabitants of rural areas still spoke a regional language other than French.[3] An important response to that situation was the Ferry Laws (1880–1887), which created a free and compulsory elementary school system in which French was the only language of instruction. Regional cultures and languages were demoted to mere "folklores" and "dialects," and children using ethnic idioms on school premises were punished.

The process of *francisation*, i.e., the assimilation of members of native ethnic minorities as well as immigrants into the French majority culture, was not entirely forcible, nor must it be attributed solely to a school system that disseminated a common culture in which "Frenchness" (*francité*) was defined officially not in ethnic or religious terms but in terms of the acceptance of republicanism, laicism, and rationalism. There was also the impact of economic development: industrialization and urbanization uprooted many of the ethnically oriented peasantry and coopted them, and their elites, into a national French system that promised advancement and prosperity. The French process of assimilation was, to all appearances, so successful that the number of ethnic-language speakers declined dramatically and an increasing number of intellectuals and politicians could pretend that there were no longer any ethnic minorities in France. In fact, most geography books published in the first half of the twentieth century speak of geographic-ecologic rather than ethnic regions, inhabited here and there by peasant folk communities with quaint customs.[4]

The spread of socialism, in particular its Marxist version, served also to delegitimate ethnic orientations; they were reactionary not only because they were associated with provincial-clericalist doctrine, but also because they reflected a false consciousness. During the interwar period, it is true, some socialist and other progressive elements who were critical of capitalist concentration and colonialism expressed sympathy for the regionalist sentiments in poverty-stricken areas (e.g., Brittany and Occitania). But after Liberation, sympathy for ethnocultural aspirations declined sharply. In part, this was due to the overreaction of right-wing (mainly Gaullist) and left-wing Jacobins to the fact that certain ethnic leaders in Brittany, Alsace, and the Flemish region had been enticed into collaboration with the German occupiers by promises of eventual autonomy.[5] More important, most political leaders were distracted from the ethnic problem by the urgent need to reconstruct the *national* political and economic systems.

OPENING UP TO THE ETHNIC REALITY

After the establishment of the Fifth Republic, French elite opinion began to show greater receptivity to ethnic concerns and a willingness to reexamine Jacobin ideology. The mystique of the French "nation-state," a state based on a great martial tradition, a globally significant language, and a culture that was widely admired and imitated, had been undermined by military defeat during and after World War II. The image of the French national culture was also tarnished by the loss of empire, in the sense that that loss led to a constriction of France's global *mission civilisatrice*. As France rebuilt its war-shattered economy, the country became increasingly aware of its lack of economic self-sufficiency. The imperatives of economic modernization implied a quest for global markets, and they also implied a gradual displacement of the old, humanistic elite that had been oriented toward French literary culture by a "technicist" elite that increasingly used mathematical symbols or—*horribile dictu*—English. The use of these nonnational languages served to undermine the prestige of French and to enhance the relative standing of Breton and other peripheral "dialects." The establishment of the European Economic Community, with its multilateral and supranational transaction patterns, put in question the old assumption that the "nation-state" was the most logical or most efficient subunit and evoked the possibility of a restructuring of the Western European geographical space along ethnocultural lines. Moreover, the greater permeability of political boundaries led to increasing transterritorial contacts between related ethnic communities—the Alsatians and the inhabitants of the southwestern Federal Republic of Germany; the Catalans of France and Spain; the Flemings of the Dunkirk area and Belgium; and the Celts of Brittany, Ireland, and Great Britain—and enlarged their field of action. Finally, there was the influx of immigrants—a consequence of decolonization and a response to the need for cheap labor—which was so massive and abrupt that rapid assimilation was unfeasible. In short, it was no longer possible to deny that French society was multiethnic.

Concurrent with this emerging social reality there was a reexamination of the hallowed historical thesis that the "integration" of the Bretons, Corsicans, and others into France through territorial acquisition implied for them a move from a politically and economically backward to an advanced position. It was pointed out, on the contrary, that that integration had brought them into a political system based on royal absolutism, had led to the loss of their elite to Paris, and had brought about the removal of control over economic resources from the periphery to the center and with it, the impoverishment of the ethnic masses. Impressed by the acquisition of political sovereignty by all sorts of "tribes" in Third World countries, French intellectuals, in particular of the democratic left, detected a parallel between the erstwhile colonial situation of these tribes and that of the ethnic communities within France, which were now often seen as victims of an "internal colonialism."[6] They believed, moreover, that the weakening of capitalism would occur by way of a dismantling of the overcentralized state and of the accompanying centralized culture that was an expression of a concentrated capitalism, and that the liberation of the citizen would be secured by three forms of "deconcentration" that would occur more or less simultaneously: administrative, economic, and cultural. The conviction that the achievement of genuine freedom implied a restoration of authenticity and autonomy—a conviction that spread among leftist *militants* during and after the events of May 1968—led to certain excesses, including the idealization of the peasantry and its local culture and the positing of various kinds of utopian schemes for economic self-management (*autogestion*), but it also led to a greater receptivity to new forms of pluralism.[7]

THE EVOLUTION OF POSTWAR POLICY

These "revisionist" ideas should be viewed not as ideological adjustments to an emerging policy reality but rather as an intellectual preparation for a policy of the future. The actual accommodation of ethnic demands, and even the official legitimation of their existence, was slow and hesitant. Before, during, and after World War I, numerous petitions by ethnoregional voluntary associations to permit the teaching of ethnic languages and ethnic culture and history were forwarded to the national authorities. On several occasions, such demands were officially endorsed on local and regional levels. For example, in 1912 the general council of Morbihan, a department in Brittany, and in 1938 the city councils of more than 300 communes of that region, passed resolutions in favor of the Breton language and transmitted them to the national government—with little effect. Similar requests had emanated from Alsace, both during the interwar period and immediately after World War II, but these invariably produced negative reactions on the part of the national government. Many Alsatian political and cultural elite figures called for the promotion of bilingualism or, more precisely, for the creation of an equilibrium among French, German, Alsatian components of culture in Alsace and in part of Lorraine—French to promote national unity; Alsatian to reflect the genuine regional folk spirit; and standard German to connect Alsatian (and Alsatians) to Germanic "high culture" and to facilitate transnational contacts.[8] If there was a "policy" with respect to Alsatian culture at all, it consisted in governmental noninterference in the publication of Alsatian- or German-language journals, in the hope that the readership of these journals would decline by attrition. Indeed, between 1946 and 1984 the circulation of the bilingual *Nouvelles d'Alsace* declined from 317,000 to 118,000 copies.[9]

In 1952, the national Ministry of Education permitted the reintroduction of High German as an elective for pupils in the last two years of elementary schools in Alsace. But this was, strictly speaking, not part of an ethnolinguistic policy. Moreover, although 84 percent of parents expressed themselves in favor of such instruction, the national elementary school teachers' union (*Syndicat national des instituteurs*) was hostile and tried to obstruct the implementation of the new policy. Gradually, especially since the early 1970s, instruction in Alsatian and High German was initiated in more than 300 communities, but these classes were organized by voluntary associations (notably the *Cercle René Schickele*) *outside* the regular school curriculum. During that period, many local school councils sent appeals to Paris, often transmitted by the general councils of the Bas-Rhin and Haut-Rhin, for the inclusion of instruction in German in the public school system and the official use of Alsatian, in addition to the teaching of regional culture. These appeals—which were to begin to bear fruit in the 1980s—were supported by selected politicians of the major parties and by the two largest trade unions, the (pro-Communist) *Confédération générale du travail* (CGT) and the (pro-Socialist) *Fédération des syndicats généraux de l'education nationale-Confédération française démocratique du travail* (SGEN-CFDT). Although the general councils were heavily Gaullist and the unions leftist, both were equally disinclined ideologically to support cultural pluralism, at least initially—the former because of fear of separatist consequences and the latter because of a lingering conviction that the promotion of ethnic culture was inconsistent with modernity and progressive democracy. But neither the Gaullists nor the leftist unions could for long ignore the growing public and (electoral) pressures. According to public-opinion surveys, between 80 and 90 percent of Alsatian households favored instruction in German.

The first, and from the point of view of symbolism the most important, official act in support of ethnocultural claims was the passage of the Deixonne Law in 1951. This law, which had been introduced by a Radical-Socialist deputy (and followed an abortive bill sponsored four years earlier by Communist and other left-wing deputies),[10] provided for the teaching, on an elective basis, of Breton, Basque, Catalan, and Occitan in the upper and lower forms of lycées. Unfortunately, the law had less than perfect practical value, since the Ministry of Education failed to provide adequate funding for the training of teachers in these languages or even the regulations needed to implement the policy. (The first regulations related to the Deixonne Law were in fact issued only 1970.) Although the very passage of the law contributed to a movement leading to practical steps, including the withdrawal of official objections to the teaching of selected regional languages on an optional basis, government policy remained hesitant and selective. For example, government circulars issued in 1970–1971 that permitted the teaching of Breton in elementary schools contained several qualifications: the language was to be taught if at least ten pupils asked for it; the courses were to be offered outside of regular school hours (during lunchtime or after school); and (as was often the case) the teacher received no extra pay.

Between the mid-1960s and mid-1970s, radio news broadcasts in Breton were introduced and gradually expanded from five to twenty minutes per day; and in 1975, a "cultural charter" was signed by the regional authorities of Alsace, the city of Strasbourg, and the national government, which committed itself to the promotion of regional culture. This promotion included the introduction of new university courses, the support of Alsatian music festivals, expanded research on Alsatian history, and limited broadcasting of Alsatian cultural themes on one of the three national television channels (FR3—France-Régions). A parallel cultural charter for Brittany was negotiated in 1977 among national and local authorities and Breton voluntary associations.

Such policies had become somewhat less risky politically because of the gradual evolution of public opinion and a lessening of resistance. This evolution was reflected in the speeches made by both President Georges Pompidou and President Valéry Giscard d'Estaing (especially during election campaigns in "ethnic" regions) in favor of the idea of defending the cultural-linguistic heritage of French ethnic communities. But little concrete policy resulted from such expressions, because these presidents were still too tightly in the embrace of Gaullism, whose ideology had put heavy stress on the intimate connection between cultural-linguistic homogeneity and political unity.

THE ELECTION OF MITTERRAND:
A NEW DEPARTURE

When Mitterrand assumed the presidency of France in June 1981, he brought with him a political party that had been going through a period of ideological and programmatic adjustments in regard to the ethnic reality. During and after the events of May–June 1968, many Socialist activists were sensitized by rebellious students and workers to the problem of the disorientation and alienation that rapid urbanization, mass industrial production, and an increasingly impersonal administrative system had been producing among the people. Their concerns had been taken up in particular by the *Parti socialiste unifié* (PSU), which argued that the French citizens' self-worth could be restored by a restoration of their autonomy and a recognition of their unique individuality, a restoration that required as much decentralization, deconcentration, and self-governance as possible in administrative, economic, and cultural spheres. While calling for the restoration of meaningful regional and local government and for "participatory democracy" in the factories, the PSU also advocated a degree of ethnocultural self-determination. In 1971, it issued a monograph entitled *Colonialisme intérieur et minorités nationales*,[11] in which it stressed the cultural-linguistic differences among various regions and asserted that the ethnics be given the right to develop their own cultural policies. Although the PSU's position was not wholly consistent—some of its pronouncements concurrently stressing the exigencies of the productive process and the suppression of economic and class inequalities as paramount—its influence on the Socialist party (*Parti socialiste*—PS) was significant, especially after 1973, when many of the PSU leaders and activists joined the PS. Thus, between the early 1970s and 1981, the need to develop a policy that acknowledged the legitimacy of the cultural aspirations of ethnic minorities was articulated in numerous Socialist speeches. Mitterrand himself, in a speech in 1974, said:

The Socialist party has always decided to choose the development of the personality. And when one considers Brittany, Corsica, the Basque country, and the Languedoc region, too, it is true that the attempt to suffocate all the means of expression of original languages—for the structures of languages are also the deeper structures of the brain, touching the very essence of being—it is true that economic colonialism . . . and a certain reflex of centralistic domination of a colonialist nature—all that should be corrected. . . . At one time the kings of France, the Jacobins, Bonaparte . . . were right . . . in their efforts to [fight against] centrifugal tendencies. . . . Very well, it was necessary to make France. But . . . the necessary unity has become uniformity, in which individual being is stamped out. . . . [Now we must respect] the right to be different.[12]

These ideas were echoed in the *Manifeste municipal socialiste* of September 1976, adopted by the PS executive committee, which referred to the need for the *autogestion* as well as for a policy that would "bring to the [local] population a structure best adapted for the expression of their identities and their cultural specificities."[13] Similarly, the *motions d'orientation* at the PS congress in Metz in 1979 called upon the party to fight against a uniform and overly centralized state and proposed legislation that would recognize for all regions, and in particular Corsica, "the right to be different."[14]

In the *Projet socialiste*, the massive "party platform" of 1980, which blamed capitalism for a "homogenization of mentalities," the PS called for a policy that would lead to "a flowering of regional languages and cultures that constitute one of the riches of the French cultural inheritance." It promised the teaching of regional languages in public schools and the use of these languages in the electronic media.[15] This was echoed just before the 1981 elections in the *110 Propositions pour la France* (no. 56), which promised specifically that "regional languages [would] be recognized and taught," and in Mitterrand's *Discours de Lorient* in March 1981, in which he declared that "to strike at a people's culture and language is to wound it most deeply."[16] In a tract issued just before the elections, the PS advanced a number of concrete proposals. Reflecting the views of the Socialist federations of several ethnic regions, the tract called for the recognition and utilization of such ethnic (private) schools as the Basque *ikastolas*, the Breton *diwans*, the Catalan *bressolas*, the Corsican *scole corse*, and the Occitan *calandretas*, with all of which the government would contract for the teaching of ethnic languages.[17]

After the elections, the Mauroy government tried as soon as possible to introduce measures consistent with these declarations, not only because it was morally bound by its preelectoral promises but also, and perhaps more importantly, because it had become clear that the majority of the Armenian, Jewish, and even Gypsy electorate had voted for the left, as had many inhabitants of the Overseas Territories; that an increasing number of regionalist *militants* in Brittany and the Occitan and Basque areas had become active in the Socialist party; and that many immigrants, though not necessarily voting, had fraternized with native French workers during demonstrations in favor of leftist politicians.[18]

Among the ethnopluralistic policies pursued under the Mitterrand presidency between 1981 and 1986, it is necessary to distinguish between those that were concerned specifically with the promotion of ethnic cultural pluralism and those, like administrative decentralization, that had a spillover effect on ethnic policies.

The decentralization policies of the first two years of Socialist rule have been widely viewed as among the most far-reaching and innovative measures of postwar France. The most important of these measures, the so-called Defferre Law, which passed the Assembly in the fall of 1981 and was signed by the president in March 1982, was aimed at effective administrative decisionmaking deconcentration. The law affirmed that "the communes, departments, and regions shall administer themselves freely by means of elected bodies."[19] It abolished the prefect, replaced him with a *commissaire de la République* and transferred the power of decision to the president of the general council, who would be elected directly by the people (rather than, as hitherto, indirectly via the cantonal elections). The city councils as well as the general councils were given greater power to collect their own revenues and make their own locally and regionally relevant decisions.

It is a matter of controversy to what extent the drafters of the Defferre Law specifically thought of ethnic cultural matters as one of the now "delegated" policy concerns; and it is equally uncertain whether that law, if left by itself, would have been effective in the promotion of such matters. On the one hand, the law gives regional assemblies the power "to assure to the region the preservation of identity," through it does not list any specific ethnic or cultural-linguistic criteria for that identity. On the other hand, the law makes a reference to the need to preserve the unity of the nation and retains for the national government the responsibility for education and "the management of scholarly establishments." Nevertheless, the ethnocultural spillover of the legislation was not long in coming. In the first place, the autonomy statute for Corsica, which was enacted in 1982 and which was regarded by many as a model for future autonomy arrangements for other regions, provided for a regional legislature that would have power to enact laws pertaining to secondary school curricula and to "determine complementary education activities aimed at preserving the Corsican language and culture." Second, the regional and municipal authorities were increasingly viewed as the natural loci of application of whatever ethnocultural measures were to be decided on a national level.

In any case, several of the study commissions that were set up by the various ministries—Culture, Education, Interior—and various agencies dealing with native minorities, immigrants, and even repatriates operated under the assumption that administrative decentralization, economic deconcentration, welfare-state measures and the regulation of the labor market could not be entirely separated from the question of cultural diversity. Among the most important of the authoritative reports were those prepared by the Queyranne and Giordan commissions, both set up by Jack Lang, the minister of culture, in 1981. The Giordan report, submitted in February 1982 and entitled "Cultural Democracy and the Right to be Different," begins with a listing of various ethnocultural regions and language communities found in the Hexagon, using it as evidence for its contention that French society is a multiethnic mosaic.[20] While not fully accepting the distinction, made on several occasions by Robert Lafont, between *nation politique* and *nation linguistico-culturelle*, and hence between citizenship and nationality,[21] the Giordan report did argue that membership in the body politic, i.e., *political* citizenship, is incomplete without being accompanied by *social* citizenship (i.e., welfare-state entitlements) and *cultural* citizenship, that is, the rights and privileges of cultural benefits and self-expression.[22] To make these last-named benefits and rights meaningful, the state must abandon its elitist position: its conception of language and culture must be based not merely in Paris but must include the regional and peasant cultures of France. The Giordan report suggests that these cultures and languages be not only legitimated, but that the government encourage their maintenance and diffusion by means of budgetary allocations to build archives, undertake research, train teachers, and subsidize projects in literature, history, grammar, music, and the arts. It also suggests that regional boundary lines be redrawn as much as possible along ethnocultural lines.

One of the findings of the Giordan Commission is the fact that not all ethnic minority cultures, no matter how long implanted in the country, had a specific geographic base; therefore, it makes a distinction between the "territorially based" cultures and those that are geographically dispersed (*cultures communautaires*). The Giordan report does not deal with specific immigrant worker communities—probably in part because the commission did not wish to invade the domain of other agencies dealing with them—although it acknowledges that some of its recommendations might partially apply to them as well.[23] One of them was the Ministry of Labor, which issued its own report advocating special schools for children of immigrants that would at once help to integrate them economically into French society *and* help them preserve a dual cultural identity.[24]

The Giordan Commission's views about France as a multicultural civilization were perhaps somewhat romantic in that they ignored the vestiges of Jacobin thinking, the widespread xenophobia, and the administrative conservatism of France, all of which served to impede the development, and could be expected in future to impede the implementation, of policies of cultural pluralism. Nevertheless, the report contained practical suggestions of an organizational nature that the government was soon to take seriously. Among these suggestions was the establishment of an administrative division within the Ministry of Culture for minority languages and cultures that would have clientelistic relationships with ethnic groups; a commission for research into minority languages and cultures; regional directorates and agencies (*cellules de concertation*) for territorially based ethnic groups, and parallel directorates for nonterritorial communities based in Paris—both of which would help implement national policies *and* send emissaries ("delegates") to the government in Paris to recommend policies; and, finally, a national committee (of representatives) of minority cultures.

The Queyranne report, entitled "Regions and Cultural Decentralization," which was issued in July 1982, was more concrete and more realistic, in the sense that it took into account existing administrative structures and based itself heavily on patterns of relations between the central government and the provinces that were already in place, among them the *conventions culturelles* that had been inaugurated during the Giscard presidency.[25] Like the Giordan report, this report, too, emphasized that ethnocultural policies must be collaborative ventures of the nation and the regions.

LEGISLATIVE AND ADMINISTRATIVE ACTIONS

The official actions that followed the Queyranne and Giordan reports were of four distinct types: (1) piecemeal measures emanating from the ministries of Education and Culture and other agencies that addressed themselves to the ad hoc needs of ethnic communities, especially with regard to language teaching; (2) policies and measures that, although not specifically concerned with ethnocultural pluralism, nonetheless had a tangible effect on it, e.g., measures pertaining to immigration, asylum, the rights of aliens, and naturalization; (3) government and private-members' bills; and (4) executive-administrative actions.

During its first year in office, the Socialist government ratified the International Human Rights Convention of 1966, which provides (Article 27) that "in states where ethnic, religious or linguistic minorities exist, persons belonging to those minorities may not be deprived of the right to maintain, together with other members of their group, their own cultural life, to profess and practice their religion, or to use their own language." At the same time, the government abolished the State Security Court, which had been set up two decades earlier to deal with sedition and which had become the venue for trials of members of radical (including separatist) ethnic organizations. The Auroux Laws (passed in June 1982) provided that even union members not fluent in French were eligible for election to labor-relations tribunals; and a citizenship law enacted in November 1983 granted naturalized citizens equal political rights by providing that they could run for any public office without having to wait ten years after acquiring citizenship.

As was suggested above, the decentralization measures were expected to figure in one way or another in the evolving policies of ethnopluralism emanating from Paris. The decentralization laws of March 1982 contained a provision (Article 93) for a special endowment fund (*dotation*) for regional and local cultural projects. But the government was slow in allocating money for the fund, and the 1986 budget (enacted well before the parliamentary elections of that year), contained no specific allocation for the fund at all.[26] The (supplementary) decentralization law of July 22, 1983 (Title II, Section 5, Articles 56–58), was fairly specific in transferring to departments, communes, and regions several types of competences in cultural matters: libraries, museums, schools for the visual and performing arts, architectural preservation, and departmental archives. In this law it was stipulated that the local authorities themselves provide the financial resources, but that the national government was to supervise the appointment of scientific personnel and safeguard the overall "quality" of the services—in short, to retain its *tutelle* (national government guardianship) in cultural matters.[27]

Cultural *tutelle* continued to be maintained by means of a plethora of regulations aimed at ensuring that national or subnational agencies concerned with culture and the arts did not go too far afield from national responsibilities and orientations.[28] Nevertheless, it has been suggested that enough competences regarding cultural matters were transferred to enable local and regional officials to promote ethnically specific cultural projects *if* the officials possessed sufficient political will.[29] Thus, departments had the power to provide technical and financial assistance to communes for cultural projects; and communes were permitted to provide supplementary educational programs and—subject to agreement by the department and the local school authorities—to use local school premises for such programs. Nevertheless, it is not clear to what extent the transfer of competences to local/regional offices has correlated with the promotion of ethnoregional culture by the local authorities. In some cases involving grants from the national government to local bodies, negotiations between Paris and the local authorities have been protracted. In other cases, Paris has provided the initiative in defining the cultural projects to be pursued locally—that is, to resort to local or regional authorities (such as the *Fonds régionaux d'art contemporain* [FRAC][30] to promote not ethnic (or peasant) culture but rather national (or Parisian elite) culture, much as André Malraux, de Gaulle's minister of culture, had done during the early 1960s with his provincial *maisons de culture*.[31]

The above suggests conflicting meanings of "cultural decentralization." For many members of the elite, from the Gaullists to the Socialists, the decentralization and "democratization" of culture has meant a process of bringing "high culture" and Parisian refinement to the provinces rather than strengthening practical peasant culture or "folklore"; that is, they wish to stress the innovative and globally relevant rather than the "hereditary" (and excessively particularistic) aspects of culture, no matter how authentic. In the view of this cultural Jacobinism, ethnoregionally specific projects should relate primarily to the safeguarding and study of local architectural styles and art collections, not for their own intrinsic worth but for their importance to French national history and as part of the nation's physical inheritance (*le patrimoine immobilier de la nation*).[32]

Among the institutional reflections of this national approach to regional culture are the *Commissions régionales du patrimoine historique, archéologique, et ethonologique* (COREPHAE). Each of the commissions has thirty members, all chosen by the *commissaire de la République*, including ten civil servants, sixteen elected officials, and four representatives of "interested organizations." The underdeveloped ethnoregional orientation of the COREPHAE is perhaps illustrated by the fact that for some of the members of that body, the terms *ethnologie* and *ethnographie*—now used widely by intellectuals and high officials—have come to refer not so much to ethnic matters as to functionally defined social types. Another consultative body with more specific responsibilities, the *collège régional du patrimoine des sites*, was established in 1984. It has twelve to eighteen members, appointed by the *commissaire de la République* as well, who are "qualified individuals," e.g., architects and representatives of private associations, but who are not necessarily chosen on an ethnic basis. There may well be conflicts between these two bodies and problems of overlapping jurisdiction, but not enough time has elapsed to provide adequate information about this matter.

In 1984, still another set of bodies was established: six *directions régionales des affaires culturelles*. These *directions* were provided with funds under the 1984–1985 budget—e.g., 15 million francs for Brittany, and 500,000 francs for a specific Occitan project in Languedoc-Roussillon for which a contract had been signed earlier between the national government and the regional authorities. It was unclear to what extent these *directions* were to be used to coordinate the activities envisaged by the numerous charters and conventions relating to regional cultures that had been signed earlier. Some of these conventions were too specialized; they authorized too limited a program and were under the direct supervision of a single ministry, which lacked the competence to deal with the regional culture as a whole. This was the case with the cultural charter of Alsace, which was signed (in February 1981) only by the Ministry of Culture, and—although it touched upon broadcasts and upon educational programs for young people—did not involve the ministries of Education or Youth or the authorities responsible for the media. Conversely, other conventions involved too many authorities, a situation giving rise to jurisdictional disputes, a thinning out of interest, and buck-passing.

It was hoped that the *commissaire de la République*, who was given specific directives to facilitate the development of regional culture, would play an important role in coordinating, on departmental levels, both old and new projects. Since that official (unlike his predecessor, the prefect) was to be responsible to the general council of the department rather than to the national government, that hope was not regarded as unrealistic. However, as decentralization was being implemented, it became apparent that the *commissaire*'s activities would be pursued not merely in behalf of ethnic cultures but of the national cultural interest as well, for this official was assigned multiple roles: (1) as the agent of central government tutelage; (2) as the liaison between national minister (e.g., of education, culture, and interior) and the regional and local authorities; (3) as the person who "confirms" decisions made by elected regional and local assemblies and who "harmonizes" these decisions with national policies; and (4) as a facilitator of dialogues between the various authorities.[33] The *commissaire*'s work was thus not much different from that of the prefect whom he replaced; in fact, the prefectures continued to exist, and the *commissaire* himself continued, by force of habit, to be referred to as the prefect.

A major attempt to clarify the direction of ethnocultural policy was the "Bill Concerning the Promotion of the Languages and Cultures of France."[34] Introduced in May 1984 by Jean-Pierre Destrade, a Socialist deputy from the Basque region (Pyrénées-Atlantiques), and cosponsored by the entire Socialist Assembly group, the bill was designed to reverse "the tradition of cultural repression [in France]" and to reaffirm "the right to be different" (*droit à la différence*), which in turn implied "the sacred right of a people to speak its language." Specifically, the Destrade bill provided that the right of ethnic minorities to the use of their language be guaranteed; that discrimination based on language use be outlawed; that for each "language of France" there be created a consultative council charged with proposing to regional and national authorities measures to safeguard and promote that language; that the regional councils be supplemented by a national coordinating council; that audiovisual centers for minority languages be set up in the various regions; and that the use of ethnic minority languages be permitted in all matters of public administration and "acts of public life," including the courts, the police, and the postal service.

The bill did not get very far because the government refused to put it on the agenda in the National Assembly, and it was soon withdrawn. The reasons for this development were complex and ambiguous. Not all Socialist deputies who signed the bill were enthusiastic about all its features; and there was still too much opposition within the ranks of the PS (in particular its CERES wing)[35] to ethnocultural pluralism as a whole to risk open debate, with its attendant threat to party unity.[36] Furthermore, the bill contained no specifics regarding budgetary allocations, an omission that made it difficult to calculate future expenses and increased the likelihood that the entire policy favoring ethnic minorities would be used as political ammunition by the extreme-rightist *Front National* and others in an appeal to the working-class supporters of the PS who were xenophobic and who—in this period of unemployment and retrenchment of the welfare state—would resent the expenditure of scarce fiscal resources for ethnocultural "frills." Perhaps, too, the sponsors of the bill did not expect it to pass but rather to serve as a spur to the government to redouble its own efforts. It has even been argued that the passage of the bill would have exacerbated tensions between the national government and local authorities, for many of the local bureaucrats and politicians harbored national ambitions and orientations and were therefore less liberal and less sympathetic to ethnoregional cultural pluralism than the Socialist politicians in Paris.[37]

To complicate matters, a small number (i.e., about two dozen) deputies of the Gaullist-Giscardist opposition had introduced a rival bill, "Concerning the Status and Promotion of Regional Languages and Cultures."[38] This substitute bill was a response to pressures exerted on some Gaullists and Giscardists by constituents in Alsace and Brittany. Most of the opposition politicians appeared to be uninvolved in the bill, while a handful of hard-liners (such as Michel Debré) fought it, expressing the fear that any concession to linguistic pluralism would strike a severe blow at national unity. It was in part to pacify these hard-liners that the opposition bill also made a strong case for the protection of the French language, which was "threatened not from within but from without," and called for the establishment of a *Commissariat général* for French and regional languages. In view of these developments, there was the growing belief that the aims of the Destrade bill could—and would—be pursued more effectively, and with less political fallout, by executive-administrative action.

The controversies surrounding the "decentralization" of culture, as part of the whole complex of decentralization policy, pointed up the gap that existed between good intentions and ideological, institutional, and budgetary constraints. It is true that the decentralization laws of 1982 empowered the municipal and general (departmental) councils to vote their own budgets; however, the transfer of revenue-gathering powers to subnational units was to take place gradually. The regional and local authorities were to obtain their revenues from real-estate, business, and miscellaneous license taxes; the return of a (progressively increasing) portion of nationally collected taxes; the issuance of bonds; a remission of local contributions toward the maintenance of the (nationally controlled) police; and direct subsidies by the national government of specific local projects.[39] The actual transfer of fiscal powers has been skimpy and cautious, a situation that attests to the second thoughts of the post-1983 Socialist leadership and of the Gaullist government since 1986 about decentralization.

ETHNOPLURALISM AND
INTEREST-GROUP PLURALISM

The promotion of ethnic policies has involved not only public authorities on national, regional, and local levels, but voluntary associations as well. A few years ago, ethnically based associations were viewed with misgivings, and ethnic "lobbying" was considered to be un-French, if not subversive. Today, the open expression of cultural demands by associations of indigenous ethnics has gained legitimacy. In October 1981, the opportunities for ethnic lobbying were extended to immigrants as well when a law was passed that permitted foreigners to form associations.[40]

The relationship between official government bodies and private-interest groups has been a complicated one in this matter. On the one hand, as a direct consequence and, in a sense, in imitation of the government's openness toward ethnocultural pluralism, trade unions began to print information in ethnic languages and to encourage immigrants or their descendants to join them. On the other hand, the voluntary associations have often taken the initiative with regard to ethnic policies and the government authorities have increasingly depended on, and even solicited, their input. For instance, the decision taken by the Ministry of Education in 1985 to grant diplomas (*Certificats d'aptitude au professorat de l'enseignement secondaire*—CAPES) to future teachers of Breton was the result of complicated negotiations with Breton voluntary associations.[41] Many of the "contracts"—generally signed for one year but renewable[42]—have involved the participation of ethnic cultural societies, documentation centers, or organizations of language teachers that existed on regional levels, e.g., the associations for the promotion of Basque, Corsican, Breton, and Occitan cultures and languages. Other contracts have been made with cultural centers that were established with the encouragement of public authorities for the express purpose of implementing ethnocultural policies. In several instances, the government paid the salaries of employees of private associations who functioned as organizers (*animateurs*) of officially endorsed ethnic projects; in other cases, the government paid teachers' salaries. Thus, in 1984, the Ministry of Education provided a subsidy of 1,285,000 francs to the *Diwan* Association for the salaries, and a contribution of 250,000 francs to the social security coverage, of Breton-language teachers; and for the academic year 1985–1986 the Ministry of Culture promised a subvention of 856,000 francs for salaries and 200,000 francs for the association's debt repayments.[43]

The role of voluntary associations has been particularly important in the case of the geographically dispersed ethnics (the *cultures communautaires*), such as the Armenians, Jews, Gypsies, Kurds, Maghrebis, and the relatively recently settled East Asian communities. The social/cultural centers of most of these communities are located in Paris, both because of the relatively significant clusters of *communautaire* ethnics in the capital *and* because the official promotion of their cultural interests can be promoted most effectively by the national government. In some instances, the government relied on well-established institutions, such as the *Centre Rachi*, which has for many years furnished Jewish cultural and educational programs. In other cases, such as that of the Gypsies, the government's commitment to the promotion of ethnic culture *required* that appropriate ethnic "voluntary" associations be created.

The enlargement of the role of ethnocultural voluntary associations paralleled, and was stimulated by, the growing importance of economic and professional associations since the 1970s, the ever-closer collaboration between them and the national and local government, and the increasing delegation of public-administrative tasks to the private sector. These developments have raised the question whether geographic subnational units—i.e., old administrative subunits such as departments—are not threatened by the emergence of new kinds of "functional" subunits, among them perhaps the ethnic community. More important, it raises the question whether the involvement of interest groups in France's ethnic policies has been "pluralistic" or "corporatist," i.e., whether the emerging ethnic policies are likely to be "vector" results of competing ethnic pressures, or whether the government's own policies will be determined independently and will serve to coopt ethnocultural associations and deprive them of their autonomy.

Present indications suggest an interpretation on the side of "pluralism." It seems clear that the official legitimation of ethnic interests and ethnopolitics is accompanied by an efflorescence of *la vie associative*—an overall growth of all kinds of interest groups and of interest-group activity in all domains. It is no coincidence that "liberal progressives" who have favored an active interest-group pluralism (e.g., Bernard Stasi, a left-of-center Christian Democratic Giscardist)[44] have also favored ethnic pluralism. The legitimation of ethnic interest groups and of their involvement in the shaping of cultural policy is likely to grow even stronger as the state relaxes its traditional monopoly over cultural matters. Such a relaxation is already reflected in a continuing decentralization of education, in the abandonment of the Socialist government's attempts to bring private school curricula under closer control of the centralized state, and in laws permitting the establishment of regional and private (commercial) radio stations and television networks.

THE MINISTRY OF EDUCATION
AND THE ETHNIC DIMENSION

The involvement of the Ministry of National Education in the promotion of ethnic minority languages and cultures has been impressive. A three-year plan inaugurated in June 1982 for the systematic development of instruction in these languages and cultures projected the participation of 110,000 kindergarten and elementary school pupils in 2,900 schools and of 4,800 teachers. The plan also included experimental bilingual classes, the preparation of eighty-one curriculum specialists (*conseillers pédagogiques*), and special training courses in thirty-two teacher-training schools (*écoles normales*), and provisions for ethnic language instruction for 13,000 students in 300 lycées. Ethnic-language instruction was to be made available in all elementary and secondary schools where a sufficient number of students demanded it. Furthermore, the ministry undertook to support ethnic language "majors," at undergraduate and/or graduate levels, at a number of appropriate regional universities: in Corsican at Corte, Catalan at Perpignan, Alsatian at Strasbourg, Basque at Bordeaux, Breton at Rennes, and Occitan at Aix-Marseille, Nice, Toulouse, and Montpellier. Support in these cases meant the appointment of new (or newly specialized) *professeurs titulaires* and of 800 other teaching personnel, as well as the preparation of curricular materials.

In addition to widening its contacts with ethnic voluntary associations, the Ministry of Education spurred on local authorities to take their own initiatives. Thus in Corsica, the Academic Commission for the Corsican Language and Culture, authorized in 1979 but dormant, was reactivated at the behest of the rector of the Corsican education district (*académie*).[45]

Between 1983 and 1985, the Ministry of Education spent over 20 million francs for the teaching of a minority languages in lycées and nearly 8 million francs to teach these languages in elementary schools. In addition, nearly 5 million francs were allocated during the period of 1984–1985 alone to voluntary associations that provided bilingual instruction. One of these associations was the *Seaska* movement in the Basque country, which had been attempting to promote bilingualism by means of the privately maintained network of *ikastolas* that extended from nursery school (using Basque only) to primary and secondary schools. In January 1982, in response to a petition signed by 8,000 individuals (including mayors and spokespersons of political parties and interest groups), the Ministry of Education began negotiations with *Seaska* that culminated, more than two years later, in a *convention* that extended official recognition to the *ikastolas* as regional agents of the government's ethnic-language programs, promised subsidies to the Basque evening school system (Gau eskola), and provided for the payment of public salaries to itinerant teachers of Basque.[46]

Some critics have accused the Ministry of Education of skimping on funds and of dragging its feet with respect to a meaningful implementation of multilingual instruction.[47] Others, in turn, have argued that instruction in minority languages does not need to be heavily financed because it cannot be more than symbolic—even for the ethnics themselves, most of whom are not so irrational as to take too much valuable time away from their study of the French language, of English, and of other more useful subjects.

If there has been footdragging within the Ministry of Education, it may be attributed to the existence of overlapping jurisdictions, the frequent absence of clear directives, and the pressures emanating from the *Fédération d'Education Nationale* (FEN) and other teachers' associations, some of which are still imbued with the ideal of a national, uniform culture and language and suspicious of the hidden political agenda behind the cultural and linguistic claims of regional ethnic elite figures. In some cases, the reservations of FEN regarding government support of ethnic culture was due not so much to opposition to minority-language instruction as such, but to other reasons. Thus, the leadership of the teachers' unions had the uncomfortable feeling that the granting of a CAPES for a regional ethnic language implied a kind of recruitment that, although officially a national competitive one, would in practice be limited to specific regional positions (and to teachers of ethnic background) while, conversely, there were "exiled" Bretons who had been specializing in more general "national" subjects who might have to wait years before being able to secure posts in Brittany.[48] More important, there was the fear that the *laïciste* orientation of the national education curriculum—and the wall of separation between state and religion—would be undermined. There has been (at least historically) and undeniable correlation between Breton (and to a lesser extent Occitan and Catalan) culture and Catholic values and folkways, and there has continued to be a connection between Jewish culture and Judaism, and Maghrebi Arab culture and Islam.[49] The Ministry of Education itself must have been torn between its desire to fall in step with the emerging pluralistic attitudes of the Socialist government—and the obvious good will of Alain Savary, the minister of education—and its responsibility for maintaining a national, republican, secular, and more or less coherent educational system.

Moreover, official footdragging has been neither systematic nor even deliberate; often, policymaking delays or failures could be ascribed to the complexity of the ethnolinguistic-geographic reality and to intraethnic confusions or rivalries, which some public officials exploited, if not actually encouraged. The facts that there are more than 10 million Occitanians—according to one estimate, at least that many inhabitants of France easily understand one or another variant of Occitan, among the most important of which are Languedocien, Provençal and Gascon—and that the Occitan geographical space occupies about a third of the total area of mainland France[50] should have resulted in an official legitimation if not active support of the language. However, the very linguistic diversity of Occitania has made a uniform and consistent language policy difficult. Indeed, the government has referred to *les langues d'oc* in the plural and to the *diversité dialectophone* of the area,[51] reflecting not merely a desire to find an excuse for the long refusal by the Ministry of Eduction to créate a *diplôme d'études universitaires générales* (DEUG—akin to an undergraduate major) in Occitan but also the reality of intra-Occitan fragmentation. Thus, there have been quarrels among Occitan scholars regarding proper orthography, and rivalries among universities (e.g., Aix-en-Provence, Montpellier, and Toulouse) as centers of Occitan studies.

The concern of the Ministry of Education with ethnic policies has been shared by other ministries and government agencies: the Ministry of Social Affairs, which has organized programs to sensitize French citizens to the reality of immigrants and their social and cultural problems; the Ministry of National Solidarity; the *Fonds d'Action Sociale*; the Secretariat of State (i.e., subministry) for Repatriates (which has facilitated meetings between native French and Muslim repatriates); the Secretariat of State for Overseas Departments and Territories (DOM/TOM); and the Secretariat of State for Communication (operating under the direction of the prime minister). This last-named office has been charged with supervising public radio and television networks, and it has been responsible for ensuring the provision of adequate broadcasting time for programs in regional languages. Typically, this has meant between one and ten hours of broadcasts per week in Occitan, Corsican, Catalan, Basque, and other languages by regional stations of Radio France; broadcasts (mostly emanating from Paris) in nine immigrant languages (including Arabic, Spanish, Portuguese, Turkish, Vietnamese, and Cambodian); and an expansion of ethnic-language television programs.

THE MINISTRY OF CULTURE: "TRAFFIC MANAGER" OF ETHNOPLURALIST PROGRAMS?

The major responsibility for the promotion of cultural and linguistic pluralism belongs to the Ministry of Culture. It has acted as the initiator and "traffic manager" of ethnocultural programs, and it served as the instrument for the innovative ideas and the passionate commitment of Jack Lang, who headed that ministry throughout the period of Socialist government. To be sure, ethnic culture has been only one of the ministry's numerous concerns. Lang had to balance his obvious desire to serve President Mitterrand and reflect Socialist policy regarding ethnic pluralism against his other tasks, to disseminate and share the national cultural patrimony with the provinces, to bring elements of high culture to the masses even while upgrading the value of mass culture, and to protect French culture as a whole against the inroads of "vulgar" American influences.

The government measures in which the Ministry of Culture has played a leading part have been promoted largely by means of "cultural development agreements" (*conventions de développement culturel*), of which more than 100 were signed between mid-1981 and the end of 1982 alone: 25 with regions and overseas departments; 10 with metropolitan departments; and 69 with municipalities.[52] The government measures have taken a variety of forms: (1) the direct subsidization of specific programs; (2) blanket lump-sum allocations to each of six *directions régionales des affaires culturelles* for programs of their own choosing; (3) grants-in-aid or matching funds agreed upon in multiannual contracts (*contracts Etat-région*), e.g., the four-year contract with Brittany involving 15 million francs to help sustain the work of Breton cultural associations, or the agreement with the region Languedoc-Roussillon for the promotion of Occitan culture for an annual allotment of 500,000 francs; (4) the provision of overall financial support to a region, with the authorities in the latter left free to decide for what purposes—cultural or other—the money is to be spent, as has been the case in Corsica since the enactment of the "autonomy" laws of 1982; and (5) collaborative projects between the national government and the cities, such as the decision taken in 1984 by the Ministry of Culture and the City of Paris for the joint financing of a museum of Jewish art, which would be a component of a great center of Jewish studies, a pet project of Jack Lang.

The specific projects supported since 1981 have been so numerous that they cannot be listed in a few brief pages. The following list is highly selective, but it illustrates the diversity of projects:

- Subsidies to publishers of Breton books and periodicals (which cost the government 130,000 francs in 1983, 85,000 francs in 1984, and 150,000 francs in 1985)
- Scholarships for research in ethnomusicology (an item for which the Ministry of Culture spent 187,000 francs in 1983 and 460,000 francs in 1985)
- Agreement with a Catalan publishing house in 1984 involving 125,000 francs for the translation of three books into Catalan
- Publication of dictionaries, grammars, and texts in Basque, Breton, Catalan, Creole, and Provençal
- Festival of Mediterranean cultures, held annually in Corsica since 1982
- Gypsy art festival at Arles (planned for 1986)
- Black theater
- *Théâtre chronique* in Corsica
- Jazz festival in French Guyana
- Festival of Jewish culture, held annually in Paris
- Armenian, Arab, Italian, and Jewish film festivals
- Dialogues on African roots
- Filming of *Shoah*

- Support of ethnological museums
- Subsidies for the establishment of ethnic libraries[53]

Recently, the Ministry of Culture, together with the Ministry of Social Affairs, established an interministerial mission for intercultural affairs, one of whose tasks was to organize "encounters" between French and Islamic cultures. In addition, the Ministry of Culture opened a Division for Regional and Nonterritorially Based (*communautaire*) Cultures as a component of the *Direction du développement culturel*, whose budget for 1983–1985 amounted to over 5 million francs. Its major responsibility was to provide "a deep cultural irrigation" of regional authorities and voluntary cultural associations.[54] Among its activities were the subvention of a Basque Cultural Center (for which a million francs were earmarked) and of an Occitan Documentation Center, as well as the support of numerous Breton projects and institutions.

Estimates for the total annual expenditures for ethnocultural projects for 1984/85 have ranged from 100 to 150 million francs. Precise figures are hard to get, not only because sums are allocated by a variety of ministries and other public bodies, but also because it is not always possible to separate "ethnic" components from expenditures for overall regional purposes or from general expenditures for culture, e.g., the promotion of "traditional" music or folk dance. Moreover, it is not easy to disaggregate the "cultural" aspects of government programs on behalf of repatriates or immigrants from measures for ordinary cultural adjustment (e.g., those promoting basic literacy) or socioeconomic adaptation.

There are Bretons and Basques who complain that the sums of money spent constitute little more than token reparations for years of cultural oppression or neglect; that the sums are just enough to mute the discontent of the ethnic communities and avert more obviously "political" mobilization; that most of the projects are essentially folkloric and not serious; and finally, that the ethnic cultures and projects subsidized are so numerous that financial resources have been thinned out. (The charge is not entirely fair, because individual small projects are incremental and because the allocation often represents seed money that arouses interest and encourages ethnic voluntary associations and local governments to make their own contributions.) At the other extreme, there are those who believe that the expenditure of *any* sums for cultural minority programs is too much, because it takes away funds needed for more important socioeconomic programs, glorifies reactionary tribalism, and helps to keep ethnic minorities economically disprivileged by maintaining them in cultural ghettos.

In a decision to allocate money, careful attention has to be paid to the type of project: it must not be so "politically" loaded as to bring out latent separatist sentiment, e.g., among Creoles, Corsicans, Basques, and Alsatians; it must not stress the most trivial folkloric aspects of an ethnic culture as to be construed as patronizing, i.e., as an insult to the ethnic elites; and finally, it must reflect a consensus within the ethnic community regarding the projects most deserving of support. Such a consensus is not always easy to achieve, because there are differences of opinion within ethnic communities as to what should or should not be stressed, e.g., among Maghrebis—Islam or Arabism? Among Jews—religion or Zionism, Yiddish or Sephardic (or Hebrew) culture? Among Occitans—linguistic or economic rehabilitation?

THE NATIONAL COUNCIL FOR REGIONAL LANGUAGES AND CULTURES

It was largely to help the government make intelligent choices regarding ethnocultural programs that early in August 1985 the cabinet issued a decree establishing a National Council for Regional Languages and Cultures (*Conseil national des langues et cultures régionales*). The creation of such a council had been recommended by an interministerial committee under the leadership of Jack Lang and including high officials from the prime minister's office, the ministries of National Education, of Research and Technology, and of Interior and Decentralization, and the Under-Secretariat for Universities.[55] The purpose of the council, as officially stated, was "to put into concrete form the desire of the public authorities to promote an effective policy in favor of cultural democracy and the acknowledgment of the pluralism of French culture." The council would be "a crossroads of ideas" and "a tool of the government for the generation and implementation of measures" of cultural pluralism. It would also serve as a link between the state and the ethnic voluntary associations that were proliferating, and for that reason it would contain both public (elected and appointed) officials and representatives of ethnic groups—or at least private "experts" on specific ethnic cultures. It was acknowledged that it would be unfeasible to make the council fully "representative." There were so many cultures and languages in France that the inclusion of spokespersons of all of them would have resulted in a body of several hundred people.[56] Instead, the council would be composed of thirty to forty members, to be appointed on the nomination of the prime minister for four-year terms—except that half of the members would initially be appointed for two-year terms in order to make possible a renewal of half the membership every two years. The council, which would meet at least twice a year, would present an annual report to the prime minister but would be consulted by several ministers and government agencies on all matters pertaining to policies of cultural pluralism. There was no line item provided for the council in the 1986 budget; the secretary-general appointed to manage the council was to be paid as an official of the Ministry of Culture, while its overall expenses were to be borne by the prime minister's office.[57]

The first meetings of the council took place in January 1986. Among the participants were thirty-seven appointed members, in addition to the prime minister, the minister of culture, the full-time secretary-general of the council, and six ex-officio members representing the ministries of Interior and Decentralization and of Education, Communications, and Overseas Territories, and the Consultative Committee on the French Language. The appointed members were predominantly university professors, but included also some journalists, writers, artists, engineers, and a handful of regional politicians. Among them were representatives of Alsace, Corsica, Occitania, the Basque, Catalan, and Flemish regions, Brittany, and the Asian, Armenian, Gypsy, Jewish, and Maghrebi communities. Prominent among the members were personalities professionally or politically involved in, and committed to, cultural pluralism: the president of the Gypsy Cultural Center of Paris; a professor of Creole studies; Jean-Pierre Destrade, the Socialist deputy mentioned earlier; Bernard Stasi, a Giscardist who had long been involved in fighting for the rights of minorities and immigrants; Pierre-Jakez Hélias, a prominent Breton writer and specialist on Celtic culture; Robert Lafont, one of the best-known Occitan intellectuals; and Henri Giordan, the researcher who had presided over the study committee whose report, as already noted, contained recommendations that continued to provide the basis for much of the work of the Ministry of Culture, including the creation of the council itself.

In his welcoming remarks, the prime minister declared that France "manifested by the creation of this organization [the fact] that it conceives itself as a multicultural society." He emphasized that if the tradition of centralism had once facilitated the unification of France, a country whose population had been very heterogeneous, and had made this unification possible by means of a common French language, today one must reject an excessive uniformity and must encourage "a quest for roots." In establishing this council, he added, "the President of the Republic and the Government . . . take note of the existence of a movement that transcends France and in France itself, transcends the different political families."[58] The prime minister reaffirmed his belief that the new policy would not threaten the prominent place of the French language and that minority languages would complement rather than compete with French. He pointed out that the installation of this council coincided with the establishment of three public organs devoted to the defense, promotion, and diffusion of that language (la francophonie).

During the first discussions in the council, the members produced a cornucopia of ambitious proposals for annual folk festivals, documentation centers, translation projects, and ethnic studies majors based on the model of the Breton major leading to a university degree (CAPES), which had been decided earlier and slated for inauguration in 1986. There were also proposals for the systematic support of "nonterritorial" languages (including such widely diffused languages as Arabic and such little-used ones as Berber and Yiddish), an expansion of ethnological research projects, bilateral and multilateral agreements concerning cultural exchanges, a national exhibition on "the regional languages of Europe," and a significant expansion of ethnic language and culture broadcasts. Finally, there were suggestions that there be more serious efforts at sensitizing the majority to the phenomenon of cultural pluralism in France and to the unique contribution of specific ethnic cultures.[59]

Within the council there appeared to be a considerable amount of good will. The members, while making a case in behalf of the cultures of "their" ethnic clientele, nevertheless did not initially behave as if the council, or the government, were operating in a zero-sum situation. Their behavior appeared to reflect the conviction that the support of the demands of one ethnic constituency would not detract from the support of those of another. Yet it was doubtful that a joint strategy would emerge within the council. Despite a common agreement by all representatives on the definition of French society as a culturally pluralistic one and, hence, on the propriety of everyone's efforts at staking ethnocultural policy claims, there were bound to be clashes. Bretons and other indigenous ethnics cannot easily accept the legitimacy of the demands of communities of immigrant stock, e.g., those of Polish extraction who might wish to cultivate *Polonité*. Catholic ethnics of various kinds might not be particularly sympathetic, for historic or theological reasons, to Jewish or Arab ethnocultural assertions. Jews and Maghrebis might be hampered in efforts to collaborate for reasons of religion and, more important, socioeconomic rivalries and foreign policy conflicts. And many French minority group members might collectively be hostile to the Maghrebis.

One of the problems articulated during the first sessions was that the existing administrative divisions of France (which the new decentralization laws did nothing to change) did not correspond to the linguistic-cultural divisions of the country, a lack of correspondence that would hamper the implementation of ethnopluralistic policies. Another was the fact that many of the people involved in the promotion of minority cultures (among them the programming staff of FR3, the regionally oriented television stations) were ignorant of regional languages and cultures. It was also pointed out that certain minority languages were disadvantaged for one reason or another: the lack of a fixed territorial base, an insufficient number of adherents of the ethnic community, a relative lack of organization and political power, and a diminution of the number of speakers of their language. Most council members appeared to be conscious of the fact that ethnic culture was not necessarily coextensive with ethnic language—that the Breton, Jewish, and *Beur* (i.e., Arab) cultures were often expressed in French rather than in

Breton, Hebrew, or Arabic (languages that many French-born ethnics no longer spoke).

After the victory of the Gaullist-Giscardist alliance in the parliamentary elections of 1986 and the formation of the government of Jacques Chirac, the future of the council was put in question. Although that body was not abolished, it was no longer funded, and its secretary-general was left with nothing to do. Consequently this position, like that of *chargé de mission* for ethnocultural matters, was phased out. Promised meetings of the council were postponed for a number of reasons, among them the need to make it larger and more "representative" (i.e., more Gaullist and conservative, and perhaps more Jacobin), and to have a more detailed and more carefully prepared agenda. Furthermore, Chirac was afraid of offending the extreme-right and xenophobic National Front, which did not want to see the national culture weakened by ethnopluralistic policies of which "foreigners," and especially Arabs, might be the principal beneficiaries, and which threatened to raid a part of his electorate. There was an additional reason for the government's inaction: Chirac was in a complicated relationship with François Léotard, his minister of culture, whose presidential ambitions competed with those of the prime minister. Therefore it was not surprising that when a council meeting finally did take place in late 1987, it broke up in disarray.

WHICH CULTURES, WHICH LANGUAGES?

In the background (though not voiced at the council meetings) was the question whether all cultures found in France deserved equal support and whether all the languages spoken by residents of that country could properly be considered "languages of France." Are Flemish and Catalan, spoken also by peoples across the border, "languages of France"? Are the languages of recent immigrants, such as Arabic or Berber, to be so considered? If Jews are seen as members of a legitimate ethnic community of France and their culture worthy of support, which language—Hebrew, Yiddish, or Ladino—is to be favored? And while the membership of the Corsicans and Alsatians in the "French nation" is not challenged, is the government to encourage the use of the Corsican language or rather of standard Italian? Cultivating Corsican, the idiom of the ethnic masses on the island, might tend to shut speakers of that language into a sort of cultural ghetto; on the other hand, cultivating Italian, the language of an intellectual elite, might bring Corsicans closer to Italy than to France. Should one choose High German or Alsatian? Which variety of Breton or Occitan is one to favor? If the choice fell to one alternative rather than the other, it might be seen as discrimination against the neglected variant; if several (or all) were supported, it might undermine the internal unity of the Occitan or Breton community as a whole.

The choices have been influenced by a number of considerations: the number of speakers of the ethnic language, the intensity of ethnic mobilization, electoral exigencies, the shape and evolution of the ethnic culture and the strength of its academic and literary traditions, the efforts of the ethnic elite, the degree of external encouragement and support, and the extent to which a particular ethnocultural policy relates to the government's conception of the national interest.

Thus, the acknowledgment of Breton and Occitan cultural claims, including the relabeling of Breton and Occitan as "dialect" rather than "language," was in large part a response to increasing political activity on the part of the Bretons and Occitans, the proliferation of ethnocultural associations, and increased Socialist voting. The fact that Provençal obtains greater official legitimation and more government support than Languedocien has to do with the widely held belief that the former has a more solidly established literary tradition. There is no way of denying the importance of the *Félibrige* literary output and, in particular, the writings of Frédéric Mistral. Conversely, Picard, a Romance language spoken in northwest France, is not (yet) taught systematically (apart from some elective courses, offered since 1982 for three hours a week in the lower grades of some lycées), largely because that language is not considered sufficiently literary and is labeled by many as nothing more than a "deformed French."[60] However, Gallo, a Romance language spoken in Haute-Bretagne and part of Loire-Atlantique, has achieved greater official support, notably with the establishment of a university chair in Rennes and (since 1983) the recognition of the language as a subject that may be used toward the secondary school diploma. The preferential treatment of Gallo might be attributed variously to greatly increased literary output in that language, the activities of voluntary associations, and—by those inclined to Machiavellian interpretations—to the idea that the recognition of three widely spoken languages in Brittany weakens the position of Breton.

Similar "prestige" considerations have applied to Chinese. When (in 1985) in response to efforts by the Socialist deputy for Paris's "Chinatown" the Ministry of Education signed an agreement with the *Association 13e sans frontières* (composed of Chinese immigrants) to subsidize the teaching of Chinese, the ministry selected not Cantonese, the variant spoken by the majority of the Chinese of the area, but the official Mandarin.[61]

The teaching of both Alsatian and High German is now supported without much hesitation because there no longer is any question about the political loyalty of the Alsatians; because the majority of residents of Alsace, including non-Alsatians, Gaullists, and leftists, seem to favor it; and because—as a pragmatic by-product—a wider knowledge of

German facilitates the export of French goods to the Federal Republic of Germany.

The proliferation of courses in Spanish and Portuguese reflects different considerations: the vast number of Iberian immigrants, the homogeneity of their communities, their seriousness about preserving their heritage, the wide availability of teachers of their languages, and, last but not least, the existence of bilateral agreements made (even before the victory of the Socialists) between the French Ministry of Education and the governments of Spain and Portugal.

The support of Maghrebi culture and the growing interest on the part of the government in subsidizing the teaching of Arabic may be attributed in the first place to the undeniable, and probably permanent, presence of some 2 million North African Arab immigrants and the recognition of their (present and potential) political importance. There is no doubt that some authorities wish deliberately to perpetuate Arab-Islamic culture among these immigrants and their descendants in order to keep them in cultural and economic isolation, emphasize their "temporary" status in France, and encourage their ultimate departure. A more important factor, however, is the existence of bilateral agreements with governments of sending countries, as well as the desire on the part of politicians to foster good economic relations with the countries of the Arab Middle East.

The government's accommodating attitude toward Jews as an ethnocultural community has a number of explanations. The influx of North African Jewish "repatriates" in the late 1950s and early 1960s more than doubled the size of the Jewish community. It led to a revival of Jewish ethnic consciousness that has expressed itself not so much in religious observance as in folklore, custom, cuisine, endogamous marriage, and transnational solidarities (including the support of Israel and of Soviet Jewry). In turn, the French intellectual elite began to abandon the Napoleonic view of the Jews as members of an amorphous collection of individuals adhering to a religious denomination and to think of them as forming an ethnic community. The Socialist government, in responding positively to that redefinition, was probably also motivated by a desire to make amends for the long history of anti-Semitism in France and the misbehavior of French authorities during World War II.[62] The support of the teaching of Hebrew—now considered by some as "a language of France"—is one aspect of that policy (with Yiddish favored to a much lesser extent, because the majority of its speakers—immigrants from Eastern Europe—have long since died and their descendants have assimilated).

It is evident that some ethnic languages and cultures can be supported more easily, and with less political risk, than others, because the majority is less hostile to some ethnic groups than to others. An accommodationist attitude toward the culture of the Bretons and Occitans is readily accepted because these communities are considered historically French and are not seen as posing any threat to French "high culture." Alsatian, Catalan, and Flemish cultures are tolerated as French because of their Christian foundations. Jewish culture is more problematic: although Jews had first come into Gaul with Caesar's legions, the vast majority of Jews in France today are descendants of recent immigrants. However, both the enormous contribution of Jews to French civilization and their patriotism are now widely acknowledged in the secular environment of France. In contrast to the Muslim Arabs, the Jews appear to be so "French" that many intellectuals—even from the moderate right—now speak of the "Judeo-Christian" civilization of France. The extreme-right *Front National* continues to have difficulty in accepting Jews as French; but that movement is so preoccupied with the numerically much larger and even more "alien" Maghrebis that it does not spend too much time opposing the support of Jewish culture. To the more conservative and xenophobic elements of provincial France (*la France profonde*) the support of Maghrebi culture means the support of an unassimilable and threatening element. It is unassimilable because of the Arabs' "oriental" physiognomies, life-style, and language, and their adherence to Islam, a religion that cannot be separated from daily life and that allegedly connotes foreign political allegiances. It is threatening because the Maghrebis are thought of as competing with natives for scarce jobs and welfare-state benefits and as contributing heavily to the rise of criminality.[63]

PARTIES, IDEOLOGIES, AND
COMPETING VIEWS OF FRENCH SOCIETY

The future course of ethnopluralistic policies in France is uncertain because it is dependent on a number of interrelated factors that are fluid and unpredictable: the support of public opinion, the distribution of political forces, and the evolution of attitudes within political parties. The ideological cleavage that was alluded to above between persistent Jacobinism—found among orthodox Gaullists and most Communist leaders—and an openness to the ethnopluralistic reality—found largely among the majority of Socialists and many centrist-progressive Giscardists—still prevails. This cleavage has been manifested on the policy level in the very measures promoted by Socialists governments between 1981 and 1986 and in the half-hearted support of, if not opposition to, those measures by the Gaullist-Giscardist alliance. On the intellectual level, the cleavage has been evidenced by discordant definitions of French society—discordances that are reflected in two books that appeared at about the same time (October-November 1985). One, the Socialist-sponsored *L'identité française*, argues for a pluralistic France and suggests a disjunction between political and ethnocultural identification, or between citizenship and nationality.[64] The other, *L'identité de la France*, sponsored by the conservative *Club de l'Horloge*, argues that a culturally pluralistic society (in particular one including Muslim Arabs) is "a negation of French identity."[65] Whereas the one book emphasizes the contribution of ethnically diverse cultures to an enriched French culture, the other stresses the role of ethnic communities as "countersocieties" and their allegedly destructive impact.

It would, however, be simplistic to suggest that differences of ideology or policy can be presented in terms of neat left/right, or Socialist/Giscardo-Gaullist distinctions. In addition to the disagreements within the Socialist party about the nature and scope of ethnocultural accommodation there have been ambivalences within the other camps as well. To some of the more devoutly Catholic elements within the *Centre des Démocrates Sociaux* (CDS), the Christian-Democratic component of the Giscardist *Union pour la Démocratie Française* (UDF), the commitment to ethnocultural pluralism has been a collateral to the belief in a pluralism of education systems. These elements have been encouraged by Pope John Paul II who, in recent discourses, declared that members of immigrant and other minorities must neither withdraw to a cultural ghetto nor let themselves be so assimilated as to lose their original culture and their identity.[66] Other Giscardists are hostile to cultural pluralism, among them members of the Republican party, the "neoliberal" component of the UDF that has often reflected the views of organized business, i.e., the sector that has played a prominent role in importing cheap and "exotic" foreign labor. To still other neoliberals, much of the argument is in the long run irrelevant. A triumphant capitalism will introduce pressures for cultural assimilation that ethnic minorities will be unable to resist and that will undo many of the policies enacted by the Socialists.

Within the Gaullist party, the *Rassemblement pour la République* (RPR), there are some differences as well. Thus, the hardnosed attitude of Michel Debré and other dogmatic Gaullists, who argue against any dismantling of the monopolistic position of French (majority) culture, is balanced in some measure by that of moderate politicians like Michel Hannoun (himself a Jew of North African origin), who would at least tolerate a *multiracial* France,[67] and by that of pragmatic politicians who must publicly favor cultural pluralism because they need the votes of ethnic minority members of their electorate.

The attitudes of Communists are dictated by a mixture of ideology, rank-and-file pressures, and electoral opportunism. On the one hand, there is the well-known Marxist belief that any policy of ethnopluralistic accommodation interferes with the class struggle; on the other hand, in the recent past Communist politicians have supported the ethnocultural demands in Occitania and other regions where those demands reflected perceptions of relative economic deprivation.[68] Communist politicians, driven by pressures from indigenous low-income workers and slum dwellers, have used racist slogans; and even Georges Marchais, the leader of the Communist party, has made unflattering remarks about certain (non-European) immigrants.[69] Nevertheless, Communists have on occasion taken a strong stand against racially or ethnically discriminatory municipal ordinances.[70]

Such ambivalences have been mirrored in the trade unions. Some officials of the CGT have been opposed to policies favorable to ethnic minorities (and especially immigrants) because they have been subject to the same rank-and-file pressures as the Communist party; others have kept an open mind insofar as they see ethnics as potential members of the union. The CFDT has been more consistently in favor of ethnic pluralism, both because such a position is in accord with its long-time advocacy of economic self-management (*autogestion*) and because it has been relatively immune from pressures of low-paid workers belonging to the majority.

At present there are no electorally significant ethnic parties. There is no technical or legal reason why such parties cannot be established, and it is possible (even under the single-member constituency system to which France has returned after a brief hiatus) that they might do reasonably well in districts where an ethnic electorate is heavily clustered, e.g., in Brittany, Corsica, and Pyrénées Orientales. However, members of ethnic minorities have a variety of interests and overlapping memberships that condition their voting behavior. As the foregoing discussion suggests, politicians belonging to various parties in ethnic regions have supported the cultural aspirations of minorities, and no single nationally oriented political party has been wholly hostile to these aspirations. The single exception is the extreme-right *Front National* ; but its leader, Jean-Marie Le Pen (of Breton origin himself), is not so much against policies of ethnocultural pluralism (insofar as these policies concern indigenous Catholic communities) as he is racist. These are the reasons why ethnic political mobilization has not translated into a categorical kind of bloc voting in which one or another major party has been used as an agency for processing ethnic claims or as a clear target of ethnic wrath.

It is probable that various ethnic groups have learned from one another how to mobilize and assert demands. However, because of the heteromorphic nature of France's ethnic communities, interethnic collaboration thus far—apart from the dialogues within the National Council on Regional Languages and other official bodies—has been modest. Efforts at collaboration have been reflected in the establishment of an interethnic radio station in Paris; study groups such as the *Cercle Gaston-Crémieux*, founded in the late 1960s by Jewish Socialists for the purpose of exchanging ideas among Bretons, Jews, and others;[71] *SOS-Racisme*, an organization set up in 1984 with some encouragement by the national government to fight racism,[72] and including in its ranks blacks and whites, Maghrebis and Jews, and a miscellany of indigenous ethnics; and the Committee for the Protection of the (Seven) Languages of France, which has been concerned only with the "native" (regional) languages but not with the "immigrant" (*communautaire*) tongues.

This is not the place to discuss ethnic "movements."[73] Suffice it to note that with some (electorally insignificant) exceptions in Corsica and Brittany, they have not been separatist or irredentist. Their demands have generally ranged from cultural-linguistic legitimation to increased regional investment, and they have been found all over the ideological (i.e., left-right) spectrum. For the nonterritorially concentrated ethnics, political separatism is, of course, a physical impossibility; for others (e.g., Bretons and Catalans), the sociopolitical values and economic benefits they share with the majority are important enough to provide little incentive for separatist solutions.

THE ETHNOTERRITORIAL-POLITICAL DIMENSION: CORSICA

The Corsican autonomy laws enacted in March and July 1982 (and supplementary laws of 1983) were viewed by many observers as models of ethnoterritorial accommodation that would sooner or later be followed in ethnically specific overseas departments and territories and selected metropolitan regions. The Corsican assembly, elected by popular vote in August 1982, was given wide powers to legislate in the areas of agriculture, coastal fishing, communications, land-use planning, transport, technological research, vocational training, education, and culture.

Pluralistically inclined optimists viewed the Corsican autonomy statutes as a practical means of providing a degree of provincial self-determination that would respond to the specificities of a "peripheral" region where ethnic consciousness, territorial demarcation, and political aspirations were most closely associated, without compromising the political integrity of France. Hard-line Jacobin pessimists, however, saw in the statutes a first step toward separatism.

Thus far, the fears of separatism have proved groundless, because there have been a number of constraints against the island's detaching itself from France. First, the national government continues to occupy the commanding heights of responsibility for public order and for the educational curriculum in primary and secondary schools. Second, the relatively poor island continues to depend on the national government—and on private investors of the mainland—for development funds. Third, the internal divisions among the 250,000 inhabitants of Corsica—between the natives and mainlanders, the Francophones and Corsophones, the assimilationists and ethnic pluralists, the Gaullists and Socialists—and the persistent arguments about the nature of Corsican culture and the role of the Corsican language in expressing it[74] ensure the superordinate status of the French language and culture and weaken the position of separatists.

A circular issued by the Ministry of Education in June 1982 promised that "the teaching of the regional language [in Corsica and elsewhere would] be provided from kindergarten to the university not as a marginal subject but as *matière spécifique*."[75] However, the practical implementation of that expression of good will proved to be a problem. The jurisdiction of the Corsican assembly in educational matters was limited to the maintenance of school buildings and to *complementary* curricular material on primary and secondary levels, and to the support of local initiatives (*animation municipale*) for theater and the staging of folklore festivals.[76] To complicate matters, a number of parallel regional institutions, among them the Corsican *académie* (rectorate), the Social and Economic Consultative Council and the *Conseil de la culture, de l'éducation, et du cadre de vie* were associated with discussions of measures of ethnic culture, and it was unclear whether these institutions served to enhance or diffuse regional decisionmaking competence. Moreover, Corsican ethnicists were not certain whether an upgrading of the Corsican language would be necessary or sufficient for the shaping of Corsican ethnic consciousness. Perhaps a third of the 110,000 ethnic Corsicans on the island no longer spoke Corsican and preferred to use French,[77] and the "foreigners"—the settlers from the mainland, the *pieds-noirs*, and the Maghrebis—could hardly be expected to learn Corsican. Finally, the congruence between ethnicity and territoriality has been put in question by the existence of a Corsican "diaspora," the more than 200,000 Corsicans who live permanently on the French mainland but who preserve their ethnic identity and return regularly to the island to cast their ballots.[78]

Under these conditions, Corsicans did not put much faith in the ability of the island's assembly to promote ethnic culture, let alone separatism or effective political autonomy. The first Corsican Assembly of sixty-one, elected in August 1982, contained only seven autonomists. Nevertheless, the government in Paris ordered the dissolution of the assembly in 1984 because of a virtual deadlock between contending forces, among them the Gaullists and the Socialists. In the subsequent elections, held in August of that year, the autonomists saw their representation reduced even further. (The separatist Corsican National Liberation Front [FNLC] had meanwhile been dissolved.) In the partial elections held in March 1987 in Upper Corsica (*Haute-Corse*), the autonomists barely held on to their three seats. That poor showing could perhaps be attributed to the fact that 42 percent of the Corsican voters had boycotted the elections.[79] While some of the abstainers were motivated by dissatisfaction over the inadequate powers of the assembly, others feared that the assembly might bring to power corrupt clan leaders who, in the process of promoting Corsican ethnic culture, would also help to revive propensities to anti-French behavior that would have a chilling effect on the island's democratic processes: political extremism, vendetta politics, banditry, assassination, and terrorism.[80] The natives' xenophobia, fed by resentment of North African Muslims who had allegedly been brought into the island by mainlanders, was expressed in such slogans as *"Arabacci fora"* (out with the Arabs) and *"La Corse aux Corses,"* which were the obverse of the National Front's slogan, *"La France aux Français."*

CONCLUSIONS AND PROGNOSES

The parliamentary elections of March 16, 1986 and the resulting replacement of a Socialist by a Gaullist-Giscardist government clearly had a chilling effect on policies concerning ethnic minorities. The Gaullist preference for cultural monism and the pressures from the *Front National,* whose xenophobia had wide appeal, and which threatened to "raid" part of the RPR-UDF electorate, made the new coalition hesitant about ethnopluralistic policies, especially as these affected Maghrebis, and caused the Chirac government to revert to some of the repressive measures vis-à-vis North African immigrants that had been used during the presidency of Giscard d'Estaing. The avowed commitment of the RPR-UDF to progressive *désétatisation* ("degovernmentalization"), to a privatization of the media, and to the continued availability of the option of private schools was not sufficiently conducive to an amplification of the Socialists' ethnopluralistic policies. Because of the oil glut, the increase of terrorism, and the growing animus against North African Muslim immigrants, the almost tropistic pro-Arabism of the French Foreign Office (and other parts of the Giscardo-Gaullist establishment) was not translated into elaborations of bilateral agreements with Arab countries that would cater to the cultural-linguistic needs of Maghrebis.

The results of the presidential and parliamentary elections of 1988 were not likely to produce major changes in the government's policies regarding ethnic minorities. Although Mitterrand was reelected as president and the PS was returned to power with the appointment of Michel Rocard, a Socialist, as prime minister, Socialist control over the Assembly was not secure enough to permit dramatic new experiments in favor of ethnic cultural policies. Moreover, the PS seemed to have shelved such policies in favor of a more rapid integration of minorities, and especially of recent immigrants and their descendants, into French society. A harbinger of that new thinking was the report of a committee of experts on a reform of the nationality and citizenship code. The committee, which consisted of university professors, public officials, representatives of ethnic minority communities, and politicians, had been appointed by Chirac in mid-1987; its report, which reflected the testimony of both the "republican" Right and the democratic Left, and of both Jacobins and ethnic pluralists, proposed a relatively liberal approach to the acquisition of French citizenship.[81] The prospects for the enactment of the proposals were enhanced by the reduced political fortunes of the *Front National* on a national level: although its leader, Jean-Marie Le Pen, received over 14 percent of the first-ballot vote in the presidential elections, his party's representation in the Assembly was virtually eliminated.[82]

The Socialists were expected to be increasingly responsive to the pressures from the *Beurs*, the descendants of Arab immigrants. The discussion by *Beur* associations in Lyons and elsewhere in 1987 about the possibility of putting up a Maghrebi candidate for the forthcoming presidential election seemed to be a largely academic exercise. However, the campaign led by the *Association France-Plus* to register *Beur* voters (most of whom were likely to vote Socialist) was impressive enough to make an increasing number of local politicians listen to *Beur* concerns. Thus far, this has not led to U.S.-style ethnic lobbying; moreover, most *Beur* pressures have been aimed less at the promotion of ethnic cultural or educational pluralism than at greater equality of political rights and better access to jobs and social benefits. To be sure, there are the pressures of agencies staffed by people appointed for specific multiannual terms, of programs equipped with an earmarked budget, and of vested ethnic interests.

A museum, once it is filled with ethnic content, cannot be easily "de-ethnicized," and the termination of instruction of an ethnic language (even if the ethnic group made little use of it) would be considered an insulting act.[83] However, there are fiscal priorities—among them the creation of jobs, the reduction of the balance-of-payments deficit, and the fight against domestic violence—that make the pursuit of ethnocultural programs appear luxuries.[84] For these reasons, most of the measures introduced or expanded under the Socialist government of 1981–1986 were likely to be maintained—among them, the programming of ethnic-language broadcasts, the affixing of dual-language street signs (as in several places in Brittany), the training of ethnic-language teachers, and the option to use Breton in dealings with public authorities.[85]

Whatever the pursuit of ethnopluralistic policies may portend for the relative position of the culture of the majority, such aspirations, and the governmental responses to them, cannot be seriously viewed as translating into a threat to the political unity of France—despite the frightening scenarios frequently evoked by Michel Debré and other adherents of a monolithic notion of *état-nation*. Nevertheless, because of the lack of congruence between *ethnie* and region, ethnic minority accommodation in France can be territorial only in a limited sense. But because, historically, culture and language have been major policy domains of the state, ethnopluralistic matters, insofar as they affect culture, will continue to concern the public authorities. What the institutional reflection of that concern will be remains to be seen.

APPENDIX

Chronology

13th–16th centuries	French expansion into and incorporation of Occitan lands
1532	Annexation of Brittany by France by act of union—Brittany at first retains own parliament and administrative autonomy
1539	François I promulgates ordinance of Villiers-Cotterets, requiring that all judicial acts be published in the language of Ile-de-France (i.e., French)
1593	Three Basque provinces detached from Kingdom of Navarre and annexed to France
1659	Treaty of Pyrenées, under which part of Catalonia is annexed to France
1713–1714	Under Louis XIV, part of Flanders incorporated into France; also, capture of Strasbourg
1740–1750	Defeat by French armies of republican defenders of Corsica; cession (in 1768) to France
1792	French Revolution—Parliamentary proclamations at first translated into regional languages; but at the same time, calls issued for the spread of a common language—French—as "the language of liberty"
1793	Establishment of primary schools where all children would learn French
1794	Rapport Barrère: "For a free people, the language must be the same for all"; issuance of a decree authorizing the appointment of a French school teacher in each non-French speaking commune
1831	Prefects of several Breton departments call upon minister of public instruction to "encourage the decline and corruption of Breton to the point where no one can understand each other. Thus, because of a need for communication, peasants will be forced to learn French"
1870	Charles de Gaulle (a great-uncle of General de Gaulle) and two others circulate petition in favor of teaching regional languages in schools
1880–1887	Ferry laws: Jules Ferry decree, in 1884, providing for general primary education and requiring the use of French
1903	Use of Breton language in church sermons forbidden
1940	Bilingual Breton-French radio broadcasts in occupied France—ended after Liberation
1951	Deixonne Law: elective courses in "local languages and dialects" in elementary and secondary schools permitted, specifically in Breton, Catalan, and Occitan

1960s & 1970s	Limited but gradually increasing number of broadcasts in Alsatian, Breton, and Basque; and teaching of these languages in elementary schools on extracurricular basis
1968	Events of May and June
1968–1981	Non-Communist left parties (Socialist party and PSU) increasingly question assumptions of cultural Jacobinism, and gradually endorse cultural-linguistic pluralism in France.
1969	School teachers' unions (SNES, in April; and SGEN, in May) call upon Ministry of Education to adapt itself to "the facts of regional culture" and to enable those who wish it to study regional languages
	During presidential election campaign, Georges Pompidou asserts that "[if elected] I will act so that the defense of . . . regional traditions and languages benefits from a real support of the public powers"
1971	Semi-monthly television programs in selected regional languages; later (1979) introduced on weekly basis
	Guichard Circular regarding the implementation of the Deixonne Law
1972	President Pompidou declares that "there is no room for regional languages . . . in France"
1974	Georges Marchais, general secretary of the Communist party, asserts that "regional languages must live where they correspond to a historical and social reality, [as] in Brittany"
	The provisions of the Deixonne Law are extended to the Corsican language
1975	Haby reforms: one hour a week of instruction in regional languages in elementary schools, and three hours in secondary schools, if at least ten students ask for it
1981	Election of François Mitterrand as president, and of Socialist Assembly majority
	Parliament passes Defferre (decentralization) laws.
1982	Parliament passes Corsican autonomy statute.
	Savary policies: funded programs of teaching regional languages
	Giordan and Queyranne reports
1984	Destrade bill "On the promotion of the languages and cultures of France" introduced in Assembly
1985	Establishment of National Council for Regional Languages and Cultures. First meeting of Council, January 1986

Major sources: Claude Gendre and Françoise Javelier, *Ecole, histoire de France et minorités nationales* (Lyon: Fédérop, 1978); Henri Giordon, "Les problèmes des cultures régionales et minoritaires aujourd'hui," *Combat pour la Diaspora*, no 11/12, 1983, pp. 13–19; *Fact Finding Report on the Breton Language* (Plymouth Meeting, Pa: U.S. Branch of the International Committee for the Defense of the Breton Language, January 1983); and *Le Monde*, various issues.

NOTES

1. See Fanch Elegoët, "L'identité bretonne: Notes sur la production de l'identité négative," *Pluriel* 24 (1980): 43–67.

2. See Jules Michelet, *Tableau de la France* (Paris: Société des Belles Lettres, 1949), 8; Christian Coulon, "Idéologie jacobine, Etat, et ethnocide," *Pluriel* 17 (1979): 3–20; and François Burdeau, "L'état jacobin et la culture politique française," *Projet* 185–186 (May–June 1984): 635–648.

3. According to Bernard Stasi, in *L'immigration: Une chance pour la France* (Paris: Robert Lafont, 1984), pages 74–75, an inquiry conducted after World War I revealed that of 38 million inhabitants of France, a third still spoke a mother tongue other than French; among these, 4 million spoke Breton, 4 million a Germanic language, and 500,000 Basque or Corsican. And of the 13–14 million, 4 million spoke no French at all. Note that these statistics do not include Provençal, Picard, or other languages derived from langue d'oc. See also William R. Beer, *The Unexpected Rebellion: Ethnic Activism in Contemporary France* (New York: New York University Press, 1980), especially pages xxi–xxiii, for statistical data; and James E. Jacob and David C. Gordon, "Language Policy in France," in W.R. Beer and J.E. Jacob, eds., *Language Policy and National Unity* (Totowa, N.J.: Rowman & Allanheld, 1985), 106–33.

4. Cf. Philippe Pinchemel, *France: A Geographical Survey* (New York: Praeger, 1973). This relatively recent book, originally published in French in 1964, makes virtually no reference to the ethnic communities in France, except for brief allusions to immigrants and to the "ancient" distinction between langue d'oïl and langue d'oc (pages 152–153).

5. See W. Safran, "The French Left and Ethnic Pluralism," *Ethnic and Racial Studies* 7, no. 4 (October 1984): 447–461.

6. See Robert Lafont, *Décoloniser la France* (Paris: Gallimard, 1971) and his *Le dénouement français* (Paris: Editions Suger, 1985), 13–16, 25–33, et passim.

7. See François Dubet, "Défendre son identité: Approche du discours identitaire," *Esprit*, no. 50 (March 1981), pp. 80–88.

8. *Par les langues de France*, CNRS, Laboratoire de Recherches Interculturelles, edited by Henri Giordan (Paris: Centre Pompidou, 1984), 30.

9. François Dreyfus, "La culture alsacienne entre la France et la R.F.A. depuis 1945," paper read at the colloquium of the Association Française de Science Politique, "L'état devant les culture régionales et communautaires," Aix-en-Provence, January 23–25, 1986 (hereafter AFSP Colloquium), page 5.

10. Cf. Safran,"The French Left and Ethnic Pluralism," 451.

11. Published in *Que Faire*, no. 819, December 1971.

12. *François Mitterrand: L'homme, les idées, le programme* (Paris: Flammarion, 1981), 114.

13. Safran, "The French Left and Ethnic Pluralism," 454.

14. *Le poing et la rose*, supplément au no. 82 (June 1979), p. 44.

15. *Projet socialiste* (Paris; Club Socialiste du Livre, 1980), 56, 252–258.

16. See Jean-Pierre Colin, "Les cultures régionales et communautaires: Un pari de l'état," AFSP Colloquium, 1.

17. Parti socialiste, *La France au pluriel*, preface by F. Mitterrand (Paris: Editions Entente, Collection "Minorités," 1981).

18. Colin, "Les cultures régionales," 1.

19. Paul Bernard, *L'état et la décentralisation*. Notes et études documentaires, nos. 4711–4712 (Paris: Documentation Française, 1983), 121ff.

20. Henri Giordan, *Démocratie culturelle et droit à la différence: Rapport au ministre de la culture* (Paris: Documentation Française, February 1982).

21. See Robert Lafont, *La révolution régionaliste* (Paris: Gallimard, 1967); and "Sur le problème national en France," *Temps Modernes* (August–September 1973): 42ff.

22. Giordan, *Démocratie culturelle*, 91–92.

23. Ibid., 53.

24. James Marangé and André Lebon, *L'insertion des jeunes d'origine étrangère dans la société française* (Paris: Documentation Française, 1982).

25. Jean-Jack Queyranne, *Les régions et la décentralisation: Rapport au ministre de la culture* (Pairs: Documentation Française, July 1982).

26. André-Hubert Mesnard, "Les problèmes adminstratifs de la mise en oeuvre d'une politique des cultures," AFSP Colloquium, 17–18.

27. Ibid., 18–19.

28. See M.R. Pesce, *Rapport "culture,"* Assemblée Nationale, first session 1983–84, number 1736, pages 89–94.

29. Mesnard, "Les problèmes administratifs," 20–21.

30. Colin, "Les cultures régionales," 16–17.

31. See Gil Delannoi, "La politique culturelle, l'héritage et l'innovation," AFSP Colloquium, 13–17.

32. Mesnard, "Les problèmes administratifs," 13f.

33. Bernard, *L'état et la décentralisation*, 115–194.

34. "Proposition de loi sur la promotion des langues et cultures de la France," no. 2157, Assemblée Nationale, 2e session ordinaire de 1983–1984.

35. The leftist Centre d'Etudes, de Recherches, et d'Education Socialistes (now dissolved). One of its leaders, Jean-Pierre Chevènement, later (in 1984) became minister of education, and in that capacity did his best to fall in line with official Socialist policy.

36. *Le Monde*, August 6, 1985.

37. Colin, "Les cultures régionales," 12–13.

38. "Proposition de loi relative au statut et à la promotion des langues et cultures régionales," no. 2711, Assemblée Nationale, 2e session ordinaire, 1984–1985.

39. See "L'administration territoriale II: Les collectivités locales," *Documents d'Etudes*, no. 2.03 (Paris: Documentation Française, October 1984), 10–13.

40. Loi no. 81.909, *Journal Officiel* of October 10, 1981. For a discussion of the consequences of the law, see Manuel Dias, "La vie culturelle et associative des immigrés," *Projet* 199 (May–June 1986): 61–66.

41. Colin, "Les cultures régionales," 17.

42. See Richard Grau, *Les Langues et les cultures minoritaires en France* (Quebec: Conseil de la Langue Française, 1985), 130–131.

43. "M. Chevènement fair les comptes," *La Bretagne à Paris*, May 3, 1985.

44. See Bernard Stasi, *La vie associative et la démocratie nouvelle* (Paris: Presses Universitaires de France, 1979).

45. *Par les langues de France*, 85.

46. Ibid., 57.

47. See the critiques in *Bro Nevez*, published by the International

Committee for the Defense of the Breton Language (Plymouth Meeting, Pennsylvania).

48. Colin, "Les cultures régionales, 17–18.

49. On the nexus between ethnicity on the one hand, and social life, family, and religious practice on the other, see L. Grand and P. Mayol, *L'invention du quotidien* (2 volumes, Paris: U.G.E., 1980), especially "Habiter, cuisiner," volume 2, pages 10–18. On *Bretonnité* and Christianity, see Louis Quéré, "Le 'pays' breton comme territoire minoritaire," *Pluriel* 25 (1981), especially pages 37–39. The (nonethnic) majority must be careful about criticizing the religious component of ethnic culture, because one or another version of Roman Catholicism has continued—even under secular republics—to be part and parcel of French culture, e.g., in the political mystique of Saint-Louis and Joan of Arc, the public festivals, school holidays, and Sunday closing laws.

50. See Pierre Bac, *La langue occitane* (Paris: Presses Universitaires de France, 1967), 15.

51. *Par les langues de France*, 62.

52. Patrick Hinge, "Régions: Les conventions de développement culturel," *Regards sur l'Actualité* 89 (March 1983): 31–32.

53. Items taken from an (unpublished) list provided by the Ministry of Culture.

54. Mesnard, "Les problèmes administratifs," 31.

55. Decree 85.1006 of September 23, 1985, *Journal Officiel*, September 25, 1985, pages 11048 (article 3). See also "La politique culturelle régionale," *Le Monde*, August 6, 1985; the somewhat critical article by Catherine Bedarida, "Jack Lang crée le conseil des tribus françaises," *Libération*, August 8, 1985; and J.P. Peroncel-Hugoz, "La politique des langues minoritaires," *Le Monde*, August 9, 1985.

56. Colin, "Les cultures régionales," 20–21.

57. Ibid., 24.

58. "Allocution du premier ministre pour l'installation de Conseil national des langues et cultures régionales le 27 janvier 1986 à l'Hôtel Matignon" (unpublished).

59. "Procès-verbal de la première réunion du Conseil national des langues et cultures régionales, Paris, 27 et 28 janvier 1986" (unpublished).

60. *Par les langues de France*, 98.

61. Philippe Bernard, "Dites '13e' en mandarin," *Le Monde Aujourd'hui*, November 14–15, 1985. Incidentally, one of the arguments of the deputy, Louis Moulinet, was that the failure by the public authorities to support the teaching of Chinese would cause immigrant families to send their children to private schools and thus help to undercut the Socialists' efforts to expand the role of the public schools.

62. French public policy toward Jews is particularly impressive when compared with that of West Germany. In that country, the policy of "making amends" (*Wiedergutmachung*) has been largely symbolic and has included the rebuilding of some old synagogues (as tourist attractions) and the establishment of Judaica institutes (with few Jews as customers)—all essentially designed for an "anthropologized" communal remnant rather than a living culture.

63. On the "unassimilability" of Muslims, See Jean-Pierre Moulin, *Enquête sur la France multiraciale* (Paris: Calmann-Lévy, 1985), passim, esp. 38. See also W. Safran, "Islamization in Western Europe: Political

Consequences and Historical Parallels," *Annals of the American Academy of Political and Social Science* 485 (May 1986): 98–112.

64. *L'identité française*, sponsored by Espaces 89 (Paris: Editions Tierce, 1985). The book is based on a colloquium held in Paris in March 1985 under the direction of Françoise Castro (the wife of Laurent Fabius, who was prime minister at the time).

65. Le Club de l'Horloge, *L'identité de la France* (Paris: Albin Michel, 1985), 206–209 et passim.

66. See the Pope's discourse in Sardinia (October 1985), cited in Colin, "Les cultures régionales," page 9.

67. Michel Hannoun, *L'autre cohabitation: Français et immigrés* (Paris: Editions L'Harmattan, 1986).

68. On the relationship between class and ethnicity and, more specifically, between economic strikes as purely class-based manifestations and ethnicity-based protests, see Jean-Claude Richez, "Référent national et mouvement gréviste," *Pluriel* 36 (1983): 52–80. On the regional-ethnic dynamics of the vintners' strikes in Languedoc, the farmers' strikes in Brittany, and workers' strikes in the Basque country, see Louis Quéré, *Mouvements nationalitaires: La question régionale en France* (Paris: EHESS, rapport CORDES, n.d.), volume 3.

69. Pierre Mayol, "Du côté de chez eux," *Projet* 171–172 (January–February 1983): 61n.

70. For examples, see "Les immigrés: Enjeu électoral," *Le Monde Aujourd'hui* (special issue), November 24–25, 1985.

71. See W. Safran, "The Mitterrand Regime and Its Policies of Ethnocultural Accommodation," *Comparative Politics* 18, no. 1 (October 1984): 59.

72. The mass demonstration in Paris in the summer of 1985, with its slogan "touche pas à mon pote," in which 200,000 young people of all kinds participated, is said to have been "orchestrated" by Minister of Culture Jack Lang. Colin, "Les cultures régionales," 8.

73. These have been explored in Beer, *The Unexpected Rebellion*.

74. See "La culture et sa parole," in *L'Archipel Corse*, supplement to *CFJ Information* (Paris: Centre de Formation des Journalistes, 1983), 39f.

75. *L'Archipel Corse*, as cited in preceding note.

76. Law of January 7, 1983. See *Regards sur l'Actualité*, no. 118 (February 1986): 29–32.

77. Michel Tozzi, in *Apprendre sa langue* (Paris: Syros, 1984), page 57, states that only 60,000–70,000 islanders speak Corsican.

78. See David Carrington, *La Corse* (Paris: Arthaud, 1980).

79. "La Corse à la dérive," *Le Point* (May 25, 1987): 174.

80. Jose Gil, *La Corse entre la liberté et la terreur* (Paris: Editions de la Différence, 1984), 139–141, 221. See also Irina de Chikoff, "Sous la loi des indépendantistes," *Figaro*, February 13, 1985.

81. *Etre Français aujourd'hui et demain*. Rapport au premier ministre par Marceau Long (2 vols.; Paris: Documentation Française, 1988).

82. Under the system of proportional representation used for the election of 1986, the FN had gained 35 seats, which were subsequently reduced to 32 because of resignations of deputies from the party. In the 1988 elections (for which France reverted to the single-member constituency system), the FN elected a single deputy—who was, however, expelled from the party after criticizing a speech by Le Pen.

83. The obligation to adhere to previous commitments is illustrated by the prominent role played by the Chirac government (and Minister of Culture François Léotard) in the inauguration, in April 1986, of a Jewish audiovisual institute and the continuation of plans to build a museum of Jewish art in Paris. See *News From France*, volume 85.09 (April 1986).

84. The new budget for 1987 (introduced in the fall of 1986) provided for a 30 percent reduction of government subsidies to health, sports, social, educational, *and* cultural associations. *Le Point* (October 13, 1986): 21.

85. However, even under the Socialists' permissive attitude, the implementation of bilingualism was uneven. In the fall of 1985, members of the association *Stourm ar Brezhoneg* were fined for having defaced road signs marked in corrupted Breton and were silenced when they tried to speak Breton in court. Information supplied by Lois Kuter, International Committee for the Defense of the Breton Language.

CHAPTER 6

Territorial Management and the British State: The Case of Scotland and Wales

MICHAEL KEATING

The British tradition of political discourse makes it difficult to talk of the state as an entity or actor in the political process. There are those, indeed, who would deny altogether the existence of such an entity as the British state, insisting that the United Kingdom is governed by traditions, understandings, and conventions—the product of the accumulated wisdom of generations. It is true that the UK possesses no written constitution, no code of public law, and no clear principles to separate the domains of the public and the private. It does, however, in the principle of the sovereignty of the Crown-in-Parliament, have a clear basis of political authority. Within the limits of parliamentary sovereignty, all manner of institutional expedients are possible, giving British constitutional practice a large degree of flexibility— but at the cost of considerable confusion and inconsistency.

The means by which the Parliament came to assume the mantle of sovereignty is itself controversial. Despite its habit of dating its origins to de Montfort's parliament of 1254, it in fact dates only from 1707 when both English and Scottish parliaments were abolished and replaced by the new body. Although the Scots Parliament had never claimed absolute sovereignty, the English principles and practices soon came to be applied to the new institution. Chief among these were the principle of parliamentary sovereignty and, as a corollary of this, the unitary state. For the Conservatives, support for the principles of unity and parliamentary sovereignty have usually posed few problems, based as they are on the legacy of tradition. More surprisingly, the British left, too, has largely failed to develop a tradition of popular sovereignty or a "Jacobin" ideology to legitimize the unitary state.[1] Instead, it has simply taken as its own the Conservatives' traditions of state management[2] and accepted without question the governing conventions. So, instead of a theory of the state, the United

Kingdom has only the "parliamentary regime," the series of conventions and traditions stemming from the central doctrine of parliamentary sovereignty.

Our subject is the politics of the peripheral nations of the UK, nations that have had their own distinct political concerns and where the balance of political forces has often differed from that in England. In order to manage the politics of the periphery within the unitary and sovereign UK Parliament, a variety of devices—constitutional, institutional, and political—has developed over the years to cope with the problem of diversity within a unitary state. A key development was the exclusion of Irish politics from the Westminster Parliament. Irish members had been a thorn in the flesh of governments in the late nineteenth century, disrupting business in their quest for home rule and land reform and leading the other parties to impose the draconian procedures that continue to sustain front-bench dominance to this day. In 1922, effective independence was given to the south of Ireland while the north was given a devolved parliament and reduced representation at Westminster. Without this settlement, the presence of fifty or more independent Irish members could have deprived most governments since then of their majority and so prevented parliamentary sovereignty effectively becoming the sovereignty of the government of the day, with its disciplined parliamentary batallions. This is a crucial point, for the disciplined party system, with governments being able to count on a parliamentary majority, is the basis for the "parliamentary regime," the procedures and conventions by which the UK is governed. Governments lacking a majority enter on uncharted constitutional waters. At the same time, the dominant party system has undermined the importance of territorial representation. Members of Parliament (MPs) are supporters of their party first and constituency representatives second, while the politics of peripheral territories can normally find expression only through the dominant executive and party systems themselves.

Further crucial developments in the building of the twentieth-century system of territorial management were the decline of the Liberals after the First World War and the integration of their Labour successors in the Westminster regime. "Home Rule All Round" has been firmly accepted as policy on the left wing of the Liberal policy, sustained by the strength of the Liberals in Scotland and Wales and by distinctive issues such as land reform, church disestablishment, and temperance, by the late nineteenth century. Home rule was formulated in the days of limited government and proposed the retention of powers over defense, foreign affairs, and a few other key items for the sovereign Westminster Parliament, while devolving responsibility for more domestic matters to subordinate parliaments in Ireland, Scotland, Wales, and even England. Some even thought that, in due course, the whole British Empire could become a commonwealth of self-governing but linked dominions, with Ireland, Scotland, and Wales enjoying much the same status as Canada or Australia. Labour took over many of the concerns of the more "advanced" Liberals and home rule was part of its program for many years.[3] After a brief flirtation with nationalism in 1914–1924, however, the commitment ceased to be taken very seriously. The postwar slump had knocked the confidence out of the Scottish and Welsh trade union movements, and salvation for the working class was now seen as lying in London, particularly after the brief experience of government in 1924. The old home rule concept itself had become largely redundant by the 1930s, with the self-governing dominions enjoying effective independence (rather than mere home rule) and the scope and complexity of government greatly increased. This was a serious problem for Labour home rulers who had to reconcile devolution of power with the party's ambitious commitments to central planning, nationalization, welfare expansion, and redistribution, all of which implied the creation of a strong, centralized state. For the Conservatives, there were fewer problems of principle. While the nineteenth century and produced some Tory romantics of vaguely Jacobite sympathies favorable to nationalism, by 1889 Balfour was stating the predominant Conservative view: "We object to Home Rule whether it begins with Ireland and ends with Wales or begins with Wales and ends with Ireland."[4]

The commitment of both major parties to the unitary state did not, however, mean the end of territorial politics or the political and cultural assimilation of Scotland and Wales. On the contrary, an elaborate system of territorial management emerged, within the unitary state, based on "administrative devolution" and the role of territorial representatives and administrators. In 1885, in response to some mild nationalist agitation and a more pragmatic concern with the inefficiency of the conduct of Scottish administration, a secretary for Scotland had been appointed. Gradually improving the status and functions of the office over the last century, the secretary now has administrative responsibility for much of domestic policy in Scotland. The secretary's role is threefold:[5] to administer those functions that, because of the Scottish legal system or traditional features, need separate management; to allow for some measure of distinctiveness in policymaking for Scotland, within the limits of overall government policy; and to act as a lobby for Scottish interests within government. The functions devolved to the Scottish Office largely concern social and environmental policy, with economic and industrial policy reserved to Whitehall departments. So, while the first and second roles involve the secretary in the use of personal administrative powers, the third depends on his or her membership in the cabinet and ability to lever resources out of other departments.

Around the Scottish Office, a Scottish level of politics has developed. Scottish interest groups put their demands to the secretary of state, and separate Scottish legislation, needed because of the separate Scottish legal system, is dealt with by Scottish committees of the House of Commons. In fact, the degree of power devolved is very slight. The secretary of state, although always a Scottish MP and a member of the governing party and cabinet, has a tightly constrained scope for independent policy initiatives. Scottish parliamentary committees, where votes are involved, are constructed on the basis of the party balance in the House as a whole, not that of Scottish MPs. The scope for differentiation is largely limited to the mechanisms by which policy is to be delivered rather than the policy itself, except in some areas of social and environmental policy where party ideology is less important and the cross-border spillover is minimal.

The system was supported by Scottish politicians, however, because what they lost in terms of Scottish autonomy, they gained in terms of access to the center. Conversely, home rule might give them their own government in Edinburgh but would deprive them of their own minister in the central cabinet and put at risk their generous representation in Parliament. It would also diminish the role of Scottish politicians and territorial administrators as privileged channels of access to the center. In my work on the Scottish MP,[6] I have shown that most Scottish MPs concentrated on domestic Scottish affairs, only venturing into the UK political arena on economic and industrial matter where Scottish interests were at stake. Some Scottish MPs, it it true, being interested in wider UK and international affairs, provided a contrast, but these were a distinct minority. The most vehement opposition to devolution in the 1960s and early 1970s came not from those MPs but from the "Scottish-centered" ones whose role would be placed most at risk in any new constitutional settlement. (The style is represented to the point of caricature by the fiercely antidevolution labour MP who in 1973 demanded that only Scottish MPs be allowed to vote on proposals to change Scottish divorce laws, or the equally antidevolution Conservative MP who joined in the same filibuster to stop Scottish divorce reform although he himself has recently used his London domicile to obtain a divorce under the more liberal English law.) This system of territorial representation was not, it must be emphasized, a challenge to the party system, but operated within it and as a part of it, with Scottish and Welsh politicians being loyal party men and women. Indeed, the ability of established parties to accommodate territorial politics in Scotland and Wales (unlike in Ireland) in this way helped preserve the hegemony of the two-party system from territorially based challenges.

By the post-Second World War period, then, all serious challenge to the constitutional order had disappeared. Conservatives were attached to the doctrine of parliamentary sovereignty and unity as an essential prop of the social order. For the left, centralization was seen as a necessary prerequisite for radical change, a view vindicated in the 1945–1951 Labour government's far-reaching programs of nationalization and social welfare. Both parties recognized the need for a distinctive approach to Scottish administration and for a special channel of access to the center for Scottish interests. After 1964, with the establishment of the Welsh Office, the same approach was extended to Wales, though the secretary of state has never achieved the status of his Scottish counterpart and the office is heavily dependent on its Whitehall "big brothers." Politicians and territorial administrators in both nations increasingly sought to justify themselves in terms of their defense of territorial interests. They could claim a great deal, especially in Scotland, where per capita public expenditure levels were some 20 percent higher than in England.[7]

THE POLITICS OF REGIONAL DEVELOPMENT

From the early 1960s, the politics of territorial management were taken a step further with the establishment of regional development policies that aimed simultaneously to accommodate the needs of national (British) modernization and growth and to satisfy demands coming from the periphery. Regional policy (which had been revived by the Conservatives who, against the British swing, had lost support in Scotland in the 1959 election) was under Conservative and Labour governments, progressively developed and extended until the late 1970s. Industrial incentives were made available to induce investors to move from the "congested" regions such as the English South-East and West Midlands to the development area of Scotland, Wales, and Northern England. The theory was that diversionary regional policy was a zero-sum game in which donor regions would win through relief of congestion, the recipient regions through new employment, and the national economy through relief of inflationary pressures and extra output. At a time of growth and full employment, the argument appeared convincing.

In addition, there was a series of one-time industrial developments in the periphery, based on the theory that they would generate spin-offs into the local economy. One can cite the vehicle plants at Linwood and Bathgate in Scotland, the "integrated" steel works, split at the last minute between Ravenscraig in Scotland and Llanwern in Wales, and the smelters at Anglesey and Invergordon. These were certainly welcomed at the time but failed to generate complementary industries, and the 1980s recession has seen the closure of Linwood, Bathgate, and Invergordon and a large question mark over the future of Ravenscraig and Llanwern.

In 1965, regional planning machinery was set up in the form of economic planning councils and boards. The councils grouped representatives of local authorities, industrialists, trade unionists, and independent experts; the boards consisted of civil servants from the main economic departments. In Scotland and Wales, the machinery was placed under the respective secretaries of state. The task of the councils and boards was to produce regional economic plans to fit into the National Plan of 1965. This was an attempt to extend to the territorial level the corporatist approach to economic management being developed at the national level, by incorporating local economic elites. That approach reflected the failure of the traditional parliamentary regime to cope with the demands of modern economic and social planning. Policymaking and policy implementation were now increasingly seen as matters for discussion and, indeed, negotiation, with the major interest groups. A discussion of corporatist approaches to economic management would take us away from our main concern here,[8] but what is clear is that its territorial expression compounded the ambiguities inherent in the practice of corporatism at the national level. For example, if, as was made clear, the regional economic planning councils were there simply to execute central policy, then why were local politicians represented? If they were there to provide a distinctive local and regional input to economic development, what could happen if this clashed with national priorities? The problem can be resolved only by assuming a consensus on the aims and means of economic planning and sufficient resources to achieve them. In the event, the problem was removed by the failure of the National Plan in 1966–1967 but in the meantime a lot of political capital had been invested in the strategy, culminating in the 1966 White Paper on the Scottish economy, with its optimistic prospects for growth. Labour was duly rewarded in winning 44 of the 71 Scottish and 34 of the 36 Welsh seats in the election of that year.

THE SHOCK TO THE SYSTEM

The argument so far has been that the British political parties in the postwar period did not suppress the territorial dimension in politics but diverted the peripheral politics into safe channels. Minor differences in Scottish or Welsh political preferences could be accommodated through administrative devolution. Economic discontent could be met by diversionary regional policies, with the Scots and Welsh constantly reminded that without the help and support of the center, they would be in a sorry state. At the same time, their ability to tap the resources of the center was their main political asset.

The system received a rude shock as early as 1966 when the Welsh nationalist party, *Plaid Cymru*, won a by-election in the formerly Labour seat of Carmarthen. In the following year, the Scottish National party (SNP) overturned the largest Labour majority in Scotland, at Hamilton. Detailed analysis of the reasons for rising nationalist fortunes are beyond the scope of this paper, which is focused on the reaction to these successes, but disillusionment with Labour's failure to sustain its grand promises undoubtedly played a part. The reaction of the Labour government was to promise more of the traditional medicine in the form of regional aid and, a little later, to set up a Royal Commission on the Constitution. Labour remained overwhelmingly opposed to any concession on the constitutional issue, arguing that nationalism was nothing more than an expression of economic discontent which would subside once Labour's economic policies began to work. Only centralized government with Scottish and Welsh representation at the center could ensure that Scotland and Wales would benefit from this expected success. Certainly, there was a subsidiary stream in Scotland, holding to the old home rule tradition, and in Wales there were moves to build on the Welsh Office with an elected assembly; but neither the national leadership nor the majority of Scottish and Welsh parliamentarians would have any truck with this.

Surprisingly, in view of their history, it was the Conservatives who made the first definite moves toward a Scottish Assembly in the 1960s. Edward Heath, then leader of the party, was impatient with the Scots' habit of always looking to the center for aid, a practice that jarred with the Conservative philosophy of self-help, and in 1968 he issued his "declaration of Perth" calling for a Scottish Assembly. The details were entrusted to a committee under Sir Alec Douglas-Home, which produced a curiously contrived scheme intended to combine the virtues of devolution with the maintenance of a unitary Parliament at Westminster. A directly elected Scottish Convention would take the second reading, committee, and report stages of Scottish bills, which would complete the rest of their passage at Westminster, ensuring the last word for Parliament. How this would work when the two assemblies were controlled by different parties was not made clear, provoking a note of dissent by Professor J.D.B. Mitchell, while Sir Charles Wilson, also dissenting, put the classic unionist case. A directly elected assembly would usurp the legitimacy of the Scottish members of Parliament and central government, leading logically only to separation. In government after 1970, Heath ignored the scheme. Scottish Conservatives were never enthusiastic about it and in 1973 their conference threw out by a large majority a resolution calling on the government to implement it.

Meanwhile, to the profound relief of both major parties, the issue had subsided, with the two nationalists losing their seats at the 1970 general election—though the SNP picked up another in the idiosyncratic Western Isles—and the Commission on the Constitution still at work.

THE POLITICS OF DEVOLUTION

The next revival of peripheral nationalism, in the mid-1970s, was not so easily seen off by the parties. The economic argument was transformed by the discovery of North Sea oil in Scottish waters, and politicians who had argued that centralized government was the only guarantee of Scotland's economic future were hoist on their own petard. It would be simplistic to attribute the revival of Scottish nationalism in the 1970s purely to the discovery of the oil, but Miller's argument[9] is persuasive, to the effect that oil removed the constraint previously preventing voters expressing their Scottish identity electorally. Certainly, the argument that, with the oil, a self-governing Scotland might actually be better off undermined the established pattern of territorial representation.

Other political developments were to place the matter at the head of the political agenda in 1974. The previous year, the SNP won a by-election in the Labour seat of Glasgow Govan and, when, in 1974, the Heath Government went to the country on the issue of its dispute with the miners, the SNP won a total of seven seats: two from Labour and four from the Conservatives, plus their existing seat in the Western Isles. The Welsh Nationalists won two seats, but their position was altogether different, representing a consolidation in the Welsh-speaking rural heartland rather than an advance across the country. So, while the SNP vote had doubled from 11 percent to 22 percent of the Scottish total, *Plaid Cymru* had suffered a small overall loss and stood at just under 11 percent of the Welsh. In late 1973, the Commission on the Constitution had finally presented its belated report, just in time for the return to office as head of a minority Labour government of Harold Wilson, who had hoped to dispose of the issue through the device of the commission five years earlier. A new election was inevitable within the year and Wilson's private pollsters were telling him that, without a move on Scottish devolution, he could lose up to thirteen seats to the SNP. Labour had three choices.[10] It could seek to suppress the territorial element in politics altogether and stress purely class of ideological, socialist issues, as advocated by some on the left. This was not in practice a viable option. Labour has never been purely a class or a socialist party, and the territorial dimension could hardly be suppressed when Labour itself had exploited it for so long, presenting itself as the party best able to bring good things to Scotland and Wales. The second option was to try and divert the issue into the economic channel, rolling out the pork barrel and stretching the scope of administrative devolution a little further. This was done. Scotland and Wales were declared development areas for the purposes of regional policy, development agencies were promised for Scotland and Wales, and the economic powers of the secretaries of state were extended a little. It rapidly became apparent, however, that this was not enough and that the third option, a concession on the self-government issue, might be necessary.

Labour had in fact been moving back to a favorable view of devolution, slowly in Scotland, more rapidly in Wales; but now the British leadership decided that a move was essential whatever their Scottish and Welsh wings thought. The Scottish conference was reconvened and voted in favor of a Scottish legislative assembly, and a firm pledge was included in the Labour manifesto for the October 1974 election. Returned to office with an overall majority of only four, Labour was obliged to act. The result was the Scotland and Wales Act, providing for elected assemblies in Scotland and Wales, the Scottish assembly with legislative powers, the Welsh one to have executive powers only.

Hitherto, as we have noted, the British parties, especially Labour, had argued that Scottish and Welsh interests were best served by centralized government, with only a very weak form of autonomy allowed on social and environmental policies through administrative devolution. Any stronger degree of autonomy would, it was argued, put at risk the privileged channels of access to the center enjoyed by the two peripheries. Forced at last to compromise on the constitutional issue, Labour now attempted, in its devolution package, to have the best of both worlds. That range of policies, currently administered by the weak devolution of the Scottish and Welsh offices would now move into the more strongly autonomous sphere of elected assemblies, while economic and industrial policy and taxation would remain centralized as before. The Scottish and Welsh secretaries of state would, however, remain in the cabinet, with the continuing role of speaking up for Scotland and Wales and administering those of their existing functions (mainly with economic implications) considered unsuitable for devolution. To reassure English MPs and unionists in general, pledges were given that nothing would be done to abridge the political and economic unity of the United Kingdom or the sovereignty of Parliament—the theme of preserving parliamentary sovereignty, indeed, became an insistent one for ministers throughout the devolution episode. The difference in treatment for Scotland and Wales was justified on the grounds that Scotland's separate legal system and need, even under Westminster, for separate legislation, made legislative devolution appropriate there, but the general view was that Scotland was getting more because its nationalists were causing more trouble and that Welsh devolution was, for the government, dispensable.

There were many problems with the proposals in terms of political strategy as much as administrative feasibility. Indeed, the administrative difficulties could probably have been resolved in time, with the evolution of the new institutions. The political flaws were to prove fatal.

Much criticism was leveled at the lack of economic powers for the proposed assemblies. Economic discontent was still widely believed to underlie nationalist discontent in Scotland and Wales—indeed, Labour's position hitherto had been that the discontent was entirely economic—yet to concede economic devolution would infringe Labour's own deep-rooted economic principles. These held that economic management should be centralized, with the interests of the periphery catered for by diversionary regional policies. Trade union spokespersons were particularly confused on this point, calling for more "economic teeth" for the assemblies and at the same time insisting on the need to preserve the economic unity of the UK.

The absence of taxation powers was another key weakness. The Kilbrandon Commission had proposed that, to ensure territorial justice among the constituent parts of the UK, the assemblies should receive all their funding from central revenues distributed through an independent Exchequer Board. This was rejected by the government on the grounds that decisions on spending levels were essentially political and could not be handed over to an unaccountable body. Instead, a block grant for the assemblies would be negotiated with the central treasury on the general basis that funds should be dispensed to permit the level of services delivery in Scotland and Wales to be comparable, allowing for differences in needs, to that in England.[11] This principle of block grants as an instrument of equalization of spending potential, while not tying down the discretion of the lower tier of government as to the allocation among individual programs, is a familiar one and in Britain has long formed the basis of the rate support grant for local government. There are, however, no examples in Western democracies of lower-tier governments entirely dependent on such grants, with no discretion at all to alter overall spending levels. The refusal of even a marginal tax-raising power to the assemblies stemmed from a combination of Labour beliefs in centralized resources distribution to ensure equity and the treasury's traditional hostility to devolved taxation. Neither stood up to detailed scrutiny. As we have seen, the existing system for distributing expenditure was not based on territorial equity but strongly favored Scotland and, to a lesser degree, Wales. The uncomfortable implication was that the new system, based strictly on expenditure needs, would involve cuts in Scotland's share of the total. Antidevolution Scots were not slow to point out the difficulties in an assembly having to make a case for higher expenditure, or even for preservation of existing levels, in such a climate under the watchful eyes of English MPs and the treasury and claimed that the old Scottish Office system, with the bargaining conducted behind closed doors, gave Scots a better deal. At the same time, antidevolution English MPs adopted the contradictory argument that devolution would enhance the bargaining power of Scotland and Wales and that any devolved taxation would give them a further advantage again. The government itself feared that any scheme that implied new taxation in Scotland and Wales would be an easy target for attack.

The role of the secretaries of state, too, created difficulties. Their retention was proposed largely to mollify those in Scotland and Wales who insisted that this privileged channel of access to the center was more important than devolved assemblies, but the secretaries of state were also to retain those Scottish Office and Welsh Office functions (mainly in the economic sphere) considered unsuitable for devolution and to exercise a tutelary role over the assemblies. The need to preserve the Scottish and Welsh presence in the cabinet was urged most insistently and, without this concession, the government would have been in deep trouble with its own supporters. Yet, it is difficult to see how, in practice, short of their administrative powers, their bureaucratic support, and their status as spending ministers, the secretaries of state could continue to cut much of a figure at the cabinet table. The role of the secretaries of state in relation to the assemblies was initially seen in terms of control, with power to veto legislation (in Scotland) and administrative proposals. In later versions, the veto power was transferred to Parliament, acting on the proposal of the secretary of state, with the latter assuming the role of looking after the assemblies' interests in Whitehall, including the negotiation of the block grant.[12]

The whole devolution scheme was constructed in a characteristically British pragmatic manner, with little regard for basic principle or consistency. Alleged inconsistencies were attacked mercilessly by opponents, notably the Scottish Labour MP Tam Dalyell with his West Lothian Question. This pointed out that as a Scottish Westminster MP he would be able to vote on a series of issues affecting England but not on the same issues as they affected his own constituency, since they would be devolved to the Scottish Assembly. The unbalanced nature of the proposals, with devolution for Scotland and Wales only, not only undermined the intellectual coherence of the scheme, it also prevented Labour from selling it as a program for improving British government and the quality of British democracy. None of this would have mattered so much if the government had really believed in the proposals itself. After all, England, Scotland, Wales, and Northern Ireland had long been governed rather differently and, with the sovereignty of Parliament unimpaired by the devolution scheme, the "political and economic unity of the UK" was no more at risk than in the past. Yet, the failure to make a positive case for devolution created the impression that Labour was merely pandering to separatist pressures, and the argument was advanced as though it were a demonstrable fact that devolution would inevitably lead to the break up of the UK and the independence of Scotland and Wales.[13] This caused particular difficulties in Wales where decentralist sentiment had been widespread since the 1960s and the Labour party had endorsed the idea of an assembly but where nationalism was largely confined to the old Welsh-speaking heartland and regarded with intense hostility by the English-speaking majority. The perception that devolution was a concession to nationalism cost it a massive loss of support.

The Conservative party, meanwhile, had retreated from its brief flirtation with devolution. Scottish Tories had been unhappy with the Douglas-Home proposals, which, as we have seen, they rejected at the first opportunity. The replacement of Edward Heath by Margaret Thatcher in 1975 led, along with a sharp swing to the right in economic and social policy, to a stance of outright opposition to devolution. This did cause problems on the Scottish Conservative benches where support for devolution had been growing as Conservative fortunes in Scotland declined. In 1975, instructed to vote against the Scotland and Wales bill, the entire Scottish Conservative front bench resigned their positions, forcing Mrs. Thatcher to call on Teddy Taylor, a repentant devolutionist and now one of its fiercest opponents, to become shadow secretary of state. The official commitment to the Douglas-Home scheme was dropped and, despite the presence of a dissident minority right up to 1979, the Conservatives pursued what was to most of them the more congenial line of uncompromising support for the unitary state.

Devolution was to haunt the Labour government for nearly five years and provide the instrument of its downfall. From the beginning, the issue was subordinated to the imperative of survival of the government with a largely unenthusiastic administration corralling its followers into line. The Scotland and Wales Bill itself, although passed at second reading, came to grief when opposition by the Liberals and Labour rebels prevented the imposition of the timetable resolution, essential if it were not to be filibustered. That might have been the end of the matter, with the government regarding its election pledge as discharged, were it not for the difficult parliamentary situation. By-election losses and the defection of two Labour MPs to form the neonationalist Scottish Labour party deprived Labour of its parliamentary majority, leaving it dependent on the goodwill of the fourteen Scottish and Welsh Nationalists, the Northern Irish members, and the Liberals, with whom a pact was negotiated. Despite the Liberals' role in torpedoing the first bill, they made another devolution bill the price of their support. Without a majority and with its own left wing in rebellion for much of the time, there was in any case not a great deal the government could do in terms of new legislation, and a new devolution bill would keep Parliament occupied while ministers concentrated on executive government and looked for a favorable moment for an election.

So, new bills were produced for Scotland and Wales, much on the lines of the old one but with slightly greater powers for the assemblies and a reduction in the controls exercised by the secretaries of state. The production of two bills this time was defended as a means of giving greater clarity to the separate proposals for Scotland and Wales but it was generally believed that the government now saw Welsh devolution as dispensable and would not be too sorry to see it defeated, as long as it did not take Scotland down with it. This did not prevent a series of damaging amendments being made to the bills.[14] As early as the first Scotland and Wales bill, the government had accepted the case for a referendum in the two regions, regarded as a way of killing the Welsh proposals, given their lack of popular support. When the new Scotland bill came before Parliament, dissident Labour members, with Conservative support, succeeded in an amendment stipulating that, to be passed, the scheme should have to gain the support of 40 percent of the eligible voters at the referendum. Given British abstention rates of around 30 percent at general elections, 35 percent at the 1975 European Economic Community referendum and 60–70 percent at local and European Parliament elections, this was a formidable obstacle, clearly intended to wreck the proposals. Yet, once the 40 percent rule had been inserted in the Scotland Act, the government made no attempt to oppose its application in Wales or to reverse the amendment at a later stage in the legislative process.

The referendum campaigns saw a shift of opinion by confused Scottish and Welsh voters to the no side to produce a massive no majority in Wales and only a small yes majority (well short of the 40 percent threshold) in Scotland. In Wales, the result was a shock for Labour, its first defeat in that country for many years. In Scotland, where polls for the last fifty years have, without exception, shown a substantial majority in favor of a Scottish assembly, the result was although more ambiguous. Conservative voters had overwhelmingly voted no after an appeal by Lord (formerly Sir Alec Douglas-) Home who insisted that this was the way to obtain an improved devolution scheme, and after the following promise by Francis Pym, the official Conservative spokesman:

> On behalf of the Shadow Cabinet we can give a clear pledge to the people of Scotland that, if the Scotland Act is rejected, the Conservative Party will not regard this as a rejection of devolution.[15]

It would, of course, be regarded as a rejection of the Labour government, providing an inducement for Conservatives to vote no. Labour voters in the majority voted yes though with a substantial dissident minority following the lead of Labour antidevolutionists who campaigned hard against the act.

The immediate aftermath of the referendum effectively confirmed the role of devolution in the government's political strategy. Fearing that they would not have the support in Parliament to push through the Scotland Act in the face of the indecisive result, ministers took the view that by framing the act and putting it to the people they had discharged their responsibility. Devolution was a peripheral concern and not an issue on which they were prepared to accept parliamentary defeat and an immediate election. As a result they lost the support of the SNP and, when the pact with the Liberals expired, could not expect to survive long. They were duly defeated on a motion of no confidence. So, ironically, devolution, which the government had played along with for five years to keep itself in office, was the immediate cause of its downfall.

TERRITORIAL MANAGEMENT IN THE 1980s

The 1979 general election saw a significant Conservative advance in Wales as a whole, while the Welsh Nationalists strengthened their hold on their two seats in the Welsh heartland. Labour, which in the mid-1960s had come close to being a genuine Welsh national party, with support right across the country and in rural as well as urban areas, fell back to its strongholds in the industrial valleys. The result was that, outside the small Welsh-speaking enclave, Wales seemed increasingly to resemble England electorally, a trend confirmed in the 1983 election when the Conservatives won fourteen Welsh seats, with Labour down to twenty and Liberals and *Plaid Cymru* with two each.[16] Combined with the decisive rejection of devolution in the 1979 referendum, this considerably eased the Conservative government's task of managing Wales.

Scotland posed problems of a quite different order. Not only had the referendum yielded a yes majority, but the 1979 general election saw a small swing to Labour, costing the would-be secretary of state and "no" campaigner Teddy Taylor his seat. The 1983 election weakened both major parties but Labour maintained a clear lead with forty-two seats against twenty-one for the Conservatives, eight for the Liberal-Social Democratic alliance, and two for the SNP. The Conservatives were thus set the task of governing Scotland on the basis of 31 percent (in 1979) and 28 percent (in 1983) of the popular vote. With the defeat of Teddy Taylor, the more emollient George Younger, an erstwhile devolutionist, was appointed secretary of state. He soon made clear the government's view that devolution was a dead issue because "most people in Scotland" (the refusal to use the term "Scottish People" is significant) were against it.[17]

Instead, territorial management involved applying the center's policy with the appropriate institutional modifications for Scotland while acting as a lobby for Scotland in Whitehall—a reversion to the traditional role, but with some important new elements. Government now insisted with great force that a formula devised for determining Scottish expenditure levels over a wide range of fields gave the secretary of state absolute discretion to shift spending from one program to another. Observers (including myself),[18] have expressed serious doubts about the reality of this, but its political implications were important. The secretary of state could no longer imply that he would like to satisfy some Scottish demand but that the treasury would not give him the money. It was officially his task to find the money for his priorities by economizing elsewhere in Scotland; the burden of managing Scotland and balancing the interests within it therefore rested firmly on his shoulders.

The secretary of state retained his role in lobbying for Scotland on matters outside his expenditure block and outside his functional responsibility altogether. Under the impact of the recession and with the government setting itself against devolution, Scottish political attention shifted back to the old concern with lobbying the center for material benefits. For the Scottish Office, this became an even more vital element of its political management role. Yet its ability to play the role had been diminished by three factors. The devolution debacle and the decline of the SNP had weakened the Scottish lobby by removing London's fear that, without material concessions, separatism will prevail. There was a feeling at the center that Scotland had cried wolf too often and that its part warnings were no more than a bluff. In any case, fear of Scottish political consequences was unlikely to sway a government whose political base was the south and midlands of England and which may have felt it had little to lose north of the border. At the same time, the impact of the recession and the collapse of formerly prosperous regions like the West Midlands and of English inner cities made it more difficult to present Scotland as a specially deserving case. This was all the more so since the devolution debates of the 1970s brought home to English MPs just how well Scotland appeared to do from the Scottish Office system.

Nevertheless, lacking other means of political expression, the Scottish lobby coalesced around the Scottish Office and, to some extent, around the Parliamentary Select Committee for Scottish Affairs, set up in 1979 in defense of Scottish material interests. A long battle has taken place over the future of the Ravenscraig steel work, scheduled for closure by the nationalized Steel Corporation. A thinly-veiled threat of resignation by the secretary of state and a cross-party lobby drawing in business and unions, the churches, and local government, gained a three-year reprieve. Later, the proposal to close the Gartcosh steel mill aroused opposition on the grounds that its closure would put Ravenscraig in trouble. Again, a cross-party lobby was formed, though the attempt to focus it on the Parliamentary Select Committee was sabotaged by two right-wing Conservatives who refused to join their party colleagues in criticism of the government. The steel issue is seen as vital for Scottish Conservatives to preserve Scotland's industrial base and, by showing that they can stand up for Scotland, to save what is left of Scottish conservatism itself. Another major battle was over the takeover threat to the Royal Bank of Scotland, the last independent Scottish clearing bank. Once again, Conservatives were to the fore because, without an independent bank, the remainder of Scottish indigenous capitalism would be in danger and, with it, Scottish conservatism.

These battles have increasingly put the Scottish Office on the defensive, unable to live up to all the expectations placed on it. At the same time, the task of applying central policies in Scotland became increasingly difficult. The secretary of state became locked in a battle with Scottish teachers. Theoretically, he could decide to concede their claim for an independent pay review, but in practical terms, he was tied by the treasury and cabinet. Rating revaluation—which occurs in Scotland but not in England—caused an outcry among his own supporters; but to change the rating system he needed cabinet approval. He clashed with local authorities whose spending he must seek to control because, for the purpose of treasury accounting, it counts as his own even where it is financed from local taxation. By the end of 1985, then, Conservative territorial management in Scotland was in deep political trouble and the party was registering unprecedentedly low support in the polls. Conservatives were calling for action to safeguard the Scottish steel industry, for separate Scottish legislation on rating reform if the English departments were not prepared to act, and for a Scottish initiative on the teacher's dispute. The devolutionary implications of this were not lost on people like Ian Lawson, a prominent figure in the Conservative campaign to save the Gartcosh mill who, repenting his no vote in 1979, joined the Scottish National party.

At this point, George Younger was transferred to the Ministry of Defence and replaced by Malcolm Rifkind, a young Edinburgh advocate with an altogether more aggressive style. Determined to rebuild Conservative fortunes in Scotland, Rifkind set himself the target of 30 percent of the vote at the next election—a modest enough goal for a party of government but which involved doubling the level of support he inherited, when his party was lying fourth in the opinion polls. Eager to break the traditional style of secretaries of state by taking bold policy initiatives, Rifkind found himself subject to the same constraints as his predecessor, the expectations on him far outweighing his powers to satisfy them. So he picked up and pursued with enthusiasm the one initiative that Younger had been able to obtain from the cabinet: the promise to replace domestic rates with a poll tax, euphemistically labeled the "community charge." Legislation for Scotland was put through Parliament in advance of the 1987 election, with only a vague promise of its extension to England, where ministers appeared much less enthusiastic. The poll tax was, as many observers had predicted, an electoral disaster. Its beneficiaries were few in number and almost certain to vote Conservative in any case, while the losers, as in most tax reforms, were distinctly more vocal. The June 1987 election saw Conservative support in Scotland slump to an all-time low of 24 percent, reducing the party to a mere ten seats. George Younger hung onto his own seat at Ayr by only 182 votes. Wales, too, swung against the Conservatives, giving them just 29.5 percent of the vote and eight sets and reversing the trends of recent years.

This was the "doomsday scenario" much discussed in the press in the days preceding the election: a Conservative victory in Britain as a whole but a rout in the peripheral nations. Given the mechanism developed over the years to manage Scottish and Welsh affairs, the question was whether the Conservatives could now govern there. At one level, the problem was purely practical, the need to staff the Scottish and Welsh Offices and the committees of Parliament from their depleted parliamentary band. Wales posed the lesser problem, despite the shortage of Conservatives there, for the Welsh sense of identity is much less institutionalized than the Scottish and there was a precedent for a Welsh secretary representing an English seat, though on that occasion he was a native Welshman. In 1987, Mrs. Thatcher was able to kill two birds with one stone by exiling to the Welsh Office her most articulate cabinet critic, Peter Walker, whose imminent dismissal had been well trailed by the Downing Street leaking machine. The gesture recalled the earlier exile of dissident minister James Prior to Northern Ireland but, considerations of nationality apart, the Walker exile may have made some tactical sense, since Walker's liberal views could help soften the government's image in Wales.

In Scotland, matters were more difficult. To appoint English ministers to the Scottish Office, while constitutionally proper, would indicate a complete change of style in governing, from the traditional collaborative mode to one in which ministers were sent north as governors-general. It would mean admitting the eclipse of Scottish conservatism as a force capable, if not of winning elections, at least of sustaining some basis of local support and producing a governing elite from within its ranks. In the event, a secretary of state was available, since Rifkind had retained his seat but, of the other nine Scottish Conservative MPs, one (Younger) was in another cabinet position, three had already resigned or been dismissed from the government, and one, an unrepentant devolutionist, refused an offer of a Scottish Office post. Of the remaining four, three had to be appointed junior Scottish Office ministers, leaving hardly any backbenchers to staff the Scottish legislative and select committees. The system of administrative devolution was just saved, but immense difficulties loomed on the practicalities of getting through a program of Scottish legislation.

Perhaps more serious in the longer term was the issue of the government's legitimacy in Scotland, given its lack of electoral support. This is a difficult issue since, in a unitary Parliament, an overall majority is all a government needs. Yet, the conventions developed over the last century had relied on a government possessing some political base within Scotland, and the increasing institutional differentiation of Scotland had posed the question of the balance of political power within the Scottish arena. Before the 1987 election, there was much talk of what would happen in the event of the doomsday scenario coming to pass. Some Labour radicals claimed that the Conservatives would lack a mandate in Scotland and spoke vaguely of plans for parliamentary disruption and even civil disobedience. The "no-mandate" argument is in fact an extremely complex philosophical issue and one that is almost impossible to reconcile with Labour's traditions and beliefs. Let us examine the propositions that might be made to sustain the no-mandate case:

1. "The Conservatives lack a majority of the Scottish vote and so have no mandate to govern Scotland." The problem here is that no party has a majority of the Scottish vote.

2. "The Conservatives lack a plurality of the Scottish vote," or, closely related, "The Conservatives lack a majority of Scottish seats." The implication of this is that any government, to be legitimate, needs a concurrent majority of seats or plurality of votes in all parts of the United Kingdom. This would make every government this century illegitimate and, even if we exclude Ireland, would make most of them illegitimate. It would certainly make it difficult for a future Labour government to rule in England. A few Labour radicals, having written off England, and with it the UK, as hopeless for Labour in any case, would not worry unduly about this, but the overwhelming majority in the party would find the argument utterly unacceptable.

3. "The 1979 referendum result favoring a Scottish assembly was overturned and the government that did this was subsequently rejected in Scotland." This argument is on firmer moral ground, though no part that believes in the sovereignty of Parliament can really challenge Parliament's right to change its mind on devolution or set whatever rule it wishes for advisory referendums. It is true that parties favoring an assembly gained some 76 percent of the Scottish vote in 1987. But to argue that the government has no mandate on education (devolved in the Scotland Act) but does on the steel industry (retained in the Scotland Act), and thus may close Ravenscraig, has no mandate on housing (devolved) but does have a mandate on the poll tax (retained), would scarcely make sense to the voters.

The no-mandate argument, indeed, resting as it does on a rejection of the authority of Westminster, is an argument for self-determination. It is not necessarily an argument for separatism, since the Scottish people, given the choice, might reject that option. It is, though, an argument for allowing Scotland to determine its own constitutional preferences—which would then have to be negotiated with London. This is, in essence, the position adopted by the all-party Campaign for a Scottish Assembly but rejected by the Labour party, which continues to adhere to the principle of parliamentary sovereignty and must therefore play by the rule that the overall majority is all that counts.

Labour's position, repeated before and during the 1983 and 1987 election campaigns, is that an assembly will come from a Labour government at Westminster, using its parliamentary majority. It would be based on a strengthened version of the 1978 Scotland Act and be elected on the first-past-the-post electoral system. Scottish interests in Whitehall and Westminster would continue to be looked after by a secretary of state and the full complement of seventy-two MPs. This position was regarded with considerable skepticism outside Labour's ranks, for three reasons. First, many people doubted Labour's ability to win a UK majority. Second, many doubted the ability of a Labour government to put through an assembly bill, given the hostility encountered in Parliament last time. Third, there was an inconsistency in Labour's claims to be in favor of devolution as a democratizing measure at the same time as insisting on the first-past-the-post electoral system that would ensure a permanent Labour majority as long as it hung onto as little as a third of the total vote. There is, of course, even greater inconsistency in claiming, in defiance of the parliamentary conventions, that the Conservatives lack a mandate in Scotland and then relying on precisely one of those conventions (that it is the majority of seats and not votes that counts) to claim that Labour has the mandate.

It follows that any campaign to discredit the government's mandate in Scotland and to demand an assembly on democratic grounds must be a cross-party one and must incorporate some form of proportional representation into the assembly proposals. Yet, this the Labour party consistently refuses to countenance, believing that it would set a precedent for proportional representation at national elections and sticking to the view that Labour will put through assembly legislation as a normal bill once it wins a majority.

There remains the problem as to how in the meantime Labour is going to demonstrate to its Scottish supporters that their vote has not been entirely wasted. In the immediate aftermath of the election, a set of policy demands was lodged, involving government recognition of their setback in Scotland. These included the establishment of a Scottish assembly, the repeal of the poll tax legislation, measures to tackle unemployment, more investment in housing, and no privatization of the Scottish electricity boards. Not surprisingly, the government refused to concede, and there, presumably, the matter will rest. Prospects may be greater at the local government level, where Labour-controlled regions and districts can resist pressure to cut services and try to continue to deliver the goods. However, this power base, such as it is, will be further undermined by rate capping, contracting-out legislation and the squeezing of fiscal autonomy through the community charge, and the nationalization of the business rate. There may be some more high-profile campaigns to highlight Labour's opposition to Conservative policy but, given the fear and distrust of Scottish nationalism on the part of the leadership, these are likely to play down the Scottish dimension. After all, to highlight their own inability under present conditions to resist Conservative policy in Scotland is to play into the hands of the SNP.

In Wales, the devolution issue is less prominent, given the decisive rejection of an assembly in the 1979 referendum. It follows, given the Welsh people's endorsement of the Westminster rules, that a no-mandate argument is a non-starter. Yet, Labour faces the same problems as in Scotland, in responding to the responsibility placed upon it as the leading party, in delivering rewards to its supporters.

Further problems of territorial management therefore face the two major British parties, problems that may prove even more troublesome than those posed by the rise of peripheral nationalism in the 1970s. At that time, the problem was the intrusion of territorial parties into the central legislature at a time of close party competition. The problem was peripheral in several senses of the word. It concerned the periphery of the United Kingdom, it was posed by "fringe" parties, and the issue was marginal to the great issues of the day. So it could be dealt with by devolutionist expedients that preserved intact the essentials of the state while allaying concern at the periphery. The hope was that "normal" two-party politics could then resume at the center. In 1987, however, the problem was posed by a grossly uneven pattern of support for the two major parties of the state. On the one hand, the governing party could no longer claim a substantial political base in Scotland and Wales to underpin the institutions of administrative devolution. On the other hand, the major opposition party had become to a large degree a territorial party, with its basis in the inner cities and peripheral territories (where it was firmly rooted), but without a realistic prospect of the return to power at the center that would allow it to meet the aspirations of its supporters. The unwritten conventions and understandings that underlay this, as they underlie other aspects of the British constitution, were based on the regular alternation of parties in power. Labour has restrained the separatist inclinations of some of its supporters with the promise of a return to power at the center and has carefully preserved a pattern of territorial management that it hoped to inherit. If this system should break down because of the unrealism of these expectations, a vacuum could be created into which separatist forces could again step.

NOTES

1. J.B. Jones and M. Keating, *Labour and the British State* (Oxford: Oxford University Press, 1985).

2. J. Bulpitt, *Territory and Power in the United Kingdom* (Manchester: Manchester University Press, 1983).

3. M. Keating and D. Bleiman, *Labour and Scottish Nationalism* (London: Macmillan, 1979).

4. *Hansard* 54:1732.

5. M. Keating and A. Midwinter, *The Government of Scotland* (Edinburgh: Mainstream, 1983).

6. M. Keating, *The Role of the Scottish MP* (Unpublished Ph.D. thesis, Council for National Academic Awards, 1975); M. Keating, "Parliamentary Behaviour as a Test of Scottish Integration in the United Kingdom," *Legislative Studies Quarterly* 111, no. 3 (1978).

7. D. Heald, *Public Expenditure* (Oxford: Martin Robertson, 1983).

8. But see J.B. Jones and M. Keating, *Labour and the British States* (Oxford: Oxford University Press, 1985).

9. W. Miller, "The Connection between SNP Voting and the Demand for Scottish Self-Government," *European Journal of Political Research* 5 (1977).

10. M. Keating and D. Bleiman, *Labour and Scottish Nationalism.*

11. D. Heald, *Financing Devolution Within the United Kingdom: A Study of the Lessons from Failure* (Canberra: Centre for Research on Federal Financial Relations, Australian National University, 1980).

12. Vernon Bogdanor, *Devolution* (Oxford: Oxford University Press, 1980).

13. T. Dalyell, *Devolution: The End of Britain?* (London: Jonathan Cape, 1977).

14. M. Keating and P. Lindley, "Devolution: The Scotland and Wales Bills," *Public Administration Bulletin* 37(1981): 37–54.

15. *Guardian*, July 28, 1979.

16. J.B. Jones and D. Balsom, "The Faces of Wales," in I. McAllister and R. Rose, eds., *The Nationwide Competition for Votes* (London: Frances Pinter, 1984).

17. Richard Rose, "Scotland: British with a Difference," in I. McAllister and R. Rose, eds., *The Nationwide Competition for Votes* (London: Frances Pinter, 1982).

18. M. Keating, "Bureaucracy Devolved," *Time Higher Education Supplement*, April 6, 1985.

CHAPTER 7

Referendums and Ethnoterritorial Movements: The Policy Consequences and Political Ramifications

ROBERT J. THOMPSON

One of the primary difficulties encountered by scholars seeking to evaluate the significance of public policy interactions with ethnoterritorial political movements is the lack of clearly comparable cases. While there is a fairly large number of ethnoterritorial groups that are politically active in the Western industrialized countries of the world, as the chapters in this book attest, the movements vary substantially in their degree of political mobilization and their demands. The conflicts also vary significantly in terms of the public policies that have been generated in response to them. The use of the referendum in the cases of Scotland, Wales, Quebec, the Jura, the Basque country, Cataluña, Galicia, and Andalucía provides something of an exception to this situation. In each of these cases a referendum was used to settle at least some of the political and constitutional questions raised by the ethnoterritorial groups active within these territories.

The overall objective of this chapter is to further our understanding of the interrelationships between ethnoterritorial political movements and the public policy processes affecting them. Thus, I compare the usage of the referendum device in each of these cases. I also consider why it was utilized, the political/constitutional contexts within which the referendum was held, the character of the ethnoterritorial movements involved, the referendum processes, and the ramifications of the referendums for the ethnoterritorial movements as well as the broader political systems. I also evaluate the referendum device as a means of resolving or coping with the ethnoterritorial political issues central to these conflicts. The accent then will be on those features of the cases that seem to have affected the referendum process or its outcome.

THE REFERENDUM AS A POLICY TOOL

Referendums offer an intriguing example of both how public policy decision-making processes can be used to cope with ethnoterritorial political demands and how those same processes may be used by ethnoterritorial movements for their own purposes. Indeed they represent significant examples of the policy interaction process for several reasons. First, as already noted, clearly comparable examples of ethnoterritorial movements and policy responses are difficult to find. Second, these cases are worthy of attention because of the political significance assigned their outcomes by both the proponents and the opponents of the issues being decided. Moreover, while the outcomes varied, in each case the results have clearly had short-term effects and potentially long-term consequences for the ethnoterritorial movements and the political system as a whole. Third, the referendums were held sufficiently long ago that some of those consequences can now be identified, but not so long ago that the results are essentially irrelevant to the policy issues currently facing the ethnoterritorial movements or their political systems.

And, finally, as a policy tool referendums differ significantly from other forms of decisionmaking commonly involved in ethnoterritorial conflicts in the enhanced position to which the decision to submit an issue to the electorate elevates that issue on the public agenda. Like other means of policymaking, be they legislative or administrative in character, the referendum can be seen both as a response to various political pressures and as a means for making a decision about future responses. To some extent virtually all forms of decisionmaking concerning ethnoterritorial issues involve public input and scrutiny in Western democratic states. A referendum, however, enhances these aspects beyond even the legislative process by its public participation elements. This is especially apparent in all of the ethnoterritorial cases considered here, where the referendum issue involved some degree of self-government for the region. Consequently, the symbolic importance of the public's participation greatly heightened the attention given the issues and the potential outcomes.

This enhanced position on the public agenda, in turn, has the potential for leading both the proponents and opponents on the issue involved to exaggerate the costs and benefits of the outcome. Especially in these ethnoterritorial cases, the outcome is perceived by both sides as being critical for their political positions and to the political system as a whole. The proponents of a greater degree of self-government tend to see the referendum itself as a confirmation of their right to self-determination. Moreover, the referendum is the appropriate decisionmaking device from their perspective because of its participatory character. Part of their basic argument generally concerns the unrepresentative—hence undemocratic—nature of the central government. Thus, the referendum itself, by definition in most political systems an extraordinary means for resolving sensitive political issues, confirms for its proponents their underrepresentation in the ordinary policy-making processes of the state. A positive outcome in the referendum further legitimizes their position by demonstrating a firm popular base. By implication, how can any government claiming to be democratic consequently fail to recognize the propriety of further grants of self-government?

Those who oppose using referendums in such cases, and/or oppose the question to be decided, also tend to inflate the ramifications of the outcomes. Generally, they see the referendum device as a means of delegitimizing the claims of the ethnoterritorial movements to represent a majority of the electorate in the region. Just as the proponents run the risk of inflating the potential benefits of self-government, the opponents run the risk of inflating the potential costs to the integrity and even unity of the broader political system. Both sides thus have a stake in making the question one of the legitimacy of their own position as opposed to that of their opponents. As a consequence, the use of a referendum in these cases brings the issues to the public agenda in a way unlike any other means of decisionmaking.

The public agenda feature of the referendum is itself usually a result of the political process through which the issues have emerged. The decision to conduct a referendum is not the first step in the policy process. Instead, it is usually among the last. Most political systems, and especially the ones to be discussed in this chapter, use referendums sparingly. Consequently, the decision to use a referendum in these politically and constitutionally sensitive cases was an exception to the general pattern of politics in these countries. It was an admission of the special nature of the problems and issues at stake. Also, the decision to hold the referendum should be seen as a policy response in its own right, as well as a decisionmaking process for subsequent responses.

The referendum, thus, generally comes after a relatively lengthy period of political gestation. When this factor is combined with the "one-shot" character of the referendum, the significance of the outcome is inflated. All sides recognize the special circumstances surrounding the use of a referendum and realize that they will not be able to call for another in the near future if their position loses. Unlike a legislative vote, a reconsideration of a referendum decision cannot immediately be implemented. As a consequence, the referendum is not an incremental decisionmaking device, although the policy results derived from its use may be incremental in their nature.

Analysts and participants should also recognize that one consequence of the public character of the referendum is a downplaying of the broader political, social, economic, and cultural concerns behind the ethnoterritorial movement in the first place. Usually the referendum involves the transfer of additional self-governing authority from the central government to units within the ethnoterritorial group's geographic base of support. This transfer alone cannot settle all of the issues central to these cases. No decisionmaking device, in fact, can settle an issue completely unless that issue is politically insignificant and extremely narrow in its implications, which is precisely the opposite of the situation in the cases of ethnoterritorial conflict under discussion here. They tend to involve multidimensional issues that will neither be settled by a favorable decision in a referendum nor fade entirely as a result of a negative outcome. Consequently, caution is necessary in anticipating the ramifications of the outcomes of the referendums, particularly in terms of their capacity to resolve the issues in contention.

The Political Implications of an Ethnoterritorial Referendum: The Partisan Participants

Before considering the specific cases it would be useful to review the hypothetical political and constitutional implications of participating in referendums for both the ethnoterritorial movements and the political systems. Keeping the range of conceivable ramifications in mind can aid in appreciating the complexity of issues involved in these conflicts and in evaluating the actual consequences that may be subsequently identified. This is a topic that is not developed evenly in the research literature on ethnoterritorial politics or on referendums. The referendum literature discusses at length the constitutional implications of the device, even if analysts differ substantially in their evaluations of those potentialities. Discussions of other possible consequences occur only sporadically in evaluations of individual cases, yet they may substantively condition the constitutional ramifications. The political implications for the partisan participants are thus important factors in the manifestation of the constitutional ramifications.

In these cases of ethnoterritorial conflict the referendum issue concerns the proposal or ratification of a devolution of decisionmaking authority from the central government to a regionally based government. The more nationalistically oriented elements of the ethnoterritorial movement, those most ardently seeking political independence or separation, tend to see the referendum and its proposals as an important, but insufficient step. They argue for participation in the referendum as a means of demonstrating broad public support for their goals. The more regionalist-oriented elements of the movement, those more concerned about securing institutionalized representation within the broader political system, probably perceive the changes proposed as the best available opportunity. They thus are more inclined to accept the proposal, at least for the time being. Both groups, though, will see a need for further negotiation because the proposals for the transfer of power are inevitably incomplete and vague regarding specific grants of authority. Differences of opinion within the ethnoterritorial movement are likely to be submerged during the referendum campaign, as each side has a stake in a successful outcome, although those differences are likely to surface after the voting is complete regardless of the outcome, as has occurred in Quebec and Spain. At the same time, the prodevolution groups—which may be broader than the ethnoterritorial groups—try to downplay the severity of the ramifications of the referendum decision. By moderating the potential extent of the proposed changes, the ethnoterritorial groups hope to attract uncertain voters who may normally identify with the partisan positions of other parties.

Organizationally, a positive vote is perceived as critical to the future success and legitimacy of the ethnoterritorial movements. Commonly, the momentum these movements have demonstrated at the polls was a factor, if not the major factor, in the decision to hold the referendum. As a result, these movements are testing their legitimacy as representatives for their region in the referendum, as well as their momentum. If their position wins majority support in the referendum, then their claim as "the spokeperson" is validated and is likely to lead to future electoral gains. Their success would attract additional publicity, members, activists, and revenues. Failure, on the other hand, would seriously jeopardize the movement's future growth. If the movement cannot demonstrate public support in this setting, then questions would be raised about the depth and intensity of its popular support. Its potential opponents would obviously seek to capitalize on this perceived weakness. The ethnoterritorial movement would have difficulty in regaining this lost momentum, as no other election is as likely to permit the movement to dominate the public agenda on its own terms. As a consequence, failure in the referendum may lead to a reorientation within the movement.

While referendum success is perceived as being critical to these movements, it is not necessarily a guarantee of future electoral gains. The grants of authority involved in the referendum are generally replete with ambiguities that must be negotiated in the future. This means subsequent elections, and the problems of competing with the other political parties to become the new party of government will persist. This transition alone is likely to entail serious conflicts for the ethnoterritorial movement, since it has usually developed as a party of opposition with no or very little experience as the party of government. The movement has thus been able to avoid the responsibility for the administration of programs or the negotiation of policy with the central government. This situation would probably also exacerbate whatever divisions might exist within the ethnoterritorial movement. Serious differences of opinion about how to proceed with the negotiations, how much to cooperate with other regionally based parties, and how cooperative the regional government should be with the central government would likely arise.

Similarly, the opposing political parties will almost certainly continue to challenge the ethnoterritorial movement in the new decisionmaking process. Groups opposed to the transfer of power and/or the referendum tend to see the entire situation as leading to the dismemberment of the central political system. In British terms, the opponents perceive the process as leading down the "slippery slope of devolution" toward political independence for the region concerned. They dispute the ethnoterritorial movement's claims that it has majority support, can therefore be more representative of the populace, can provide more efficient, less bureaucratic government, and can run the economy better. The opponents, conversely, tend to believe that the region cannot sustain itself economically and, therefore, cannot support new levels of governmental institutions. As a means of making this point, the opponents would likely try to broaden the issues or stakes involved in the referendum. They attempt to divide voter attention by bringing in other partisan issues so that their supporters might not be lured away by the ethnoterritorialists. Also, by bringing in other issues they will attempt to demonstrate the inexperience and inability of the ethnoterritorialists to govern a complex, modern society effectively. They portray the ethnoterritorial movement as being composed, at best, of naive idealists or, at worst, crazies bent on the destruction of the political system. By casting this broad net the opponents seek to demonstrate the narrowness of the ethnoterritorial movement's political base. Moreover, their own organizational base and popular support is less vulnerable than the ethnoterritorial movement's. Since their *raison d'être* is a wider set of traditional political issues and their supporters have tended to establish reasonably long-term patterns of partisan identification, neither success nor failure in the referendum is likely to affect their electoral fortunes substantially. They obviously stand to increase their support if they can demonstrate a real weakness of the ethnoterritorial movement among the populace. However, they are not likely to gain the votes of the ethnoterritorialists without some degree of sympathy to the cause they just campaigned against. Most probably, the ethnoterritorial movement's less committed supporters will become unreliable voters fluctuating between parties, causes, and candidates. Failure in the referendum is also not likely to alter drastically the traditional parties' position. They can fall back on the politics of the new arrangements and use their normal base of support to compete effectively. They will still be in position to participate in the bargaining as the local representatives of the dominant parties in the central government.

In summary, while the outcome of the referendum may have extremely broad political ramifications, such events are unlikely, especially in the short run. This assessment is based in part on the cases that yet need to be discussed, but it is also a recognition of the complexity of the issues involved and the inability of the participants to separate the referendum from those broader concerns. This tends to mean that the likely consequences of participation will not be as great—neither in benefits, nor in costs—as the participants will argue. Many of the region's problems will persist even if the proposals are approved in the referendum. The risks of participation, though, are probably greater for the ethnoterritorial movement, whose legitimacy is at stake, than for the system-wide parties.

The Constitutional Implications of an Ethnoterritorial Referendum:The Governing Institutions

Another dimension to the question of the impacts of referendums in ethnoterritorial conflicts concerns the referendum device itself as a decision-making instrument. For all of the political systems involved, with the exception of Switzerland, the referendum is not a commonly used decision-making process. In fact, it is generally a tool regarded with substantial trepidation by central governments. Central government institutions and elites tend to fear both the short-term political consequences and the long-term constitutional ramifications of such an all-or-nothing process.

The topic of referendums and the advisability of their use in deciding public policy questions received considerable attention during the late 1970s from both politicians and scholars. This interest was a consequence of the fact that referendums had been recently used for a diverse and controversial set of issues, ranging from such matters as membership in the European Economic Community to changes in the taxation/expenditure policies of the American states.[1] Determination of the effects of the referendum on governmental authority is obviously a complex matter, as Vernon Bogdanor's review of the British referendum debate over time illustrates.[2] To a large extent, one's view of the consequences depends on one's position on the issues of the day and evaluation of the effectiveness of the government/parties in power to cope with those issues.

David Butler and Austin Ranney, however, have compiled a summary of the major arguments for and against the use of the referendum[3] (see Table 7.1). As these arguments have been voiced by a number of individuals under varying circumstances, a discussion of them may serve as a means of contrasting our cases and assessing the referendum's effects on the governmental institutions of the political systems. The main thrust of the differences of opinions has centered on the question of how much the electorate should be involved in the making of public-policy decisions. Detractors of their use primarily argue that referendums decrease the power of legislatures by removing those bodies from the decision process, thereby weakening their authority and legitimacy. Referendum proponents, on the other hand, argue that the referendum is a democratic device that permits more extensive public participation in making of important decisions. Much of the discussion depends on the constitutional nature and traditions of the particular political system. Britain, for example, has unitary system with a strong

Table 7.1 Theoretical Arguments "For" and "Against" the Use of Referendums

FOR	AGAINST
1. Legitimation	1. Referendums weaken the power of elected authorities because they threaten their control over the political system.
a. "'...all political decisions should be as legitimate as possible.'"	
b. "'...the highest degree of legitimacy is achieved by decisions made by the direct, unmediated vote of the people.'"	2. The problems facing modern governments are numerous, complex, and demanding. Ordinary citizens, for various, reasons, are not able to make wise decisions on them.
2. Direct Democracy	
a. All of the issues of a controversy are faced in a referendum unmediated by political parties or special interest groups.	3. Every vote counts the same in a referendum, thus there is no measurement of the intensity of the beliefs expressed.
b. Referendums bring the decision process close to the people.	4. Democratic decision processes should aim for a general consensus amongst the public, not force a decision between limited alternatives.
c. Referendums are public decisions publicly arrived at—the more open, the better.	5. Referendums are likely to be less protective of minority rights because they cannot measure the intensity of beliefs.
d. The popular will is accurately expressed in a referendum.	
e. Open government will end public apathy and alienation.	6. Referendums weaken representative government by causing it to lose power to the public, to decrease in public respect, and to be less attractive to outstanding candidates.
f. In a referendum the public interest is served, not merely a sum of special interests.	
g. In a participatory system the citizen's human potentials are maximized.	

Source: David Butler and Austin Ranney, eds., *Referendums: A Comparative Study of Practice and Theory* (Washington, D.C.: American Enterprise Institute, 1978): 24–37.

tradition of parliamentary sovereignty. This heritage does not allow much room for direct participation. The system is structured around political parties and the government's control over the decision-making process. Switzerland, on the other hand, has a long tradition of extensive public participation and decentralized political structure, which is compatible with the use of referendums in deciding both major and minor public issues.

Nor are all referendums of a single character. Butler and Ranney identify four types of referendums, differing on their initiation source and the extent to which they transfer control over the making of laws from elected representatives to the voters.[4] The first type is government-controlled referendums, which includes those cases in which the government has the sole authority to decide to submit a question to the electorate and to define the rules of the process. Three of our cases—Scotland, Wales, and Quebec—belong to this category. The second type includes constitutionally mandated referendums. The government controls the proposal of the amendment and its wording, but cannot adopt the constitutional amendments unless they are approved by the voters. The Spanish cases of Cataluña, Euskadi, and Galicia belong to this group. The third type of referendum has no representative example among our cases. It includes those referendums held at the behest of popular petitions aimed at voiding an act passed by the government. In other words, an affirmative majority in this type would negate an action already taken by the government. The fourth type includes those referendums held at the initiative of the public that are designed to add a new law or amendment. In this category an affirmative majority results in the adoption of the proposed legal change. The cases of Andalucía and the Jura region in Switzerland seem to belong to this category. (As can be seen, these typologies are listed in ascending order in terms of the extent to which they transfer decisionmaking power to the voters.)

Finally, the major reasons identified for holding referendums differ, although the differences are not applicable to all of our cases. Butler and Ranney found that referendums have generally been held for three reasons: constitutional requirements, a need for legitimation of the decisions to be approved, and as a means of transferring decisionmaking authority.[5] The latter two reasons are applicable in each of the eight ethnoterritorial cases in this study. Referendums, however, were not constitutionally required in the British or Canadian cases. They were held primarily as legitimating devices. Ironically, though, the fact that they were held may well have established a constitutional precedent for any future self-government legislation.

THE REFERENDUMS

The willingness to hold the referendums on ethnoterritorial issues in each instance signified a potentially consequential change in central government policy toward the ethnoterritorial movements and a possible transformation of the center's administrative structure. Given the significance of these referendums for the political systems, as well as for their ethnoterritorial movements, an understanding of what occurred in each case needs to be developed prior to assessing the consequences of the referendums. This section will, therefore, systematically address five major factors central to evaluating the effects of the referendums: the development of the ethnoterritorial issues, the structural context of that development, the origins of the referendum proposal, the campaigns, and the election outcomes.

The British Cases—Scotland and Wales

The decision to hold a referendum on devolving legislative powers to assemblies in Scotland and Wales must be set against the institutional framework of the United Kingdom and the political conflicts of the decade preceding the vote. Institutionally, Britain is probably the second most centralized system to hold referendums on ethnoterritorial matters. It is a unitary state with centralized decisionmaking authority residing with Parliament. At the same time, the system has historically allocated substantial administrative responsibility to various local government bodies, although it has avoided organizing functional responsibilities along territorial lines.[6] The major political parties, however, have generally been divided along territorial lines since they were organized. Each of them has maintained separate organizations, particularly in Scotland. There has been, as a result, some degree of distinctive political representation of Scotland and Wales within the unitary structure of the British system.

Consistent with the principle of parliamentary sovereignty, referendums as a decisionmaking device have not been used historically in Britain. The idea of the referendum had, however, received serious consideration at various times in British political debates from the late 1800s on as a potential means for resolving different constitutional issues.[7] The first and only systemwide use of the referendum, however, was in 1975 when the issue was Britain's continued membership in the European Economic Community (EEC).[8] None of the major parties, though, were willing to commit themselves to future referendums based on that experience. The referendum had allowed the political parties to disagree internally (especially the Labour party) over the issue of EEC membership without the division becoming so intense that it spilled over into issues. The EEC referendum was regarded by party leaders as a unique exception to the normal pattern for resolving political questions.

The historical connection of Scotland and Wales to the British political system is also an important factor in the development of their ethnoterritorial movements.[9] Although both Scotland and Wales have been politically united with England for a long time, Wales since the thirteenth century and Scotland since the early eighteenth, each has retained a sense of distinctiveness—a sense of national self-identity. In Wales this distinctiveness has a strong culture content, closely linked to the usage of the Welsh language. In Scotland the sense of identity is strong but more difficult to pinpoint as linked to a primary basis. Language as a cultural symbol did not perform a unifying role of significance for the Scots. Scotland was, however, guaranteed the separation of its religious, legal, and educational institutions. Moreover, the Act of Union also assured Scotland, as a region, political representation in Parliament, representation that was subsequently furthered institutionally by the establishment of the Scottish Office in 1885. Wales was not to achieve this status until the mid-1960s. Thus, Scottish distinctiveness is based upon a wider range of cultural, socioeconomic, and historical factors, none of which individually appears to have been overly dominant.

Political agitation for increased governmental autonomy for Scotland and Wales has been active since the mid-nineteenth century, but it did not attain electoral prominence until the 1960s. In both cases a political party scored electoral successes that enabled those parties to claim and be recognized as the political representatives for Scottish and Welsh nationalism. The Scottish Nationalists, though, were much more successful than were the Welsh. In the October 1974 general election the Scottish National Party (SNP) won eleven parliamentary seats with 30.4 percent of the popular vote, making it the second largest party in Scotland. The *Plaid Cymru* (PC), on the other hand, was able to elect only three MPs with 10.8 percent of the Welsh vote. These electoral victories were followed by polls in Scotland showing high public support for the devolution of governmental power to a Scottish Assembly, although not for the SNP's stated goal of independence. The Scottish independence option reaches a high of 24 percent in the mid- to late-1970s, but was generally nearer the 15 percent mark. Broader, less drastic structural changes, however, had consistent majority support among Liberal, Labour, and SNP voters, with a substantial minority of Conservative identifiers also supporting devolution.

The reaction of the major British political parties and, consequently, the governments was basically one of neglect until the 1974 elections. Both parties responded to the SNP and PC after their initial success in the sixties, but discontinued their interest once the Nationalists failed to make as large an impact in the 1970 general election as had been feared. Not until the SNP threatened the Labour party's precarious position in the later elections did devolution became a serious issue. The Labour government then began its four-year-long push to secure passage of devolution legislation granting assemblies to Scotland and Wales that culminated in the holding of the referendums.

One economic factor that influenced the political situation of the 1970s was the discovery and development of the North Sea oil fields at the same time that the British economy in general was having serious problems. Scotland had had a lower growth rate and higher unemployment than England as a whole, and particularly the southeastern region around London. For some of the more fervent Nationalists the claim that the oil was Scotland's provided a basis for arguing about the past mismanagement of the Scottish economy and was a resource base for promising better times ahead under a separate Scottish government. For their opponents, the oil revenues issue was seen as an example of the narrow self-interest base and lack of economic realism of the Nationalists. In general, though, the potential economic benefits of the oil provided a serious context for consideration of the SNP's potential significance by the major parties and the central government, a context absent in the case of Welsh nationalism.

The decision to use a referendum in determining whether or not the Scottish and Welsh devolution bills would be implemented was not of the Labour government's choosing. The government was forced to accept the referendum in exchange for the support of some of its own backbenchers in passing the bills. During the parliamentary debate of the bills, however, an amendment was imposed requiring that a majority of those voting, and a 40 percent of the total eligible electorate, vote affirmatively in the referendum in order for the legislation to be implemented. If such an affirmative majority was not secured, then the secretaries of state for Scotland and Wales were required to resubmit the legislation to Parliament, which would then decide whether to proceed. This amendment generated intense controversy, especially in Scotland, as there was considerable uncertainty over how many persons should be counted as eligible to vote given the inevitable errors in the voting rolls. The government, however, did indicate that it would seek to resecure Parliament's approval for the legislation if the 40 percent figure were not met, as long as there was a sufficiently wide affirmative margin among those actually voting.[10]

The positions of the major political actors in the referendums were somewhat confusing.[11] There were no government-funded umbrella campaign organizations as existed in the EEC referendum. As a result, the campaign was very much a free-for-all contest with each group responsible for raising its own funds. The SNP and *Plaid Cymru* both campaigned for approving the Labour government's devolution proposal. The Labour party was divided on the issue despite the Labour government's position, and individuals were permitted to campaign according to their personal preferences. Thus, an odd situation developed in the Labour party with some of its affiliated unions contributing money to the pro-campaign, while some Labour MPs played a major role of the opposing side. The Conservatives were similarly divided, although to a lesser degree since more of their supporters opposed the bills. Still, some prominent Conservatives, particularly in Scotland, campaigned for devolution. Umbrella organizations were also organized for both positions, but they had considerable difficulty in cooperating with one another as the Nationalists dominated the pro-groups and the Conservatives dominated the antis.

The actual campaigns reflected this uncertainty of overlapping political loyalties. The anti-devolutionists got off to a much earlier start, developing a well-organized campaign that tended to override the positive groups. The pro-forces, consequently, were put in the position of addressing the agenda established by the anti-devolutionists. The pro-groups also had substantial problems campaigning for the same objective. The Labour party in Scotland, for example, had difficulty explaining why its supporters should support something desired by the SNP when it had campaigned vigorously against the nationalists and separatism only months before in several parliamentary by-elections. The pro-forces also seemed to have assumed that the substantial lead in public-opinion pools for some form of devolution would lead to a sufficiently large turnout and positive vote in favor of these particular devolution bills. This, especially, seems to have occurred in Scotland where support for devolution had consistently held a large margin in the public-opinion polls.[12] In Wales, however, that the majority would be a negative one was fairly clear from the start.[13] Furthermore, in both regions, the entire process was complicated by the fact that a general election would obviously take place in the near future and the outcome of the referendums would be an important factor influencing how the Labour government would face the electorate in the Scottish and Welsh constituencies.

The results of the March 1, 1979 referendum were not at all favorable from the nationalists' perspective (see Table 7.2 for the results of all of the referendum cases). The Welsh vote was overwhelmingly negative. Only 20.3 percent of those voting supported the devolution act. The Scottish vote was affirmative, but only by a small margin: 51.6 percent to 48.6 percent. Measured in terms of eligibility, however, the Scottish margin fell substantially below the 40 percent requirement: 32.8 percent to 30.8 percent.

These results left the Labour government little discretionary room for interpretation. Even so, before it could decide to act, the SNP withdrew its support from Prime Minister Callaghan's minority government. This triggered a series of events leading to a vote of no confidence and the 1979 general election won by the Conservative party.[14] In the subsequent Parliament the SNP's representation fell from eleven to three MPs and that of the *Plaid Cymru* fell from three to two. The new Conservative government repealed the devolution acts shortly after taking office and no additional consideration has been given to the topic since. The overwhelming Conservative victory in the parliamentary elections thus ended official consideration of devolution for as long as Mrs. Thatcher heads Conservative cabinets.[15]

The 1979 election also signified a renewed interest in economic issues that has not abated since and that is likely to continue to deflect the activity of individuals who might otherwise be concerned with devolution. In addition, both major parties, but most especially the Labour party, have been engaged in very significant internal conflicts, and devolution has not been one of the important concerns involved in the debates. Thus, there has been no one left in Parliament in a position or with the willingness to press for

Table 7.2   Ethnoterritorial Referendums and Results[a]

Referendum	Date	% Yes	% No	% Turnout	
United Kingdom					
Scotland	3/1/79	51.4	48.6	63.6	
Wales	3/1/79	20.3	79.7	58.8	
Canada					
Quebec	5/20/80	40.6	59.4	85.0	
Spain[b]					
Euskadi	10/25/80	90.3	5.1	58.7	
Cataluña	10/25/80	88.1	7.8	59.7	
Galicia	12/21/80	71.0	20.9	26.2	
Andalucía	2/28/81	55.4	4.0	62.7	
Switzerland[c]					
Berne Canton - entire	7/5/59	22.4	77.6	NA	
Berne portion		11.1	88.9	NA	
Jura portion		48.1	51.9	83.0	(approx.)
Northern districts		69.4	30.6	NA	
Southern districts		26.0	74.0	NA	
Laufen		26.9	73.1	NA	
Berne Canton - entire	3/1/70	86.5	13.5	38.0	(approx.)
Jura portion		90.2	9.8	NA	
Jura	6/23/74	51.9	48.1	90.0	(approx.)
Northern districts		73.9	26.1	NA	
Southern districts		34.2	65.8	NA	
Laufen		25.8	74.2	NA	
Southern districts	3/16/75	28.9	71.1	98.0	(approx.)
Laufen[d]	9/14/75	17.0	83.0	57.4	
Switzerland	9/24/78	82.3	17.7	41.5	

Sources: United Kingdom: Denis Balsom and Ian Mcallister, "The Scottish and Welsh Devolution Referenda: Constitutional Change and Popular Choice," *Parliamentary Affairs* 32 (Autumn 1979): 394–409, Canada: Henry Giniger, "Quebecois Defeat Sovereignty Move by Decisive Margin," *New York Times*, May 21, 1980, p. 1, Spain: *Keesing's Contemporary Archives*, April 11, 1980, p. 30181; April 24, 1981, p. 30827; July 18, 1980, p. 30357; and December 18, 1981, p. 31250, Switzerland: Kurt B. Mayer, "The Jura Problem: Ethnic Conflict in Switzerland," *Social Research* 35 (Winter 1968): 736; *Keesing's Contemporary Archives*, July 10, 1971, p. 24706; September 2, 1974, p. 26699; June 9, 1975, p. 27169; October 20, 1975, p. 27404; and April 6, 1979, p. 29541.

[a]All referendum results have been displayed so as to indicate percentage favoring or disfavoring further autonomy for the territory involved.
[b]Spanish percentages do not equal 100 percent. The difference between the yes and no totals and 100 percent is due to the percentage of ballots cast that were blank or spoiled.
[c]All Swiss results structured to indicate the percentage favoring or disfavoring Jura's separation from Berne, or, where appropriate, districts joining the Jura.
[d]On 9/7/75 a further referendum was held for the border communities of those districts that were to be geographically between the new Jura Canton and those remaining with Berne. Eight communities voted to join Jura. Five declined.

devolution. This situation changed somewhat during the 1987 election, but only moderately so.

Coincidentally with this sidetracking of official interests in devolution, the SNP itself has undergone some difficulties. The aftermath of the referendum has brought internal fighting over leadership positions and the formation of a splinter group within the party, both of which had been uncharacteristic of the party's more recent past.[16] Information on continued public backing of the SNP is difficult to obtain, although there are indications of continued support. On the other hand, the public-opinion polls still indicate substantial generalized support for devolution. Ironically, the factors that might swing some of that sentiment toward the SNP, or at least toward devolution, are the very economic issues that have deflected interest thus far. If the Conservative government cannot deal with the regional economic problems of Scotland and Wales, then a situation may be created upon which the Nationalists can capitalize. This occurred to a minor degree in the 1987 election with erosion of the Conservative party's support in Scotland.[17]

At best, though, the Scottish and Welsh Nationalists are still in a very weak position electorally and organizationally. Their legitimacy as the major spokesmen for their regions has never recovered from the referendum loss, nor have they been able to rebuild their popular or organizational base. Moreover, their continued success is still dependent upon the actions and strategies adopted by the larger system-oriented political parties. If devolution is to come to Scotland and/or Wales, it is likely to be a result of decisions made by the Labour party or some Labour-Liberal coalition. These parties continue to express general support for the concept and did so in the 1987 general election as a means of appealing particularly to the Scottish electorate. The SNP and *Plaid Cymru's* role is likely to be minimal, although a legislative assembly would provide a more hospitable forum for them.

The Canadian Case—Quebec

The immediate situation in Quebec that led to the referendum was substantially different from that in Scotland and Wales. The Parti Québécois (PQ) controlled the provincial government of Quebec and was, consequently, able to authorize the referendum itself without being dependent upon a decision of the federal parliament. Moreover, the PQ government came into power in 1976 on a platform that included a promise of a vote on the nature of continued relations with the rest of Canada. The party had only been organized eight years before, built from various small nationalist groups and Liberals dissatisfied with their party's unwillingness to push for stronger provincial powers. Since its beginnings the PQ has been perceived as the voice of French-Canadian nationalism.[18]

The Quebec context also differed from the British ones in the political and institutional opportunities afforded the French-Canadians. As the majority language group (>80 percent) in Quebec (although a minority in the whole of Canada), the French-Canadians have long experienced political representation and accommodation within the federal system. They were able to dominate the province politically, as well as play a major role in federal politics through their support of the Liberal party. As Chapter 3 notes, however, after 1960 French Canadian desires for increased provincial powers intensified sharply, particularly in those areas that would protect and further the economic opportunities of the French-speaking majority. Historically, the English-speaking majority occupied the more dominant economic positions within the province and the French Canadians began to react to this situation. As a means of securing this protection, the PQ advocated renegotiation of the federal relationship, and calling the referendum was a major step in the PQ's plan to fulfill that goal.

The question of holding a referendum in Quebec thus differed from the British cases because of Canada's federal system. The matter was outside the control of the central government. The setting of a date for the referendum was pushed back several times, but the provincial government eventually decided to hold it in 1980. The ground rules for the campaign established by René Lévesque and by the PQ government were fairly extensive. Each alternative in the referendum wording would be permitted a single umbrella campaign organization. The government would provide sums of money to each group. Groups would also be able to solicit a limited amount of private contributions from individuals, but not from businesses or business groups. Three days after the issuing of the referendum notice a provisional committee composed of those members of the National Assembly concurring with the referendum alternatives would be formed. This committee would decide the representation of various parties and other groups on a national committee and choose major officers. The national committee would then be responsible for conducting the referendum campaign. This rule forced the anti-sovereignty-association groups to function largely under the wind of the Quebec Liberal Party and its leader, Claude Ryan, which was not especially satisfying for all of the negative groups. The positive forces, however, were closely aligned with the PQ, making cooperation easier.[19]

The Quebec referendum is also of interest in terms of its purpose, as it differed from most of the other cases. In placing this measure before the Quebec people the PQ government was not asking for acceptance of an already-negotiated administrative or constitutional change but, rather, permission to negotiate for sovereignty-association. The meaning of this goal was never completely articulated, but was often discussed as an arrangement allowing for political sovereignty while maintaining an economic union with the rest of Canada. If the referendum measure passed, the PQ government would commence negotiations with the federal government for this new status. Before any changes would be effective, however, another referendum would be held.

The actual campaign was an intense one, possibly more so than occurred in Scotland or Wales.[20] From the beginning, the no-forces generally held the lead in public opinion polls. They seemed to have worked out some of their earlier organizational problems and concentrated their campaign on the adverse effects of separatism. Fears, particularly of adverse economic consequences, were also stressed by the business community. Several other provincial government premiers intervened, trying to make clear their objections to the referendum's passage. Probably most important, though, was the active campaigning of the Prime Minister Trudeau. His heavy involvement against sovereignty-association stressed the seriousness of the change being contemplated. The referendum thus placed the French-speaking voters in a bind by forcing them to choose between their two favorite politicians, Trudeau at the federal level and Lévesque at the provincial level. Moreover, the choice was complicated by Trudeau's promise to seek further constitutional change if the referendum failed. The pro-forces campaigned much the same as they had prior to the call for the referendum, stressing the need for a new status for Quebec and denigrating the charges of potential harmful effects. Lévesque also had to appease the extreme separatists within his own organization who found the referendum proposal too mild.[21] The final results of the May 20 vote were somewhat surprising. The no-option had held a lead in the polls, but the final margin was greater than expected: 59.5 percent no to 40.5 percent yes. Even French-speaking Quebecers voted against the measure, 52 percent to 48 percent, with the other language groups voting over 90 percent against it.[22]

The Parti Québécois was hurt considerably less by its defeat in the referendum than were either the Scottish or Welsh nationalists, already possessing governmental power at the time. Also, even if approved, the referendum would have only authorized the provisional government to begin negotiations. The results did mean that Lévesque and the PQ felt compelled to drop the sovereignty-association issue for the time being, concentrating instead on the other problems facing the province. This shift of focus, however, was still not a complete one, because the debate over Quebec's economic problems, the language policy, and the constitutional status of Canada's intergovernmental relations inevitably continued to place French Canadian concerns on the public agenda.

The PQ agreed during its victorious 1981 election campaign not to raise the sovereignty-association issue for several years. There were party members, though, who were not satisfied with accepting the results of the referendum. As long as Lévesque was the dominant leader of the party and actively pressuring the federal government for alternate means of ensuring and/or increasing the province's autonomy, these internal disagreements were manageable. In March 1985, however, a group of militants broke away from the party forming a pro-sovereignty movement and subsequently, in August, a separate political party. In between the two events, Lévesque resigned from the premiership and the party leadership. The provincial elections held in December 1985 saw the PQ defeated by the Liberals.[23]

Throughout this period, though, the PQ as Quebec's governing party was much better situated than the SNP or *Plaid Cymru* to raise public issues and to pressure its rivals, both provincially and nationally, to accommodate the province's concerns. As Chapter 3 clearly illustrates, the PQ was quite effective in pursuing its goals even with the referendum loss. The PQ was aided in this process by the intergovernmental conflicts present within Canadian politics as well. The other provincial and national leaders may have opposed the PQ's positions on constitutional questions, but their own intense defenses of provincial government prerogatives contributed to the legitimacy of such positions. The PQ lost the 1985 elections, but by the time it did, it had played a major role in redefining the stands of the provincial Liberal party and the national Conservative party. They may not have succeeded in getting all of their demands accepted, but they were quite successful nonetheless.

Since its 1985 defeat, however, the PQ has lost some of its ability to be identified as the party of French Canadian nationalism. The Liberals have undertaken policies which have also enabled them to make an effective argument on this point. In addition, the PQ has also developed deep divisions over the independence question. These divisions intensified after Lévesque's resignation. Approximately a week after his death in November 1987, the split reached a sufficiently intense point that Pierre Marc Johnson, Lévesque's moderate successor, resigned as the party's leader, and militants desirous of pushing for Quebec's independence were returned to leadership positions.[24]

The Spanish Cases—Cataluña, Euskadi, Galicia, and Andalucía

The Spanish referendum case differ from both the British and Canadian cases in origin. The Spanish referendums were part of a larger process of decentralizing and democratizing Spain in the wake of Franco's death.[25] As such, these referendums do not stand alone. They were part of the process that included the writing and approval of the new constitution, as well as the election of the new parliament.[26]

The Spanish cases also differ from the other cases because of the extreme centralization of governmental authority that characterized Franco's Spain. All of the other political systems examined were either federal in nature (Canada and Switzerland) or at least more institutionally pluralistic (United Kingdom) and did not need to rely upon official violence. Yet, this degree of centralization was not always the case in Spain. The various regions constituting the Spanish kingdom had historically retained some of their regional institutions and privileges. While there was a tendency for the privileges to be restricted during the latter half of the nineteenth and early twentieth centuries, the trend was not entirely undirectional. During the Second Republic, however, the pattern was reversed. Cataluña and Euskadi (the Basque provinces) were permitted to establish autonomous governments after the parliamentary states were approved in regional referendums. Galicia was also granted autonomy, but was unable to experience it because of the Civil War. The movements responsible for the creation of the autonomous governments were heavily based on the language and culture of the regions.[27] The extensive repression of regional cultures and political sentiments under the Franco government converted these open public movements into clandestine, conspiratorial groups. As a result, Spain has undergone a continuing series of terrorist acts against the symbols and individuals representative of the Madrid government, most notably, but not exclusively, in the Basque region. Through these acts of violence and other political activities, such as continued political support by nonviolent local politicians for regional governments, it was apparent after Franco's death that if Spain was going to have democratic government, then some form of accommodation with the regionalist groups was required. Without such an accommodation no new constitution would be approved, there would be no abatement of the terrorists activities, and no democratic government would be likely to survive. As a consequence, provisional autonomy statutes were approved for Euskadi and Cataluña in 1977, with ten more regions being granted preautonomy statutes within the next year. Additionally, negotiations proceeded during the writing of the constitution as to the means by which the regional governments would be established and the powers they would be allocated. The subsequent referendums on creating autonomous regions were thus a fulfillment of obligations made by the central government during these preceding negotiations.

A final set of noteworthy differences between the Spanish cases and those of Scotland, Wales, and Quebec concerns the breadth of public support behind autonomy. First, in each of the Spanish cases there were multiple political parties aligned with the ethnoterritorial demands. This contrasted with the other cases where there was a single predominant ethnoterritorial party. Second, these parties represented diverse political ideologies in each region, with only the far right not sharing the ethnoterritorial desires. Moreover, these parties drew their backing from all social classes, further illustrating the breadth of support for regional self-government. And finally, the Spanish cases were distinct because of the high degree of unity shown by the regional parties in their confrontations with the central government.

Unlike the British and Canadian cases, the use of the referendum device was not entirely novel to Spanish politics. The new democratic government had used them on several occasions to register public backing for its changes. The first was held in December 1976 to introduce democratic reforms and dismantle the Francoist governmental structure, and a second one in December 1978 for the approval of the new constitution. Both referendums were government-controlled referendums. Essentially, the government alone had the initiative for their proposal and execution. On the other hand, the four ethnoterritorial referendums to date have been held in fulfillment of the autonomy process previously agreed to in the drafting of the new constitution.[28] Three of these have been for the approval of an autonomy statute: the October 1980 referendum in Cataluña and Euskadi and the December 1980 referendum in Galicia. The other, the February 1980 referendum in Andalucía, was for obtaining autonomy via Article 151 of the constitution.

As indicated earlier, the new government recognized the special necessity of granting autonomous powers to the Basques and Catalans in order to maintain their support and to end the political violence in those regions, particularly Euskadi.[29] The Basque General Council, which had begun work with the passage of the pre-autonomy statute, was responsible for preparing a draft autonomy statute which the Constitutional Committee of the Spanish Parliament subsequently approved in July 1979. The government then set October 25, 1979 as the date for the referendum for approval of the statute by the Basque electorate. The referendum campaign lasted a month, with the *Partido Nacionalista Vasco* and other nationalistically inclined parties, as well as the Spanish Socialist and Communist parties, calling for a yes vote. Only the radical *Herri Batasuna* party called for abstention since the statute did not recognize the right to national self-determination. The other extreme of the political spectrum, the far right, called for a no to stop the disintegration of Spain. Large numbers of police units were sent to the region, fearing acts of political terrorism that would negatively affect voter turnout. However, while ETA-militar rejected the statute because it did not recognize the Basque people's right to self-determination and secession from Spain, the group ceased its activities for a period of time covering the referendum, although the group made it known that this was due only to a "technical truce." ETA politico-militar, on the other hand, expressed its approval of the statute as a first step towards independence, urging the Basques to vote yes.[30] The statute received a solid yes vote with an approximate 60 percent turnout and was later ratified by Parliament. The subsequent elections to a Basque Parliament were held in March 1980 and overwhelmingly elected regionalist party supporters.

The referendum in Cataluña followed a similar process.[31] Catalan legislators prepared a draft statute, which was approved in August 1979 by the Cortes. The Catalan referendum was set for the same day as the Basque referendum and the campaign began with all the Catalan parties, as well as the Spanish affiliated parties, backing the statute. Because there was little opposition, the campaign in favor of the statute was languid. Furthermore, the majority of the Catalans were known to support autonomy. The statute was approved with a high percentage of yes votes. As in the Basque case, the regionalist Catalan parties subsequently fared well, winning most of the regional parliamentary seats, whereas the government party, the UCD, won only 18 of 135 seats despite the intense campaign it carried out, which included a visit by Prime Minister Suarez to the region.[32]

As Clark notes in Chapter 2, the limits of the government's willingness to extend autonomy to the other regions became apparent during the process followed for the autonomy of Andalucía. The UCD altered its regional policy and backed away from rapid decentralization to the other regions by mobilizing its resources during that campaign to urge the people to abstain from voting in the referendum. It argued that if the autonomy process were to continue for all the regions demanding it, the next few years of Spanish politics would be nothing but referendums and local elections that would disrupt the governmental process and affect its handling of more important issues, such as the economy.

The *Junta de Andalucía*, the pre-autonomous governmental body of that region, as well as all the other parties in favor of autonomy, reacted strongly to the government's new policy and pressed for a date to be set for the referendum. In view of the government's advocation of a boycott of the referendum, the president of the junta threatened to resign if his demand for a referendum in February was not met. Finally it was agreed that the referendum would be held on February 28, 1980.

The case of Andalucía differs from the Basque and Catalan cases principally in that the latter had, before the Civil War, completed the process of autonomy and had been granted a statute. Therefore, all that was necessary to regain their autonomy was to submit a statute to the electorate in a referendum, have it ratified by the Cortes, and then proceed to elect an autonomy parliament. This same procedure also applied to Galicia. All other regions wishing to become autonomous would have to follow a different procedure. First, they had to determine if they could obtain autonomy via Article 151 of the constitution (which allows the region to begin the autonomy process immediately) or via Article 143 (which allows the process of Autonomy to begin after five years have elapsed).[33] To this end, a referendum had to be held in each of the provinces of the region wishing to become autonomous and the yes vote had to win by a majority defined as a percentage of the total electorate of the province. If a majority was obtained, the region would then be able to proceed, via Article 151, to the drafting of a statute which would then be submitted to the region's electorate in a second and final referendum.

In the February referendum for Andalucía, all the provinces save two, Almería and Jaén, registered the required majority of yes votes. The positive vote in Almería was only 42.1 percent, while it was 49.3 percent in Jaén. (The Jaén vote was later contested and ruled a positive majority.) The UCD was pleased by the results although it paid dearly, losing much of its support in the region. The other parties that had called for a yes vote, and the *Junta de Andalucía*, accused the government's supporters of irregularities and would not accept the referendum results for the province of Almería. After months of negotiations between the reticent government and the junta, an agreement was reached in October 1980 that allowed Andalucía to become autonomous without having to wait for a period of five years. The controversy was resolved by a modification in the Law of Referendums permitting the Cortes to recognize provincial initiatives for autonomy in the event that the vote failed to produce the necessary majority for some reason. Thus, other evidence of the province's desire for autonomy could be substituted for the election results. Through this process the results from Almería were annulled. Andalucía was then able to follow the procedures of Article 151. The referendum on the autonomy statute was subsequently held on October 20, 1981, receiving an 89.4 percent positive vote from those who turned out. The abstention rate was 46.4 percent, up from 37.3 percent in the February 1980 referendum. Nevertheless, this positive vote permitted the elections to the regional parliament to be held in May 1982.[34]

The last of the referendums for approval of a statute was held in Galicia, the third of the historic regions of the peninsula.[35] Once again the process was complicated and delayed by the UCD. The UCD proposed an autonomy formula practically devoid of political content and closer to a simple administrative decentralization. The Socialists and other Galician parliamentarians rejected this proposal, insisting on a statute similar to that of Basques and Catalans. After a year of negotiations the statute for Galicia was approved by the Constitutional Committee of the Cortes in November 1980 and the date of December 21, 1980 was chosen for the referendum.[36]

The electoral campaign was brief, lasting only fifteen days. The UCD, the Spanish Socialists and Communist parties, and the majority of the Galician nationalist parties campaigned in favor of the statute, with the more extreme left- and right-wing parties opposing it. The results of the referendum were discouraging because of inordinately high rate of abstentions, 73.9 percent.[37] The fact was allowed those who opposed autonomy for Galicia to declare that proceeding with the adoption of the statute and implementation of autonomy was undemocratic when only 14.5 percent of the possible electorate had given their approval to the measure. Despite the low turnout in the autonomy referendum, elections to the Galician regional parliament took place on October 20, 1981.[38]

As Clark discusses in Chapter 2, the situation that followed the referendums in the Spanish cases differed substantially from that in Quebec and the United Kingdom because the next step in the autonomy process was one of negotiation over the transferal of authority to the new regional governments. This process has been under way basically since the referendums were held, but progress in the negotiations has been slow. Cataluña and Euskadi have generally been the test cases. The arguments and patterns of power transferal arrived at in those cases have served and will serve as precedents for the other regions. The process of establishing autonomous regional governments has been complicated by several matters. First, the range of powers and authority to be transferred is theoretically quite extensive, covering almost all aspects of domestic policymaking. The actual transferal, however, is a matter of negotiation between the regional and central governments. Consequently, while the range of powers is potentially great, so is the room for interpretation and disagreement during the negotiation process. In addition, the fulfillment of autonomy has been complicated by the political climate within Spain. Rightist groups have not favored autonomy. This has placed considerable pressure on the central government to move cautiously in the negotiations, especially given the continued use of terrorism by the Basque militants. This situation particularly makes negotiation on law enforcement questions difficult. The process of bargaining has also been complicated by the instability of political party relations—again, especially in Euskadi. The new result has been movement on some policy questions like broadcasting in the regional language and education, but stalemate in other more complex policy areas.

The Swiss Case—Jura

Although the ethnoterritorial politics involving the Jurassien districts of Switzerland's Berne Canton did not receive a separate chapter in this book, the referendum to which they led has several distinctive facets that may be useful to note in this comparative exploration of the impacts of referendums. First, unlike the other cases, the case involved trying to separate from a subunit (a separate canton) of the Swiss Confederation. The other cases involved a separation or decentralization directly from the central government. Given the extensive authority of the Swiss cantons, however, creation of a Jurassien canton from Berne would allow it autonomous powers comparable to those sought in the other cases. Second, one should remember that referendums are frequently used in Switzerland, making them a more familiar and accepted means of settling political issues than has been the norm in our other examples.[39] Finally, the number of referendums is significant. Because of the particular manner in which the Jurassien case developed, five major referendums have been held since 1959. In all of the other cases, except Andalucía, there was only a single referendum specifically on the question of self-rule.

The Jurassien situation dates to the Congress of Vienna in 1815, which gave the old bishopric of Jura to the Berne Canton. The basis of the distinctiveness between the two areas principally involves language differences.[40] The majority of the old Berne Canton are German-speaking, while a majority of the Jura's population are French-speaking. This language difference also tends to coincide with a religious one, particularly for the northern districts of Jura. They are predominantly Catholic and the southern districts of Jura are largely Protestant. Over the years since Berne's acquisition of Jura there have been repeated instances of disputes between the two language groups. One researcher has noted, for example, that in at least three previous conflicts the question of separation has been seriously raised.[41] The earlier efforts were successful in receiving official recognition of the French-speaking people, as well as institutionalizing some forms of governmental representation. However, while the earlier disputes sufficient to maintain a sense of distinctiveness and the idea of possibly creating a new canton, no organization dedicated to that objective has sustained until the current controversy developed.

The contemporary conflict began in 1947 when a French-speaking individual was denied an important cantonal position because he did not speak German. This controversy was followed by twelve years of agitation for a referendum on separation from Berne. Initially some concessions were made to the Jurassiens, but they proved insufficient to blunt the extensive ethnoterritorial demands. Moreover, that this time the *Rassemblement Jurassien*(RJ) was created and sustained, an organization whose purpose was the attainment of these objectives. This was not the only Jurassien group formed in response to the controversy, but it came to be the principal one fairly quickly. The RJ differs from the other ethnoterritorial organizations within our study in that it is not a political party.[42] The group's members may belong to any of the regular electoral parties; consequently, it does not run candidates under its own label. It does, however, effectively pass the word around about the separatist sentiments toward various candidates, thus making it exceedingly difficulty for antiseparatists to be elected.

By collecting more than enough signatures the RJ was able to force a referendum in July 1959 on the question of whether the Jurassien people should be able to determine their fate. The measure failed overwhelmingly in the canton as a whole and by a narrow margin in the Jurassien districts. However, in the French-speaking Catholic districts of Jura the measure received a large positive vote, with almost the reverse occurring in the French-speaking Protestant districts. The German-speaking Catholic district of Laufen voted against the measure by a 3-to-1 margin, establishing a basis for its own later separation from the Jura.

The Berne government believed the referendum's outcome to have settled the conflict, but that was not the opinion of many Jurassiens. Agitation continued during the 1960s and would occasionally even involve acts of violence on the part of several small Jurassien groups. Finally, in 1967, the central government established a commission to make recommendations on the future of the Jura. This commission recommended a referendum on self-determination. The assistance of the federal government was then requested. A federal commission on the problem made further recommendations that were essentially accepted by the Berne government. As a result the Berne parliament passed the necessary enabling legislation for a second rederendum.

The referendum process for Jura differed from our other cases in several respects but largely because of its protracted nature. In a sense the process was the consummate example of using the referendum as a means of political participation.[43] The protracted nature of this situation arose because of the language incorporated into the legislation adopted in the March 1, 1970 referendum on granting the Jura the right to hold a referendum on self-government. This measure was approved by a wide margin, because of support by the Berne government, and because of Jurassiens both supporting and opposing separation. While the measure did not grant self-government to the region, it did establish the procedures for reaching that decision. First, a referendum would be held for all the Jurassien districts on separation. Second, those districts opposing separation would hold a second vote on remaining part of Berne. Third, those communes on the border between those districts separating and those not separating would vote to determine their own course of action. Fourth, the district of Laufen would be permitted to vote on the issue of remaining with Berne, being part of Jura, or joining a third canton, since Laufen would be physically isolated from the old Berne canton by the separating districts. And, finally, the entire set of changes would have to be adopted in a national referendum, because adding a new canton would require amendments to the federal constitution.

As is indicated by the above provisions of the referendum legislation, separation of at least the northern districts of Jura was clearly anticipated. Nevertheless, the Berne government attempted to forestall Jurassien separation by offering additional administrative devolution to the region. When this effort failed, the Berne government gradually backed out of further extensive involvement in the referendum process. The pro-separation forces were particularly led by the RJ, while the anti-separation forces were led by the Union of Jurassien Patriots (UPJ). These two organizations were largely responsible for gathering the necessary petition signatures that instigated the legal process of conducting the referendums and then the actual campaigning itself, a situation that contrasts with the active governmental involvement characteristic of most of our other cases.

The referendum on the question "Do you favor separation from Berne?" was finally held in June 1974. As expected, the northern districts voted yes and the southern ones voted no. Although the RJ bitterly opposed the division of the Jura, the southern districts held their referendum on remaining with Berne the following March and overwhelmingly opposed leaving the old canton. Several communes on both sides of the probable borders then held their subsequent referendums. The final vote approving the creation of the Canton of Jura was held in September 1978 and the canton formally came into existence of January 1, 1979. Full legal separation would not occur, however, until November 1984 when both the Berne and Jura parliaments reached agreement on the complexities of financial separation.

One significant aspect of the Jurassien referendum process as compared with the other cases is the high emotional content of the entire situation. Throughout this series of elections, tensions remained fairly high between opposing groups, especially those living along the borders. The Spanish cases, particularly Euskadi, have seen extensive violence, but it has generally been directed against governmental officials. Here the conflict was between villages and neighbors. Thus, while the device of the referendum is a common one for the Swiss, in this instance the acceptability of the results may have been less than usual because of the intermingled residence of the participants. In fact, the disputes continue even into the mid-1980s. Two villages, Velerat (70 inhabitants) and Ederweiler (150 inhabitants), continued to dispute their boundaries even though both were physically separated from their preferred canton.[44] Vellerat wants to become part of Jura, while Ederweiler wishes to remain part of Berne. Ironically, the Jurassien parliament refuses to trade villages with Berne despite the preferences of Ederweiler's German-speaking residents. Jura hopes to be able to integrate the village into the new canton.[45]

Summary

This section of the chapter has surveyed the cases in terms of the basic political aspects likely to have been influential in the development of the referendum issues and for the consequences of the election results. By focusing on the development of the ethnoterritorial issue and the structural context of that development, on the origins of the referendum proposal, and on the campaigns and their results, I have attempted to draw the reader's attention to the comparability of the policy situations faced in the various cases. This is consistent with this book's assumption that the political process itself is a critical variable in the generation of future ethnoterritorial demands and policy responses.

A number of similarities and differences have been noted in the historical backgrounds of the ethnoterritorial groups and issues, the types of organizations articulating their positions, the manner of interaction with the central government, and the responses of the central authorities. The eight referendum cases further differ in the ways in which political systems have attempted to deal with their common policy concern, illustrating the varying roles for political parties, governmental officials, and interest groups in the referendum process. Furthermore, these cases demonstrate the diversity of rules under which a referendum may be conducted. The Swiss case is an example of an elaborate set of follow-up procedures, while the Quebec case serves as an example of extensive campaign rules. The Andalucian case illustrates the potential for conflict over the rules themselves when the outcome differs from that anticipated when the rules were initially formulated, while the cases exemplify situations of minimal regulation. Finally, these cases also demonstrate that there is no certainty of outcomes, as evidence by the events in Scotland and Quebec.

Obviously, no two cases, not even the cases occurring without a single political system, are entirely comparable. Nevertheless, the basic objectives of the major ethnoterritorial participants and the central governments are substantially similar. In each of the cases the ethnoterritorial movements believed the referendum, even when they were not the initiator, to be a critical step in their efforts to achieve added grants of self-government. They recognized the necessity of demonstrating their level of support against the broader population within the framework of the referendum rules. Each case also involved a substantial comparability of basic demands for a greater degree of self-government by the ethnoterritorial population. The particular institutional arrangements clearly varied in the degree of self-government that would be granted, but each provided the basis for a redistribution of institutional representation and responsibility for the ethnoterritorial groups involved.

The central government officials also viewed the referendums as a necessary, though not necessarily welcome, policy step in their efforts to cope with the ethnoterritorial issue. In each case they sought to accommodate aspects of the demand for self-government and institutional restructuring with their objective of maintaining the essential unity of the overall political system. In some cases, particularly Euskadi and Cataluña, greater institutional representation for those regions was seen as a necessary move in order to preserve unity. Even where the central authorities opposed the ethnoterritorial movements on policy grounds, a substantial degree of accommodation occurred in the staging of the referendums.

CONCLUSIONS: POLITICAL CONSEQUENCES AND CONSTITUTIONAL RAMIFICATIONS

The preceding discussion has surveyed the development of the referendum cases and their electoral outcomes. Now it is necessary to return to the basic concerns of this chapter—the political consequences and constitutional ramifications of ethnoterritorial referendums. As indicated earlier, the various participants in the referendum processes argue that the stakes in the elections are enormous for the ethnoterritorial movements and the political systems as a whole. The validity of those claims needs to be assessed, not simply accepted at face value.

Political Consequences

As noted, there are multiple possible political consequences that may result from participating in a referendum for both the ethnoterritorial movements and their opponents. The impacts of the referendums on these parties can be examined in terms of three basic sets of questions. The first concerns the impacts for the ethnoterritorial movements and the political saliency of their cause. The second focuses attention on the broader, system-oriented political parties and the issues with which they are primarily concerned. The third concerns the impacts of the referendums and their outcomes for future political debates on ethnoterritorial issues.

When the ramifications for the ethnoterritorial movements are considered, the immediate question that comes to mind is what difference winning or.losing the referendum makes. Does participation increase or decrease the intensity of the ethnoterritorial conflict? Did the referendum aid in lessening the tensions involved or did it lead to their resolution? How did winning or losing affect the parties and movements claiming to represent the ethnoterritorial population? These are especially important questions given the fact that for three of the cases covered the ethnoterritorial parties were on the losing side of the elections.

While equally good data on these and the other questions that will be considered here are not available for each case, the easiest case for which to evaluate the political impacts of the referendum is that of the Jura. The referendum results did lead to the creation of a new canton, and even though the process of establishing it has not been entirely smooth, the tensions involved did subside. Also, the loose organizational character of the RJ provided an easier basis for other, more traditional bases of political parties to reassert themselves once the canton was approved.

The results of the referendums in Scotland and Wales are also relatively easy to assess. Neither nationalist party has been able to recover its pre-referendum status. The SNP did increase its number of parliamentary seats (by one) and votes in the 1987 general election, but this can be attributed more to the collapse of the Conservatives than a resurgence of support for devolution or independence. In these cases, then, the referendums did not resolve the issues involved (from the nationalists' point of view), but they did play a role in significantly decreasing their intensity and political saliency. The nationalist parties were the major losers; they have not been able to establish a broader base of support beyond the ethnoterritorial issues in the decade since the referendums. Both the SNP and the *Plaid Cymru* are at the mercy of the Labour and Conservative party agendas. Unless something drastic happens to either of those parties, neither nationalist party will be able to assert itself as it did in the 1970s.

In the case of Quebec, the referendum did not resolve the ethnoterritorial conflict, although it did reduce the level of tension present in the province. The decisive nature of the outcome also helped channel the political debate over ethnoterritorial issues into the broader debate over the constitutional nature of Canadian intergovernmental relations. This shift contributed to the continuing legitimacy of French Canadian concerns. Similarly, the shift helped the PQ remain as a legitimate representative of the French Canadians in a way that the SNP was not able to maintain the Scots. It also, however, prevented them from being able to claim effectively that they were the sole legitimate representative. When the Liberals were returned to office in 1985, they argued that they were more capable of protecting the province's overall interests than the PQ had been.

The political consequences of the referendums in Spain were inseparably linked to the broader process of establishing a functioning democratic political system in Spain. The affirmative votes to approve the regional governments in Euskadi, Cataluña, Andalucía, and Galicia led to the complicated process of negotiating and establishing the appropriate legal authority to make decisions. In that sense, the outcomes did decrease the intensity of the immediate ethnoterritorial issues by channeling public attention into the new political system. Divisions between the militants, the new regional authorities, and the central government continued particularly in the Basque country. The continued use of terrorists acts clearly demonstrated that the most militant groups would be satisfied only with complete independence. The importance of continuing to protect regional interests, though, was not lost on the other ethnoterritorial parties. Even as they participated in the governing process, they maintained pressure on the central government for definitions of power and grants of authority that would further enable their governments to better reflect the regions' concerns.

These cases are also good examples of a meshing of interests between more moderate ethnoterritorial parties and the central government. Central government elites recognized the necessity to grant the principal regions in Spain some autonomous decisionmaking authority. Failure in the referendums would have posed a potentially disastrous threat to the stability of the new democracy. It would have forced a serious division between the militant groups (especially in Euskadi), the moderates, and the central government—especially the military. The advocates of democracy might well have found the resulting conflicts impossible to deal with effectively. As it is, the resulting process accommodated some ethnoterritorial demands, postponed negotiation on others, and bought time for the central government to establish itself.

For the broader, systemwide parties the political consequences were also not as domestic as anticipated. Nor did the matter of being on the winning or losing side of the referendum uniformly affect the impacts on the broader parties. In the Jura, the establishment of the new cantonal government led to a revival of interest in basic issues and parties along lines similar to those that existed before the ethnoterritorial issue became so critical. This was also aided by the fact that the RJ did not function as a political party per se, but through the existing ones. The prolonged nature of the decisionmaking process also helped maintain the salience of other issues and parties.

In Scotland and Wales, the failure of the referendums enabled the Labour party to reassert its claim to be the better representative of regional issues at the national level. It is a claim, however, that has largely been untested, since the Conservatives have remained in power nationally since 1979. In 1987, the Labour party recommitted itself to devolution. Labour's support for devolution has been greatly aided by the collapse of Conservative electoral support, especially in Scotland. Both Labour's increased support and the Conservative's deceased support, though, has not been due to the sustained influence of ethnoterritorial issues, but rather the importance of national issues such as the economy, unemployment, and the general relative economic decline of the northern and western areas of the United Kingdom overall.[46] In a very real sense it has been the Thatcher government's return to the broader issues of economy and government authority that has provided the SNP with its limited opportunity to grow again. The Conservatives are sufficiently unpopular that even the SNP becomes a possible outlet for voter dissatisfaction, even if it cannot reclaim the prominence of a decade ago. The broader issues of importance to voters throughout the United Kingdom have once again reasserted themselves.

The failure of the referendum itself did not immediately alter the relative political position of the parties in Quebec, but it did help shift the focus of the debate between them. With the referendum over, the debate shifted to constitutional issues (see Leslie's discussion in Chapter 3) and the performance of the PQ as a governing party. This enabled the Liberals in Quebec the opportunity to regain the government by again broadening the issues. They were able to be seen as effectively representing the province nationally and as leaving a more appealing set of economic policies. In this way, the failure of the referendum contributed to their resurgence. Had it passed, the political agenda for the next several years would have been dominated by political and constitutional fallout of the PQ government's attempts to implement sovereignty-association. Very likely other issues might well have been dominated by that fallout.

The impacts of the referendum outcomes for the systemwide political parties in Spain has already been alluded to. It bought them some time to focus on the problems of establishing the new government. It did not, however, make that an easy task, as they had to organize regional parties that reflect regional and national interests, and the process of implementing regional autonomy has been a very complex one. Those difficulties, for example, helped lead to the demise of the UCD. Overall, though, the process has enabled broader systemwide issues to be addressed, and has strengthened the position of those parties, such as the Socialists, capable of balancing themselves on this tightrope.

Finally, one consequence of the referendum process affects the political parties, both ethnoterritorially and systemwide, and has ramifications for the constitutional processes of the countries as well. Even in the cases where the referendum issues failed, ethnoterritorial issues are now accorded the status of being serious, legitimate political issues. This is something that not all of the systemwide parties and central governments were necessarily willing to acknowledge before the referendums. Now, however, they are accepted as legitimate, although not necessarily preferred, political issues that the government must address in some manner. This consequence is, in itself, a kind of political victory for the ethnoterritorial movements in Scotland, Wales, Spain, and Quebec. It is a symbol they are not likely to forget even if, as in Scotland, Wales, and Quebec, their preferred position in the referendum failed to win majority support. Their concerns are recognized as being politically valid ones to be heard.

The Constitutional Ramifications

What implications do these referendums have for the basic operations of the constitutions of the political systems? As noted previously, the constitutional ramifications of referendums were explored by David Butler and Austin Ranney.[47] The experiences of the eight cases surveyed in this chapter can serve as a limited empirical test of the validity of the major arguments.

If one takes each of the arguments for and against the use of referendums in turn, it becomes clear that neither set of arguments is completely sustained by our cases. For example, the principal argument for referendums centers on their legitimation role. The use of referendums in our cases has clearly served to sanction publicly various courses of action arrived at by political officials. This has been especially important in the Spanish cases where ethnoterritorial issues are intricately connected to the viability of the new democratic government. Without some form of accommodation being extended to the ethnoterritorial groups it is doubtful that the system could have been maintained. In the British and Canadian cases the referendums have served the purpose of registering the voters' uncertainty over the legitimacy of the proposed changes, which further served to inform formally both the politicians and the nationalists of the public's perspective. Second, these referendums have brought the decision process closer to the people by directly involving them in the supposedly final stage. That involvement may be especially important in these types of issues where the goal is one of self-determination. Letting the public decide important aspects of how that is or is not to be achieved lends substantial credence to the outcome. Moreover, the results of these referendums and their campaigns do appear to reflect the popular will in terms of its general support for change. Although in some cases, Quebec and Scotland, what is reflected may really be confusion as to how change should be accomplished, not the level of support for change in general. This combination of legitimization, involvement of the public, and accurate reflection of public sentiments is probably a major reason why the intensity of the conflicts appears to have lessened somewhat since the referendums. There has been a general acceptance of the outcomes, for whatever reasons.

While the above three arguments for referendums were sustained by our eight cases, six other arguments were not. Three of these were for the use of referendums and three against. The argument that all major issues of a controversy will be dealt with in a referendum is not borne out by these cases. In each, various issues and problems were omitted from the campaigns and in some instances other factors impinged upon the decision process. The idea that in referendums public decisions can be publicly arrived at is also not sustained. This overlooks the fact that many important aspects of the issues at hand have to be dealt with both before and after the referendum itself. The voting thus takes on an advisory and ratifying role with much still being left for officials to decide. Third, the argument that referendums will end public apathy and alienation appears to be overstated. In fact, one of the curious aspects of these elections is the lower than expected voter turnout that occurred in several instances.

The first of the arguments against referendums that was not supported by these cases is the belief that referendums will weaken the power of elected officials. In none of these cases does this actually seem to have occurred. A good argument may be made, instead, that they have strengthened governmental authority in Spain by further legitimizing the new democratic institutions. In Quebec and the United Kingdom the holding of the referendums may well have helped the respective legislatures avoid the charge of imposing unwanted change upon the majority population in the ethnoterritorial territories. From that perspective their authority may have been enhanced. The second argument concerning the inability of referendums to measure the intensity of belief misses the mark. None of the governments in these cases has failed to note the intensity of beliefs exhibited in the campaigns. The alternatives allowed the voters may be only affirmative or negative in nature, but the results leave room for the officials to interpret their meaning and plan for the next step, witness the Jura case. Furthermore, these referendums would never have been held unless the governments had not already been aware to a large degree of the intensity of ethnoterritorial opinions.

The third argument against referendums is that they may weaken representative institutions. This argument is very close to the one claiming that referendums will weaken the power of elected officials and it is rejected for the same reasons. Representative institutions need not be weakened by the holding of a referendum. They may be granted increased legitimacy in the eyes of the public and their stature as decisionmaking bodies may be enhanced, especially if the decision to hold the referendum is perceived as being an extraordinary circumstance requiring a broad sampling of public sentiments.

Three of the remaining arguments cannot be adequately dealt with empirically as they are primarily value statements. There is no satisfactory way to say that referendums serve the public interest or maximize the citizen's human potential. Neither can one really answer the argument that referendums are bad devices because of the inability of ordinary citizens to make wise decisions, although the evidence suggests there was a sophistication among voters high enough in these cases to cope with the complexities involved. In any event, seldom is a decision known to have been wise until long after it has been made.

The remaining two arguments, that referendums force a decision, not forge a consensus, and that they may endanger minority rights, are both important questions. In reference to the first, it should be remembered that the making of all decisions requires some forcing of a deadline. On no known public issue of importance or controversy is a decision ever likely to be made if the political system waits for the consensus to be created behind a set of alternatives. Furthermore, even less understanding of public sentiments is likely to result on the part of official decisionmakers if the alternatives are not put before the public in some manner. One may argue the wisdom of the timing of the forced choice or its planning, but at some point a decision will have to be made. The last point on the matter of minority rights simply cannot be answered well given the current material and can conceivably be a significant moderating factor in the advisability of referendums.

Moreover, as the Jura example illustrates, the referendum procedure can be adapted so as to protect pro-union minorities within a separating region, at least when the latter are themselves territorially concentrated and live adjacent to the remainder of the political unit in which they wish to remain. Hence, the Jura case is an example of the referendum device in the context of "dual minorities"—the French-speaking Catholic minority in the Jura area of the canton of Berne, and the French-speaking Protestant minority in the southern Jura. Both were able to protect their interests democratically given the referendum formula adopted in the Berne Canton of Switzerland, a country with a long history of avoiding zero-sum, pure majority-rule politics in addressing political concerns. Finally, in our cases other protections are also afforded the minorities and other powers are available to the local majority such that the holding of the referendums themselves is not likely to affect their status. The outcomes may encourage or discourage some actions, such as in the implementation of language laws in Cataluña, Euskadi, or Quebec, but the evidence is unclear as to how much.

Thus, overall, the consequences of holding these referendums for the political system, beyond the administrative changes that may occur as a result of the decision itself, are fairly moderate. The use of referendums in these cases does not appear to weaken governmental authority. In fact, the benefits of increased legitimacy that the government acquires by dealing with these issues in this accommodative manner overrides the questions concerning potential negative impacts. One possible exception to this generalization involves the real fear behind many of the anti-referendum arguments—the fear that the use of referendums will become the primary way in which the political system copes with controversial issues. Certainly this apprehension was present in Britain. The use of referendums in these conflicts probably does not necessarily establish a precedent that would be difficult to avoid at some latter date. That may be the situation for Quebec, but not so for the British cases. Likewise, the Spanish cases considered serve as examples for the other regions desiring autonomous powers. However, the question of whether the precedent applies to other areas of public policy is an entirely separate matter that depends upon the constitutional structure of the political system and the broader changes it it undergoing. In the British case there may well be a spillover effect as additional referendums on other issues have been suggested by various politicians, but that would be a change in the British system due only in part to the Scottish and Welsh referendums.

In determining whether these consequences are more directly related to the politics of the referendum process or the contextual conditions from which they arose, I believe weight must be given to the latter. The experiences of these cases leads me to conclude that the longer-term factors are more likely to determine the positive or negative consequences than are the political conditions associated with the referendum process. Again, as with the consequences for the ethnoterritorial movements, this does not mean that the referendum process is insignificant. I conclude that the manner in which decisions involving these issues are finally reached may well be as important as the decision itself. Conflicts concerning the right to self-government decided in a democratic system may well require the kind of legitimation provided in a referendum. Moreover, since these conflicts involve a broad range of issues, the openness of the referendum process may be important to resolving them.

Referendums as Policy Tools

Thus, how effective is the referendum as a policy tool available to governments concerned with ethnoterritorial conflicts? The conclusion in terms of our eight cases is that it was a reasonably effective device. It did not resolve the conflicts central to these cases, but that was not its function. It was, instead, to provide legitimacy to a set of proposed changes and to involve the public in the decisionmaking process. These purposes were served fairly well. Moreover, in evaluating the referendums the potential alternative tools should also be considered. The Franco regime in Spain testifies to the inability of oppression to resolve these conflicts and, as indicated before, an arrangement unilaterally imposed by the central government may generate further resentment regardless of the intentions behind it. These do not exhaust the alternatives, but all of the others would likely involve some form of accommodation or cooperation between the central governments and the ethnoterritorial groups. The referendum appears to be a means of establishing such a pattern of accommodation. Its success is probably dependent upon an acceptance by the primary actors involved of basic democratic values and a willingness to abide by the outcome (which is something that would obviously negate the utility of a referendum in all ethnoterritorial conflicts). It may be difficult for the parties involved to retreat from the positions taken during a referendum campaign, but it may also make violence a less attractive alternative. Does it encourage further ethnoterritorial demands? Its use probably does encourage further demands in the short run, both elsewhere in a multinational state and, especially, in a newly created regional government where much will have to be clarified. But it may also place some limitations upon the scope of those demands. A referendum is also likely to help in maintaining a basis for political dialogue which in itself is not a small accomplishment.

CONCLUSIONS: CONSEQUENCES AND RAMIFICATIONS

The preceding discussion has surveyed the development of the referendum cases and their electoral outcomes. It is now appropriate to return to the basic concerns of this chapter—the political and constitutional ramifications of ethnoterritorial referendums. As indicated in the earlier sections, the various participants in the referendum process argue that the stakes in the election are enormous for the ethnoterritorial movements and the political systems as a whole. The validity of their claims needs to be assessed.

There are three basic conclusions about the impacts of referendums that are indicated by the date presented above and the events that have transpired since the votes were taken. First, it is clear that the claims of the participants about the benefits and costs of the referendums were significantly exaggerated. In none of the cases were the consequences as drastic as the participants, on either side, anticipated in their campaign rhetoric. The discussions by Clark, Leslie, and Keating in Chapters 2, 3, and 6 bear out this conclusion as well as the evidence considered here. Second, the political systems covered in this analysis were responsive to the ethnoterritorial movements in these cases. There were substantial differences in the outcomes and the willingness of the central governments, but in all of the cases the political systems provided mechanisms by which the ethnoterritorial movements could get their basic issues before the voting public. It should be remembered that in a democratic system responsiveness does not mean concurrence with demands; it means listening and providing opportunities for public discussion and decisionmaking on the issues. Third, whatever the outcomes of the referendums, the outcomes themselves become important components in subsequent ethnoterritorial political activity. In a very real sense, it is not proper to talk in terms of a "resolution" of the issues critical to the ethnoterritorial movements, no matter what the outcome of the referendums. The holding of the referendum and its results may "resolve" some aspects of ethnoterritorial conflict, but the basic issues will remain because they are multidimensional in nature. No political solution alone can resolve the cultural, linguistic, and socioeconomic dimensions frequently central to these conflicts, even if it adequately settles the political dimensions.

These conclusions are consistent with the overall theme of this book in that they argue that the political process and policy responses are extremely important independent, as well as dependent, variables in ethnoterritorial conflicts. In addition, arguing that the referendums as a policy response have not, and will not, resolve these conflicts is not to trivialize their political significance. It is rather a recognition of the process character of ethnoterritorial politics in particular and ethnic politics in general.

NOTES

1. For the most recent extensive considerations of referendums in general, see David Butler and Austin Ranney, eds., *Referendums: A Comparative Study of Practice and Theory* (Washington, D.C.: American Enterprise Institute for Public Policy Research, 1978) and Austin Ranney, ed., *The Referendum Device* (Washington, D.C.: American Enterprise Institute for Public Policy Research, 1981). Also see David Butler and Uwe Kitzinger, eds., *The 1975 Referendum* (New York: St. Martin's Press, 1976); Anthony King, *Britain Says Yes: The 1975 Referendum on the Common Market* (Washington, D.C.: American Enterprise Institute for Public Policy Research, 1977); Gordon Smith, "The Referendum and Political Change," *Government and Opposition* 10 (Summer 1975): 294–305; and Gordon Smith, "The Functional Properties of the Referendum" *European Journal of Political Research* 4 (March 1976): 1–23.

2. Vernon Bogdanor, *The People and the Party System* (Cambridge: Cambridge University Press, 1981).

3. Butler and Ranney, *Referendums*, 24–37. Also see Nevil Johnson, "Types of Referendum," in *The Referendum Device*, 19–32.

4. Butler and Ranney, *Referendums*, 23–24.

5. bid., 18.
6. Keith Thomas, "The United Kingdom," in Raymond Grew, ed., *Crises of Political Development in Europe and the United States* (Princeton: Princeton University Press, 1978), 74–82. R.A.W. Rhodes, "Intergovernmental Relations in the United Kingdom," in Yves Meny and Vincent Wright, eds., *Centre-Periphery Relations in Western Europe* (London: George Allen & Unwin, 1985), 33–78.
7. Bogdanor, *The People and the Party System*, 9–66.
8. King, *Britain Says Yes*; Butler and Kitzinger, *The 1975 Referendum*; and Anthony King, "Referendums and the European Community," in *The Referendum Device*, 89–112.
9. For discussions of the history of Scottish and Welsh nationalism see H.J. Hanham, *Scottish Nationalism* (Cambridge: Harvard University Press, 1969); Reginald Coupland, *Welsh and Scottish Nationalism: A Study* (London: Collins, 1954); Michael Keating and David Bleiman, *Labour and Scottish Nationalism* (London: Macmillan, 1979); Jack Brand, *The National Movement in Scotland* (London: Routledge & Kegan Paul, 1978); Vernon Bogdanor, *Devolution* (Oxford: Oxford University Press, 1979); Keith Webb, *The Growth of Nationalism in Scotland* (Glasgow: The Moledinar Press, 1977); Kenneth O. Morgan, *Wales in British Politics* (Cardiff: University of Wales Press, 1970); Alan B. Phillips, *The Welsh Question* (Cardiff: University of Wales Press, 1975); John Osmond, *Creative Conflict: The Politics of Welsh Devolution* (London: Gomer Press and Routledge & Kegan Paul, 1977); and H.M. Drucker and Gordon Brown, *The Politics of Nationalism and Devolution* (New York: Longman, 1980).
10. See Ivor Benton and Gavin Drewry, "Public Legislation: A Survey of the Sessions 1977/78 and 1978/79," *Parliamentary Affairs* 33 (Spring 1980): 174–186; and Vernon Bogdanor, "The 40 Per Cent Rule," *Parliamentary Affairs* 33 (Summer 1980): 249–263.
11. See the chapters in John Bochel, David Denver, and Allan Macartney, eds., *The Referendum Experience: Scotland 1979* (Aberdeen: Aberdeen University Press, 1981) for a thorough discussion of the campaign.
12. Mark V. Kauppi, "The 1979 Scottish Referendum Results: Explanations, Rationalizations, and Protestations," paper presented at the sixth annual meeting of the Rocky Mountain Conference on British Studies, Colorado Springs, Colorado, October 26–27, 1979; and Denis Balsom and Ian McAllister, "The Scottish and Welsh Devolution Referenda of 1979: Constitutional Change and Popular Choice," *Parliamentary Affairs* 32 (Autumn 1979): 394–409. The Balsom and McAllister article contains a summary of opinion poll results for both Scotland and Wales between 1976 and 1979.
13. For a consideration of the Welsh referendum see David Foulkes, J. Barry Jones, and R.A.Wilford, eds., *The Welsh Veto: The Wales Act 1978 and the Referendum* (Cardiff: University of Wales Press, 1983).
14. James Callaghan, *Time & Chance* (London: Collins, 1987), 558–563.
15. Rob Edwards, "Beware the Tories, Promising Devolution," *New Statesman*, July 17, 1987.
16. H.M. Drucker, "Crying Wolfe: Recent Divisions in the SNP," *The Political Quarterly* 50 (October–December 1979): 503–508.
17. David Butler and Dennis Kavanagh, *The British General Election of 1987* (London: Macmillan, 1988).
18. See John Saywell, *The Rise of the Parti Québécois, 1967–1976* (Toronto: University of Toronto Press, 1977); Edward M. Corbett, *Quebec*

Confronts Canada (Baltimore: The Johns Hopkins University Press, 1976); Kenneth McRoberts and Dale Postgate, *Quebec: Social Change and Political Crisis* (Toronto: McClelland & Stewart, 1976); Donald V. Smiley, *Canada in Question: Federalism in the Seventies* (Toronto: McGraw-Hill, 1976); Kenneth McRoberts, "Internal Colonialism: the Case of Quebec," *Ethnic and Racial Studies* 2 (July 1979): 293–318; James William Hagy, "Le Parti Québécois in the 1970 Elections," *Queens' Quarterly* 77: 261–273.

19. Martin Lubin, "Pro-Canada Elements in the Forthcoming Quebec Referendum," paper presented at the Canadian Studies Program of the annual meeting of the Western Social Science Association, Lake Tahoe, Nevada, April 26, 1979.

20. Hagy, "Le Parti Québécois in the 1970 Elections"; Raymond Hudon, "The 1976 Quebec Election," *Queen's Quarterly* 84 (Spring 1977): 18–30; Richard Hamilton and Maurice Pinard, "The Bases of Parti Québécois Support in Recent Quebec Elections," *Canadian Journal of Political Science* 9 (March 1976): 3–26: and Martin Lubin, "System Maintenance in Quebec: The Parti Québécois," paper presented at the annual meeting of the Northeastern Political Science Association, New Haven, Connecticut, November 22, 1980.

21. Henry Ginizer, "Division in Quebec Growing as Vote on Status Nears," *New York Times*, March 9, 1980; "New Chapter for Trudeau," *The Economist* (April 5, 1980); Henry Ginizer, "Quebecers Wooing the Undecided Vote," *New York Times*, May 11, 1980; "The Answer Is Likely to Be Fuzzy," *The Economist* (May 17, 1980); and Patrick Brogan, "Confusion Abounds over Real Aims as Quebec Votes Today to Determine Relations with Ottawa," *the Times* (London), May 20, 1980.

22. Patrick Brogan, "Separatists Accept Resounding Quebec Defeat but Given Promise of Rewritten Constitution," *the Times* (London), May 22, 1980.

23. "'Profound Change' in Quebec," *Newsweek*, December 16, 1985. Also, "Canada," *Keesing's Contemporary Archives* (April 1985): 33524–33525; (November 1985): 33984–33985; and (January 1986): 34096.

24. John F. Burns, "Quebecer Is Out as Party's Leader," *New York Times* (November 11, 1987).

25. For discussions of post-Franco Spanish politics see John F. Coverdale, *The Political Transformation of Spain After Franco* (New York: Praeger, 1979); Raymond Carr and Juan Pablo Fusi, *Spain: Dictatorship to Democracy* (London: George Allen & Unwin, 1981); and Richard Gunther, Giacomo Sani, and Goldie Shabad, eds., *Spain After Franco: The Making of a Competitive Party System* (Berkeley: University of California Press, 1986).

26. Richard Gunther, "Constitutional Change in Contemporary Spain," in Keith G. Banting and Richard Simeon, eds., *Redesigning the State: The Politics of Constitutional Change* (Toronto: University of Toronto Press, 1985).

27. The impacts of these continuing regional differences is discussed by Juan Linz in his "The Party System of Spain: Past and Future," in Seymour M. Lipset and Stein Rokkan, eds., *Party Systems and Voter Alignments: Cross-National Perspectives* (New York: The Free Press, 1967), 197–282 and "Within-Nation Differences and Comparisons: The Eight Spains," in Richard L. Merritt and Stein Rokkan, eds., *Comparing Nations: The Use of Quantitative Data in Cross-National Research* (New Haven: Yale University Press, 1966), 267–319.

28. César Díaz López, "Centre-Periphery Structures in Spain: From

Historical Conflict to Territorial-Consociational Accommodation?," in *Centre-Periphery Relations in Western Europe*, 236–272.

29. For background on the Basques see Stanley Payne, *Basque Nationalism* (Reno: University of Nevada Press, 1975); Marianne Heiberg, "Insiders/Outsiders: Basque Nationalism," 16 (1975): 169–193; Milton da Silva, "Modernization and Ethnic Conflict: The Case of the Basques," *Comparative Politics* 7 (January 1975): 227–252; John Llewelyn Hollyman, Basque Revolutionary Separatism: ETA," in P. Preston, ed., *Spain in Crisis* (London: Harvester Press, 1976), 212–233; William A. Douglass and Milton da Silva, "Basque Nationalism," in Oriol Pi-Sunyer, ed., *The Limits of Integration: Ethnicity and Nationalism in Modern Europe*, Research Reports, No. 9 (Amherst,: Department of Anthropology, University of Massachusetts, 1971), 147–186; and Marianne Heiberg, "Urban Politics and Rural Culture Basque Nationalism" in Stein Rokkan and Derek W. Urwin, eds., *The Politics of Territorial Identity: Studies in European Regionalism* (Beverly Hills: Sage Publication, 1982), 355–388.

30. Robert P. Clark, "Basque Socialism at the Polls: An Analysis of Four Post-Franco Elections," paper presented at the Conference of Europeanists, Washington, D.C., October 1980; Tim Brown, "Basques Expect Resounding 'Yes' to Home Rule," *the Times* (London), October 25, 1979; "Vote as you care," *The Economist* (October 27, 1979): 53–56; "Spanish Basques Vote to Restore Home Rule," *New York Times*, October 28, 1979.

31. For background on the Catalan case see Oriol Pi-Sunyer, "The Maintenance of Ethnic Identity in Catalonia," in *The Limits of Integration*, 111–146; Oriol Pi-Sunyer, "Elites and Noncorporate Groups in the European Mediterranean: A Reconsideration of the Catalan Case," *Comparative Studies in Society and History* 16 (January 1974): 117–131; and Norman L. Jones, "The Catalan Question Since the Civil War," in *Spain in Crisis*, 234–267.

32. James M. Markham, "Madrid's Leader's Party Makes a Poor Showing in Catalonia Election," *New York Times*, March 21, 1980; and G. Shabad and R. Gunther, "Language, Nationalism and Political Conflict in Spain," paper presented at the Conference of Europeanists, Washington, D.C., October 24–25, 1980.

33. Harry Debelius, "Andalusia Adds Its Voice to the Growing Clamor for Autonomy," *The Times* (London), January 16, 1980.

34. See Dina Titus, "Recent Decentralization in Spain: A Look at the Andalucian Autonomy Movement" paper presented at the annual meeting of the Southwestern Political Science Association, Dallas, Texas, March 26, 1980.

35. César Díaz López, "The Politicization of Galician Cleavages," in *The Politics of Territorial Identity*, 389–424.

36. *Avui* (Barcelona), November 6, 1980.

37. Philip B. Taylor, Jr., "Autonomy and Public Policy in Catalunya. Is Spanish Centralism Really Weakening?," paper presented at the annual meeting of the Southwestern Political Science Association, Dallas, Texas, March 25–28, 1981.

38. "Spain," *Keesing's Contemporary Archives* (December 18, 1981): 31250.

39. Jean-François Aubert, "Switzerland," in *Referendums*, 39–66; and, Hanspeter Tschaeni, "Constitutional Change in Swiss Cantons: An Assessment of a Recent Phenomenon," *Publius* 12 (Winter 1982): 113–130.

40. See Michel Bassand, "The Jura Problem," *Journal of Peace Research* 20 (1975): 139–150 and "Le séparatisme jurassien: Un conflit de classes et/ou

conflit ethnique," *Cahier International de Sociologie* 66 (1976): 221–246. Also see David B. Campbell, "Nationalism, Religion and the Social Bases of Conflict in the Swiss Jura," in *The Politics of Territorial Identity*, 279–308.

41. Kurt B. Mayer, "The Jura Problem: Ethnic Conflict in Switzerland," *Social Research* 35 (Winter 1968): 707–741.

42. Bassand, "The Jura Problem," 141–144.

43. Jurg Steiner, "From Regionalism to Statehood: The Formation of the Jura Canton," paper presented at the Second Conference of Europeanists, Washington, D.C., October 23–25, 1980.

44. "Switzerland," *Keesing's Contemporary Archives* 31 (February 1985): 33423.

45. "Switzerland," *Keesing's Contemporary Archives* 30 (July 1984): 33001.

46. Butler and Kavanagh, *The British General Election of 1987*, 327–328.

47. Butler and Ranney, *Referendums*, 24–37.

CHAPTER 8

Pathways to Accommodation and the Persistence of the Ethnoterritorial Challenge in Western Democracies

JOSEPH R. RUDOLPH, JR.
ROBERT J. THOMPSON

Writing more than fifteen years ago in an *Occasional Paper* for the Center of International Affairs, Erik Nordlinger provided a catalogue of six general devices available to governments for managing ethnic conflict, ranging from the purposeful depoliticization of sensitive issues to outright concessions to communal demands.[1] At approximately the same time, Walker Connor published his landmark article "The Politics of Ethnonationalism" in the *Journal of International Affairs*, in which he commented upon the difficulty of dealing with the phenomenon. There is, Connor suggested, an inherent danger that ethnonationalism will feed both on "adversity and denial" and "on concessions"—on the former out of frustration and on the latter because the "permissive perpetuation of the nation's cultural manifestations or of political structures that reflect the nation's distribution become constant reminders of separate identity and rallying points for further demands."[2] Between their two works, Nordlinger and Connor highlighted the principal concerns of our study: the extent to which ethnoterritorial demands can be contained; and which policy responses are most likely to do so, and at what costs.

ETHNOTERRITORIAL MOVEMENTS AND PUBLIC POLICY: EXPANDING THE POLICY OPTIONS

Viewed from today's vantage point, the ethnopolitical phenomenon with which Nordlinger and Connor were concerned represented a highly significant development in Western political systems. This phenomenon has subsequently, as we have seen, engulfed much of those systems' political energies and rewritten many of their political orders. However, from the outset it attracted considerable attention, occurring as it did in developed states believed to have successfully integrated, accommodated, or repressed their national minorities, and challenging as it did some of the then-basic assumptions of politics in the Western world—for example, that national integration is a one-way street (once integrated, regional groups stay integrated) and that in the modern world, class and status have generally replaced such older bases of political association as ethnicity, language, and region. Yet, as we noted at the outset of our study, most of the earlier works on these ethnoterritorial movements focused on the historical and socioeconomic contexts within which they became politically salient in individual countries and/or on their broad impact on individual political systems (new linkage groups, new sets of periphery-center issues, new institutions). The result of this mode of research was twofold. First, the comparative elements tying the movements together tended to be underemphasized at the same time that, paradoxically, there was a broad assumption that all these center-periphery conflicts were of the same sort that deflected attention from the rich *variety* of ethnoterritorial movements to be found in the Western world. Second, the policy dimension was likewise underemphasized, with the effect that a major basis for comparing and differentiating these movements and for exploring the centrality of politics in their rise and evolution frequently received only sketchy attention.

Differentiating the Movements

The studies assembled here make clear that from the beginning there was considerable diversity within the ethnopolitical movements that have emerged in developed, Western societies during the postwar era. However, viewed from the perspective of the political center, these movements appeared similar, insofar as they all posed peripheral demands against the center. As a result, often only the most obvious distinctions between ethnoterritorial movements were noted—for example, between movements pursuing their objectives violently (the ETA, the IRA) and those taking system-participatory routes (like the SNP in Scotland or the FDF in Brussels), or between organizations with an essentially cultural set of objectives and movements with much more political sets of objectives (e.g., the Welsh Language Society, with its concern for the preservation and promotion of the Welsh language versus the *Plaid Cymru*, with its pursuit of Welsh independence or, at least, autonomy). More subtle distinctions of the type drawn in this book were rarely made, though as the previous chapters indicate, these can be of considerable importance and variety, including: (1) intraregional differences (Safran, for example, speaks of a "continuum of ethnic consciousness" within France's distinct ethnic communities, while Clark identifies several intraregional differences separating competing, regionalist parties and ethnonational organizations in Spain's Basqueland);

and (2) intracommunal divisions (i.e., differences separating an apparently single national group inside a country, such as those between Canadian francophones outside of Quebec and the French-speaking nationalists of Quebec, a principal focus of Leslie's essay).

More unusual still in earlier studies were analyses of the differing pressures on politicians at the center to respond to regional developments, depending on how much those developments effected *their* influence (for example, the relatively low pressure on Tory leaders in Britain, with a comfortable majority in Westminster based on their seats in England, to respond to developments in Scotland, in comparison to the pressures felt by Labourites, with their party's dependence on Celtic Britain for systemwide competitiveness.[3] Similarly ignored were the unequal pressures on politicians at the periphery to go along with or oppose regionalist demands (as indicated by Keating in his discussion of the sitting Scottish MP's reluctance to support devolution, and by Clark, who notes the unwillingness of politicians in Navarra to join the other Basque provinces in a Basque homelands region in Spain).

On the other hand, viewed from the perspective of policy demands and the policy process, the different tactics and goals of ethnoterritorial organizations and other actors caught up in ethnoterritorial politics become both apparent and more easily subject to comparative analysis. As the contributions to this book also indicate, in terms of their *tactics*, ethnoterritorial movements can be better grouped along continuums of violence/disobedience and of participation than dichotomized into these two categories. Some movements have been and remain willing to take lives in pursuit of their objectives, which frequently include some form of nonnegotiable demand for regional separatism. Others have been willing to undertake violent but non-lethal measures, such as kidnapping and bank robbery, to advance their cause. Still others limit their targets to property. Breton and Alsatian regionalists during the Gaullist period might be cited as falling into this category, as would the Free Wales Army in Wales during the sixties. And, some have contented themselves with disrupting legislative sessions or even boycotting elections and refusing to take the seats they have won in assemblies.

Under the rubric of system-participatory organizations, diversity also exists. Some movements have pressed their demands within the (regional wing) structure of system-wide parties. Some have acted essentially as lobbying groups in their respective political processes. Some have been willing to engage in occasional civil disobedience or even to form temporary alliances with the more extreme, system-challenging groups. Most obviously, many have found it desirable to organize into regional political parties in order to extract concessions within the existing political system.

Overall, there appears to be an important connection between the strategy adopted by the government at the center to deal with the demands of the territorial and cultural periphery and the means selected by the ethnoterritorial actor. In his recent study of extremists among ethnoterritorial groups in Western Europe, Raphael Zariski concluded that "state discrimination, state violence, state repression, state concessions and reforms, timely or otherwise . . . tend to be the decisive factors in the situation."[4] Our studies suggest nothing to discount this finding; political violence was higher than at present in both Spain and France when their governments were pursuing what Leslie labels a "rejectionist strategy" in his discussion of government options. At the same time, a closer reading of our (limited) sample suggests that the relationship between government policy and ethnoterritorial tactics may be as much circular as causal. Where the system provides neither outlets for expressing autonomous demands nor encouragement that they will be considered, clandestine organizations are perhaps unavoidable, and they may inevitably be forced to choose separatism as a goal and political violence as a means. Yet, to a degree, the more violent such organizations become, the more the center is apt to adhere to its rejectionist viewpoint, lest violence be rewarded. Also, if the system is only rejectionist on issues of regional autonomy but is otherwise open for political discourse (de Gaulle's France, but not Franco's Spain), the more extreme the violence undertaken by the movement (i.e., Breton bombers) and the more the likely the movement is to estrange itself from rank-and-file regional support and remain too small to force the government to reassess its rejectionist approach. Reciprocally, the more closed the system in general and the more repressive it is to autonomist pleas in particular, the more likely it is that violent ethnoterritorial movements will be able to generate enough regional support that the government may weigh favorably the costs of accommodation against those of continuing a strategy of rejectionism and repressionism. And finally, the more open the system to change or, at least, to discussion of change, the more ethnoterritorial organizations may choose the legitimate, participatory avenues to system change.

The *goals* of ethnoterritorialists have similarly differed, both in space and time. Not only have movements within the same region and organizations in different regions varied in terms of their demands against the center, but individual organizations have altered their demands over time, depending on their relative strength, their immediate needs, and the center's willingness to compromise. Frequently, ethnoterritorial parties have even succeeded, at least temporarily, in integrating class issues and general economic dissatisfaction into their list of demands, as the chapter on Belgium indicates.[5] However, what has set these organizations apart from other political organizations in their countries (and has provided the term for referring to them) has been the persistence of the ethnoterritorial element running through their goals. This is true whether we are speaking of (1) essentially *output* demands of a "favorable policy" nature (such as "economically" grounded demands for a steel plant for Wallonia or culturally rooted demands for a television station for Basque Spain); (2) demands focusing on a reorganization of the *authority* arrangements in the state (representation of Quebec in the Canadian cabinet or the linguistic-territorial representation of Flemish Belgium on a proportionate basis in the Belgian civil service); (3) demands with a *regime* focus, seeking to restructure the state along federal lines; or (4) demands challenging the definition of the political community and calling for the creation of an independent and united Ireland, a free Scotland, or an independent, united Basque state in the European Community.[6] Beneath the specific differences in policy demands lies the central theme of payoffs in territorial terms. Significantly, where clashes have occurred between the ethnoterritorial goals of regionalists and extraterritorial communal goals (for example, between enhancing Quebec's power in the Canadian federation and promoting the well-being of Canadian minorities elsewhere in Canada), the ethnoterritorial goal has tended to prevail and regionalists have remained . . . regionalists.

It is this territorial dimension of the policy demands of ethnoterritorial groups that also permits comparisons of ethnoterritorial movements and those political processes responding to them. However, at least two other factors are also important for comparative purposes: the bargaining agenda, which has grown increasingly similar throughout the multinational states of the Western world; and the prevailing political culture/environment, which places similar restraints on bargaining throughout the developed democratic world.

Throughout our case studies, most action has recently taken place in the policy field between leaders at the center willing to bargain and within-system, ethnoterritorial spokespersons pursuing bargainable objectives of an essentially authority- and regime-centered nature ("enhanced participation" and "decentralist" options, in Leslie's terminology). Not since Franco's Spain has any state in the First World altogether refused to bargain with ethnoterritorial organizations—most states having reached the conclusion that accommodation in some form is less costly than across-the-board rejectionism as an approach to ethnoterritorial demands. Similarly, except for some diehard ETA groups in Spain and wings of the IRA in Northern Ireland (where broad-based Protestant opposition to concessions to regional Catholics has made accommodation a difficult strategy for the British to pursue), ethnoterritorialists have dropped their separatist rhetoric and limited themselves to a realistic, operational list of objectives. At the same time, ethnoterritorial organizations have generally gone beyond output demands throughout the Western world, except for France, where ethnoterritorialists operate in the context of strong national sentiment for the French *patrie* and where concessions to ethnoterritorialism have been so long in coming that any favorable policy from the center towards regional languages or finances is seen (at least for now) as significant. In short, policy negotiations currently take place in an arena where bargaining is difficult—because it does require the center and/or its leadership to surrender some of its authority to regional elites or to the regions, at the risk that concessions will feed separatist tendencies and lead to the dismemberment of the state—but where bargaining is nonetheless possible.

The political environment inside Western democracies, for its part, tends to keep the policy process within these perimeters. The general commitment to an open society and such democratic rules of the game as freedom of speech and association—now found in Spain as well as in Belgium, Britain, Canada, Switzerland and France—provides opportunities for ethno-territorialists to challenge freely the existing political system within the constitutional order. As noted, they have tended to avail themselves of these opportunities by mobilizing the ethnoterritorial community, engaging in lobbying activities, organizing demonstrations, and founding ethnonationalist political parties.

At the same time, the existing political environment also places brakes on the development of ethnoterritorial movements in a variety of ways. The fact that electorates in the Western democracies are already organized behind ideologies or along social class lines, and are subject to pressures that not only cut across class lines but communal lines as well has made it difficult for ethnoterritorial parties to capture and realign, on a durable basis, a sizable segment of the regional electorate. Similarly, most ethnoregional populations share a dual allegiance and dual sense of identity similar to that of the regional groups in France. They are French *and* Alsatian, British *and* Welsh, Spanish *and* Catalan. The relative weight accorded to the regional identity versus the systemwide one may be greater in the regions of Spain than in those of France, greater in Wallonia than in Wales; but in all states patriotism focused on the country is a barrier to separatist movements to an extent that is not true of ethnoterritorial movements in many of the newer, developing states of the world. Finally, the literate and educated nature of Western societies has made it all but impossible for ethnoterritorial movements to pursue their frequently nationalistic rhetoric. Simply stated, regional populations can understand not only the emotional appeal of independence, but also the advantages of union (e.g., economy of scale) and the often very high costs of regional autonomy (reduced representation at the center, reduced financial resources). And they have been willing to vote against devolution schemes (in Scotland, in Quebec) when the costs have seemed excessive or disproportionate to the autonomy being offered. No region wants independence at the price of becoming the Western world's most economically backward area.

On the other hand, and balancing the books somewhat, neither is a sophisticated regional electorate likely to perceive in exaggerated terms of importance purely symbolic concessions by the center, or minor, favorable policies by the center towards the periphery. Hence, just as it is in the interest of the ethnoterritorialists to place negotiable issues on the agenda for discussion, so it is in the interest of the center to respond to authority- and regime-oriented demands, and even at times to engage in preemptive agenda setting of its own on matters of substance. To pursue a rejectionist strategy or tokenist approach may feed the very ethnoterritorial movements and sentiment that the center is trying to control. To accommodate thereby becomes preferable, albeit almost always on the basis of minimally acceptable concessions.

Delineating the Policy Options

The case studies presented in this book reflect not only the growing presence of ethnoterritorial issues in the policymaking processes of Western democracies, but also the development of an expanding array of policy responses to ethnoterritorial demands. Nordlinger's original list of six policy possibilities was in actuality a mixture of two different lists. The first consisted of three *approaches* to managing ethnoterritorial demands (consociational management and depolitization of sensitive issues; compromise on divisive issues; and concessions to communal demands): The second offered three specific, essentially authority-related devices intended to control future ethnonational conflict (including the members of rival communities in the governing coalition; adhering to the rule of proportionality in the military and in determining bureaucratic leadership; and conferring a mutual veto to the rival communities in matters of a sensitive nature).[7] Both lists of options have subsequently been expanded, to a large part as the result of the work of analysts like Arend Lijphart, who has done much not only to differentiate consensual and majoritarian approaches to conflict management in general (as Clark notes) but also to detail the workings of consociational management in particular.[8] Yet to a considerable extent, the lists have also been steadily expanded by the work of political practitioners who, in responding to the demands confronting them, have fashioned an interesting assortment of devices for responding to ethnoterritorial demands.

As Table 8.1 indicates, an array of approaches can be listed under both the "rejectionist" and "managerial" policy headings. The former can range from the violent repression of ethnoterritorial expression in Franco's Spain to the "studied ignorance" approach to be found in all our states at some point in time (perhaps most conspicuously in the Jacobin French state with its unwillingness to acknowledge, as Safran summarizes it, the irrelevant primordialism and reactionary particularism of its ethnoterritorialists), to the democratic dismissal of the demands of ethnoterritorial minorities in the majoritarian policymaking processes of a democracy, as

Table 8.1   Ethnoterritorial Demands and Public Policy: Policy Options

Approach	Policy
Rejectionist	Repression of ethnoterritorial spokesmen
	Ignore ethnoterritorial issues on the government agenda; ridicule spokesmen for ethnoterritorial causes
	Dismiss ethnoterritorial demands via the state's majoritarian decisionmaking system
Managerial	Traditional consociationalism: depoliticize sensitive issues to keep ethnoterritorial matters off the public agenda.
	Delay responses: appoint commissions to study ethnoterritorial demands; delay debate until after elections, etc.
	Symbolic concessions to ethnoterritorial demands
	Substantive concessions to ethnoterritorial demands
	Output-oriented concessions to ethnoterritorial demand:
	Favorable policies of a cultural nature: support of regional development funds; porkbarrel projects for declining regional economies; etc.
	Favorable policies of an economic nature: creation of regional development funds; porkbarrel projects for declining regional economies, etc.
	Authority/Leadership-based concessions:
	Creation of an officially bilingual state to open government employment, court systems to (regionalized) linguistic minorities
	Adoption of proportionality formulae to govern leadership and employment opportunities in the bureaucracy, in the military, etc.
	Adoption of parity formula to govern the composition of the national cabinet
	Adoption of concurrent majority devices of a warning bell and mutual veto nature to govern law-making in sensitive areas
	Cooptation of ethnoterritorial elites in the decisionmaking process at the center
	Scheduling of referendums on the issues of transferring autonomy to regions
	Regime Modification concessions:
	Administrative decentralization
	Regionalization: the transfer of law-making authority via a dual mandate system in which regional assemblies are constituted out of regional representatives to the central parliament
	Devolution of financial and legislative autonomy to directly elected regional assemblies within a unitary state
	Federalization: the transfer of independent law-making authority to regional governments, or enhancement of the power of existing federal units

illustrated by Thatcher's Britain. Similarly, management techniques, while tending more towards a consensual/accommodative approach to ethnoterritorialism, need not necessarily be of that ilk. They can—and have— ranged from the systematic effort of traditional elites to keep sensitive issues off the public's agenda (traditional consociational management) to the appointing of study missions and the making of symbolic gestures as means of seeming to respond to ethnoterritorial demands, to substantive policy responses of an output-, authority-, or regime-centered nature. The list in Table 8.1 is by no means exhaustive, nor is it meant to be viewed as deterministic of the inevitable progression of ethnoterritorial bargaining in any state. It is, however, meant to be a representative listing of the range of responses to ethnoterritorial demands available in the developed world.

Examples of each of the enumerated policy options can be found in the previous chapters. All have been a part of the political processes of the developed Western states during the past twenty years, although—again— most policy has proceeded from somewhere within the accommodative options indicated on the table's latter two categories. Of these options, proposed and enacted constitutional reforms involving the transfer of central authority to regional bodies via schemes of decentralization (France), regionalization (Belgium), devolution (Britain), and federalism-enhancement (Canada and Spain) deservedly received the most attention. Constitutional change is always significant, especially when it involves a redistribution of authority in once self-consciously unitary states (Britain, France, Spain) or the revision of a very old constitutional system (Belgium). Moreover, in the long term those constitutional revisions that have been enacted will undoubtedly have the most significant effect on the political process of any of the accommodation options utilized in these states. Still, the significance of regime modification as a means of accommodation should not obscure the intriguing nature of some of the other options that have recently been used.

As Thompson notes, the use of referendums in dealing with the ethnoterritorial factor in Canada, Spain, and Britain injected an unusual element into the traditional nature of politics in these countries—one which widened the participants in the decisionmaking process to include regional voters on the key issue of the constitutional relationship between the region and center. To be sure, in the Juras and Spain referendums were in part used as means of measuring, building support for, and fine-tuning constitutional changes pertaining to a regional autonomy system to which the center was already committed. However, the referendum device had the effect everywhere of allowing the electorate to resolve the highest order of political questions— those involving the nature of the regime. Most interestingly, as Leslie and Thompson indicate in Chapters 3 and 7, the referendum response to ethnoterritorial demands is an option in its own right as well as a part of a broader decisionmaking process involving constitutional change. And even when scheduled by the regional group (as in Quebec) the referendum is a response that can work against the ethnoterritorialists much more easily than against those opposed to devolution. If centrists lose and a referendum on home rule passes, it is only one step in a process involving the transfer of government power, and—anyway—there are always other issues that wed politicians at the center to regional voters. But if ethnoterritorialists lose on the issue of regional self-rule, at the best their momentum will be considerably slowed and differences within the regional movement will almost certainly break into the open as rival factions within the region seek a scapegoat.

The tactic of coopting ethnoterritorialists into a position of decision-making responsibility can also be a costly one for ethnoregional politicians. Not only can they no longer avoid taking stances on controversial issues outside the ethnoterritorial domaine, or sidestep the responsibilities of governmental failure, but their ability to criticize the center is reduced. Meanwhile, they may find themselves playing hardball politics with a set of politicians at the regional (in Canada) or national (Belgium) level who see the policy-bargaining process as an ongoing game in which cooperation is measured in utilitarian payoffs. And the policy payoffs on which the ethnoterritorialists depend can be withheld by their new friends at any time and to the detriment of the ethnoterritorial organizations, as the ethnonational parties who joined the governing coalitions in Belgium discovered.[9]

Finally, and perhaps most interesting from U.S. perspective, there has been the use of the dual mandate system by the center to manage ethnoterritorialists. The system of dual official appointments, in which a public official can be simultaneously a mayor (and spokesperson for a urban area like Paris) and the prime minister of the country (and hence responsible for the national welfare) is unknown in the U.S. political system, though it is a major part of European systems of government.[10] It takes on an unusual twist, however, when used in an ethnoterritorial context to mute ethnoterritorial demands by giving official, regional spokesperson status at the center in order to subject them to additional sets of pressures. Thus, as Keating noted, the administrative spokesman for Scotland sits in the British cabinet, subject to principles of cabinet responsibility and party discipline. In Belgium's devolution process, as we have seen, the membership of the regional assemblies was to be drawn from the representatives elected to Parliament from Wallonia, Flanders, and Brussels, respectively, and the representatives of the linguistic councils are the members of Parliament, regrouped on the basis of language. Even France's recent essay into what Safran describes as devolution within *tutelle*—a national guardianship system—has the potential of creating a dual mandate system for France's periphery. The commissioner of the republic in the field, an agent of tutelage in the grand French tradition, is also the chief official spokesperson *for* the regions at the center. Similarly, although Safran notes that it has not yet happened, there is the potential that the quasi-official spokesperson for the regional communities *in* the regions will be those ethnoterritorialists who receive central funds under Article 93 of the 1982 Decentralization Law—that is, those the central government chooses to recognize as the spokespersons for France's territorialized, cultural enclaves.

ETHNOTERRITORIAL MOVEMENTS AND PUBLIC POLICY: EVALUATING THE POLICY OUTCOMES

Measuring political performance in any field is persistently one of the hardest tasks of political analysis. We will therefore undertake that task with respect to the developed world's policy responses to ethnoterritorialism with the trepidation it fully deserves. More precisely, the conclusions in this section are offered only within the context of the following cautionary remarks.

First, as Leslie cautions in Chapter 3 (on Canada), idiosyncratic variables can have a profound effect in determining what works and what does not in dealing with a given ethnoterritorial demand. What will suffice in one country may not succeed in accommodating ethnoterritorial demands in another; likewise, what will accommodate a set of demands in a given country at one point in time (for example, administrative devolution) may not be deemed adequate at another. Thus, our conclusions are offered very much as statements of strong *tendencies* of policy responses to ethnoterritorial demands, not as fixed rules of ethnopolitics.

Second, when speaking of the success of such policies, it is well to keep in mind that accommodating—or neutralizing—the political force of ethnoterritorialism involves two elements: ethnoterritorial sentiment; and the ethnoterritorial actors mobilizing and exploiting it. A persistent theme throughout this book has been the decline of self-appointed ethnonationalist organizations—to a degree as a result of events in the policy realm—but a continuing, often very strong presence of ethnoterritorial sentiment, readable in public opinion polls and in the declining vote of centrist parties in the ethnoterritorial areas of their respective states. It may be that policies capable of capping and reducing such sentiment have not yet been developed. It may also be that from the standpoint of politicians at the center, capping and reducing the strength of ethnoterritorial organizations itself constitutes adequate performance and policy success.

Third, as hard as it is to analyze political performance in general, involving as it does both objective and subjective elements, we believe that it is especially hard to evaluate performance when dealing with policy in ethnopolitical areas—both because of the difficulty of identifying adequate measuring devices and because of the peculiar obstacles to policy making in this field. Thus, whereas in such policy fields as managing the economy and protecting the environment, the measurement of policy performance is often objective (the changes in inflation rates, unemployment, pollutants in the air over a given period), the test of the success of ethnopolitical policies is almost entirely subjective (whether people *feel* the concession is adequate) and subject to constant reevaluation over time. Moreover, the issue of what is an adequate amount of time for a policy to succeed may be particularly hard to answer in ethnopolitical matters. From the perspective of a regional group, outraged that its homeland has been exploited through a system of internal colonialism or its language denigrated by a political majority speaking another tongue, any delay may seem unreasonable—especially if television cameras are rolling and newspapers are announcing the latest public opinion polls on the matter as though they are scores in international soccer matches. On the other hand, because ethnoterritorial demands tend to challenge the *legitimacy* of the existing order, and because no one wants to hear that the political process they love is illegitimate, from the perspective of the majority population and its leadership, the demands of ethnoterritorialists may appear particularly ungrateful and objectionable, and any concession to them may be viewed as excessive.

Above all, the evaluation of policy performance is complicated by the nature of ethnoterritorial demands. As we have noted, they rarely remain at the level where they can be satisfied through favorable governmental policies. Rather, they tend to revolve around authority and regime types of demands that require decisionmakers to do more than relinquish some of the resources over which they have control. They are being asked almost inevitably to yield some of their own influence and the power that they control—precisely the types of demands to which political systems are least likely to be responsive. Yet, while this observation may help us to understand why so many states delayed responding to the ethnoterritorial challenge until the growing force of ethnoterritorial sentiment, manifested in communal violence, or the increasing electoral strength of ethnonationalist political parties forced the policymakers "to do something," it does not help us evaluate policy. The fact that it is difficult to get any concession at all in some policy areas may not be entirely irrelevant in evaluating a policy's success in achieving its intended objectives, but there are no bonus points in political analysis for policies simply because they have emerged in areas where policymaking is particularly difficult.

Ethnoterritorial Policy and Ethnoterritorial Movements

At the most basic level, the ethnoterritorial movements and the leaders at the center who have confronted them each had two general goals. The ethnoterritorialists' goals have consisted of a desire to extract meaningful concessions from the center on behalf of their respective communities and—on the part of some though not all ethnoterritorial organizations—a desire to profit from these concessions. For their part, the leaders at the center have been primarily concerned with halting and eventually reducing the centrifugal force of ethnoterritorialism in general and the influence of ethnopolitical organizations in particular. Secondarily they have embraced a desire to avoid making any concessions to the periphery. In both camps there have been groups for whom the second goal was as important as the first—factions inside the ethnonationalist parties, and groups at the center for whom the unity of the state has bordered on the religious. However, there have always been ethnoterritorial organizations of a cultural rather than political nature, and governing officials at the center have, overall, been willing to sacrifice some of their commitment to their second objective in order to obtain their primary one. Thus, these goals, in the priority assigned to them, seem as reasonable a basis for evaluating the success of the ethnoterritorialists and of the accommodation policies as any that can be devised.

The previous chapters strongly suggest that, on balance, the ethnoterritorialists have succeeded in their primary objective. In some instances they have also succeeded in their secondary goal, although often at a much higher cost than they intended or than they might rationally have been willing to pay had they foreseen it. Throughout our case studies, the organizations *have* generally succeeded in obtaining meaningful concessions from their governments. Furthermore, while it can be argued that concessions of an output variety are not always significant (it is by no means evident in Safran's chapter how committed to regionalization the government of France is today, though it has certainly gone further in making concessions to ethnoregional groups in the Hexagon than anyone would have predicted a decade ago), concessions to demands for greater regional or communal access to the decisionmaking process and greater regional control over regional affairs may be viewed as prima facie evidence of successful ethnoterritorial politics. Far from representing symbolic or token responses to regional demands, these reductions of the center's authority and constitutional reorganizations involve the very type of augmentation of regional power that the center long delayed in Belgium, has sought to minimize in democratizing Spain, and has often resisted strenuously in Canada (e.g., Trudeau's policy of opposing further decentralization when he was Canada's prime minister). Even in Britain, where the struggle for devolution has run aground, Keating, in Chapter 4, suggests a far greater attentiveness to regional sentiments in Scotland, even on the part of the Conservatives (for example, in staffing administrative positions), than could have been expected to have occurred without the rise of the SNP in the seventies.

The past decade has not, however, bestowed any equivalent, enduring benefits on the ethnoterritorial organizations. Rather, it has been particularly hard on the ethnonational parties of Belgium, Britain, Canada, and, to a lesser extent, Spain, even though in the short term it appeared that it would be otherwise. The seventies had witnessed the FDF, RW, and VU joining the governing coalitions in Brussels, the SNP successfully bartering its support of Labour's 1974–1979 government for a devolution bill for Scotland, the PQ capturing government in Quebec, and the PNV achieving political power in Spain's newly created Basque autonomous community. Yet these initial successes, as the preceding chapters document, were followed by setbacks, some of which are attributable to outside variables (for example, global recessions overshadowing regional issues). But some of the setbacks are also attributable to the dynamics of policy processes affecting those caught up in them. It appears that as policy moved from more general, essentially output responses to ethnoterritorial demands to more specific *policy moments* (referendums, offers to ethnonationalists to participate in government) and power-sharing forms of accommodation (cooptation of regionalist leaders, regional devolution), the tendency was to intensify the divisions present within the ethnoterritorial movements and to weaken their capacity to maneuver in their respective political processes.

Our studies suggest throughout that the problems associated with government are, in general, very difficult for ethnoterritorial parties to master. Contradictions abound: how to retain the advantages of outsiders when in the government; how to practice the compromise-laden "art of the possible" when the acquisition of power has itself resulted from articulating regional demands in uncompromising terms; how to satisfy pragmatic program objectives without alienating purists and ideologues inside the party. The problems of such parties have been specifically treated elsewhere as well as in this book and need not be reviewed here.[11] What can be stressed is the pattern. The Belgian ethnonationalists suffered internal splits and electoral decline immediately following their respective turns in the government in Brussels. The SNP's support of the Labour coalition sparked divisions inside the SNP which only accelerated when the 1979 general elections saw the SNP's vote in Scotland drop off sharply from its performance in the 1974 British elections. The PQ's hold on the Quebec electorate and internal cohesiveness begin to erode following its defeat in the Quebec referendum. As for Spain, Clark, in Chapter 2, documents the drop-off in the PNV's electoral support (to the benefit of more intransigent Basque regionalist parties) and the increased power of party hard-liners following the decision of that party's moderate leadership the mid-1980s to trim party rhetoric on home rule in order unblock a pending transfer of power from Madrid. Other variables also played roles in the setbacks of these organizations, but the overall pattern supports the obvious conclusion that—far from achieving their goal of using the policy process to advance their private interests—the ethnonational parties suffered from the opportunies to experience political power that opened to them.

Policy and the Actors at the Center

Although repelling the ethnoterritorial challenge was the principal goal of leaders at the center in our case studies, it is difficult to give them credit for the decline of the regionalist parties given the normally reactive and grudging nature of the accommodation policies they pursued and the frequently unforeseen nature of the consequences of those actions.

In all of our case studies where the ethnoterritorial movements took the form of regionalist parties, their decline was much more an indirect by-product of the accommodation process than the expected result of it. Leaders of the systemwide parties invariably feared that concessions would heighten separatist pressures. Consequently, they long refused to deal with regional demands, and the decentralization of power process that eventually led to a weakening of the ethnonationalist parties was very much the incremental product of several stages of concessions, not the result of a bold policy initiative by the center aimed at the ethnonationalists.

Nor should it be overlooked that those concessions that were forthcoming often were enacted over strenuous opposition, coming as they did at the cost of such cherished goals as retaining a centralized, unitary state (Belgium, Britain, and France), avoiding the enhancement of provincial power (Trudeau's Canada), and discouraging separatist tendencies (Spain). Yet, institutional reforms in these directions have been avoided only in Thatcher's Britain, where the governing Conservatives have found it politically unnecessary to introduce the new devolution bill they promised in campaigning in Scotland against the pending devolution bill. Elsewhere, except for France, the degree of power passing to ethnoterritorial institutions has been substantial, largely because the output variety of accommodation devices most acceptable to the leaders at the center proved to be unsuccessful in containing ethnoterritorial sentiment in Western states.

Most importantly, the policies undertaken to disarm ethnoterritorial challenges have had tremendous side costs for the center in most of the systems we have examined. In Britain, Belgium, Spain, and Canada, much of the last two decades has been devoted to a time-consuming process of constitutional reform, during which other problems have multiplied and after which these countries have found it difficult to return to the *ordinary* political agenda. Sometimes the reforms themselves have continued to burden the center (for example, the duty of Belgian MPs to staff as well regional-communal assemblies). And, beyond these costs to the formal policy process, the costs of responding to ethnoterritorial politics have also mounted in terms of the weakening of existing, national party systems.

But, to return to our point of departure, were these the costs of policies that reduced ethnoterritorial sentiment, or the price of "merely" dealing with ethnonational organizations?

ETHNOTERRITORIAL POLICIES AND THE FUTURE OF POLITICS IN MULTINATIONAL WESTERN DEMOCRACIES

Our authors' response to the ethnoterritorial question seems to be unanimous: ethnopolitical sentiment is still a significant political force despite a generation of efforts to cope with it. It still paralyzes Belgian politics, it troubles cabinet formation in Britain, it still prods constitutional developments in Canada, it underlies language policy in France, and it can be regularly read in the 60 percent to 70 percent of the vote which has recently gone to "rejectionist" parties in elections in Basque Spain. Other factors have undoubtedly played a role in keeping such sentiment alive, but in general our studies suggest that ethnopolitical sentiment is too diffuse an object to be immediately affected by policy change (as opposed to ethnonational parties, which are too directly a part of the policy process to escape entirely the intended and unintended results of policies altering the nature of the political arena). Moreover, our authors suggest at least four major reasons why ethnopolitical sentiment is likely to remain a part of the public and governmental agendas and the policymaking processes of multinational Western democracies in the foreseeable future.

1. *Postindustrial Polities and Ethnoterritorial Politics.* As Clark reminds us in Chapter 2, on Spain, most Western states are either in or entering a postindustrial phase of development earmarked by the prominence of the service sector in their economies, the educated nature of their citizenry, and the importance attached to quality-of-life issues—including enhanced political participation—in their political agendas. Indeed, many analysts tied the resurgence of ethnonationalism in Western countries during the sixties and seventies in part to a postindustrial explanation: the search by ethnically self-differentiating regional communities for greater control over their political fate. The continued evolution of Western countries in post-industrial directions contains similar implications for the ethnopolitical factor on Western agendas. Clark suggests a twofold scenario. First, postindustrial means a loosening of centralized institutions created during the industrial period and a new definition of the individual, usually within the context of more localized opportunities for participation in government. Safran's discussion of the present tie between political decentralization and the new definition of individualism in the ideology of the French Socialist party fits this mold. But, second, the popular expectations concerning this loosening

tend to outstrip the objective process of decentralization, producing tensions which—in ethnically distinct, territorial communities—can take an ethnoterritorial hue, stimulating ethnoregional consciousness, and generating renewed support for ethnoterritorial political organizations.

2. *The Supranational Connection.* The process of harmonizing regional politics in multinational states that are simultaneously meshing into Europe's evolving supranational community provides another policy window for ethnoterritorial politics in the present and future of many Western European states. For Spain, Clark suggests that membership in the European Community (EC) will increase pressures at the center to reduce regional autonomy and recentralize in order to fulfill newly contracted obligations to Brussels to bring Spain's internal policies into harmony with those of other EC states. If so, EC membership may, in turn, stimulate the fears of Basques and other autonomous communities that they will lose many of their recent gains and generate a new round of defensive ethnoterritorialism and increased tension between Madrid and the periphery. Alternately, once in the European Community, Spain's autonomous regions may find in the supranational connection a new opportunity for asserting regionalism and, like the regions of other multinational members of the EC before them, lobby in Brussels for the EC's regional and energy development funds as alternatives to the purse strings of the central government. To be sure, existing EC policy is to respond to such efforts only where the regions are lobbying with the approval of their respective capitols. However, because most states are normally revenue-hungry and because it is much harder to justify denying regionalists the money of others than the money of the central treasury, membership in the EC carries with it a new policy framework, a new set of policy dynamics, and new policy options for regions. And of all the "regionalists" in Western Europe, those most likely to be mobilized are the ethnoregionalists.

3. *Political Ambiguity and the Unfinished Policy Agenda.* Still another reason for assuming that public opinion and public policy will continue to flow in ethnoterritorial channels can be found in the character of the recent political changes indicated in our studies. Public agendas were not cleared of ethnopolitical issues; they were reshuffled to lower the saliency of those issues, frequently by means of political compromises that left much of importance "to be done" at the traditional, "later date." The scope of powers to be devolved to Spain's regions, the special status of Quebec (again before Canada's politicians in the Meech Lake Accord), the status of Brussels, whether France's administrative districts should better coincide with the state's ethnocultural divisions—these and other sticky issues remain as unfinished aspects of the accommodation processes of Western states. They will maintain political interest in regional matters and retain ethnoterritorial issues on the governmental agendas until they are finally addressed—if, indeed, they can ever be fully addressed.

One key to understanding the policy options of the recent past is the political ambiguity that became an accepted part of them. Spain needed to federalize to democratize, so centrists and regionalists alike were willing to accept federalism as a basis of constitutional reform in post-Franco Spain. But, Clark informs us, to the center federalism meant basically administrative decentralization; to the Basques it meant regional autonomy. Never mind. Definitions could be sorted out later. But now *it is later* for Spain, as well as for other Western states, and the issues of what to do with the Basques, the Bruxellois, the Québécois, and others are still pending. Moreover, when they are attacked it will probably be by a similar surgical process that cuts from each issue its most difficult element and defers *it* for later treatment, in order to facilitate a more immediate agreement.

As we have elsewhere noted, both ethnoterritorial spokespersons and public authorities at the center walk thin lines in negotiating ethnoterritorial demands. If they seem too ready to negotiate with regional minorities, the politicians at the center face reproach from the dominant groups in their states and the possibility that the ethnonationalists will escalate their demands; if they seem too reluctant to negotiate, ethnoterritorial sentiment may increase and perhaps even take a violent form. Meanwhile, if the ethnoterritorial leadership seems too willing to strike deals, especially deals that reduce regional representation at the center or result in the inclusion of ethnonational leaders in ruling coalitions, then they risk being attacked at home for selling out the regional cause or having those at the center harden their own demands. On the other hand, if the ethnonationalists adopt too uncompromising a position, they may lose their moderate supporters inside their region and weaken their bargaining position. Given the delicacy of the situation, both sides have found it preferable to bargain across a wide, general policy plane—not locking themselves until the last moment into any particular policy device and leaving the detailing as open as possible—in order to find marketable policies for their separate constituencies. "Nothing ever seem[ed] to satisfy completely, and both sides frequently seem[ed] to "slide" into accommodation devices as much as consciously agree upon them because of common assessments of the need for them or their intended results."[12] But the legacy of this approach to ethnoterritorial policymaking has been to keep the government agenda in a continuing state of unfinished business, which yields policy opportunities to ethnoterritorialists on an ongoing basis.

4. *Ethnopolitics and the Contemporary Political Processes.* Finally, ethnoterritorial sentiment and politics are especially likely to remain a part of western political processes because of the manner in which their policy-making systems are now constituted.

Because they are open systems, they can expect regionalized movements to ebb and flow with regional situations. They can also expect that not only will politically salient ethnoterritorial issues surface from their larger, territorially demarked communities, but that smaller ones (like the Andulucians in Spain, Germans in Belgium, francophones outside Quebec in Canada, perhaps the Welsh in Britain) will piggyback on the pressure of their fellow, political "minorities" and press for their own policy gains.

They can also expect a continuance of ethnoterritorial politics because of the importance, extraconstitutionally, of their party systems to policy-making and because of the regionalized nature of the power of some of the parties in these states (Labour's dependency on the Celtic regions of Britain, the importance of Quebec to the Liberals' systemwide competitiveness in Canada, the importance of Wallonia to Belgian Socialists and Flanders to Belgian Catholics, and so on). Given the vulnerability of such parties to ethnoterritorial attack, party systems are apt to remain highly plugged into ethnoterritorial sentiment. They cannot afford to become estranged from it when ethnonational competitors can be presumed to be ready to exploit regional dissatisfaction and where elections roll around, at best, every four or five years, and often a good deal sooner in systems depending on coalition governments to make them work.

Nevertheless, perhaps the most substantial reason for expecting that ethnoterritorial matters will remain an engrained part of the policy agendas of Western states lies in the revised nature of their institutional arrangements. Even where administrative decentralization has been the primary response of the center to the region (France and, to a lesser extent, Britain), regional officials and politicians now define their role dualistically to include, at the least, a strong obligation to lobby for their respective ethnoterritorial communities in their country's political process. Where devolution has been the policy response, and regionalists are able to project their demands from institutionalized bases—Quebec in Canada, the Basque autonomous community in Spain, the Cultural Council for French-speaking Belgium—it is even less possible to insulate the center from regional politics. This would be especially true when, as noted in the discussion of Belgium, the center itself depends upon coalition governments composed of parties dependent upon these regions; however, as Keating observed, matters can also be difficult in even a two-party system when an asymmetry exists in which the national minority party is the majority party at the regional level and the national majority party is in the minority in the region. Furthermore, even more far-reaching reforms are now being discussed in most states, including a formula in Canada that will give Quebec the power to appoint a third of the nine justices on Canada's Supreme Court. These are not institutional arrangements that exorcise ethnopolitical sentiment or demands. At best, they domesticate them to fit into existing constitutional arrangements even as those arrangements are being streched to accommodate ethnoterritorial issues and to provide a new setting for the ongoing discussion of ethnoterritorial politics as a permanent part of the agenda in today's multinational, Western democracies.

NOTES

1. Erik Nordlinger, *Occasional Papers in International Affairs No. 29*, (Cambridge, Massachusetts: Center for International Affairs, 1972).

2. Walker Connor, "The Politics of Ethnonationalism," *Journal of International Affairs*, v. 27, #1 (1973): 1-21, p. 21.

3. Reciprocally, it might be argued that one reason Trudeau had the luxury of following his philosophy and rejecting decentralist options vis à vis Quebec was that the PQ was only interested in regional power and did not threaten the Quebec vote in national elections upon which the Liberal party depended. Especially with Trudeau as the Liberal party's leader, the Quebec vote was secure.

4. Raphael Zariski, "Ethnic Extremism Among Ethnoterritorial Minorities in Western Europe: Dimensions, Causes, and Institutional Responses," *Comparative Politics*, v. 21 (1989, forthcoming).

5. See, for example, Joseph R. Rudolph, Jr., "Ethnonational Parties and Political Change: the Belgian and British Experience," *Polity*, IX, No. 4 (1977): 401-426.

6. I remain indebted to John K. Wildgen for suggesting some time ago this fourfold basis for differentiating among ethnoterritorial demands. JR.

7. Nordliner, Occasional Papers in International Affairs No. 29.

8. See, for example, Lijphart's *Conflict and Coexistence in Belgium* (Berkeley: Institute of International Studies, 1981).

9. See especially Maureen Covell, "Ethnic Conflict and Elite Bargaining: The Case of Belgium," *West European Politics*, IV, No. 3 (1981): 197-218).

10. The closest equivalent to the system in the United States is perhaps the unofficial black caucus in the United States Congress, composed of black Congressmen and Senators who stake out positions in the field of civil rights which *may* go beyond the immediate mandates of their constituents.

11. In addition to the chapter on Belgium, *infra*, see also the coeditors "Ethnoterritorial Movements and the Policy Process: Accommodating Nationalist Demands in the Developed World," *Comparative Politics*, XVII, #3 (April, 1985): 291-311, 300-302.

12. Ibid., 308-309, 309.

Bibliography

L'Administration territoriale II: Les collectivités locales. October 1984. *Documents d'Etudes*. No. 2.03. Paris: Documentation Française.

Alcock, Antony E., Brian K. Taylor, and John M. Welton, eds. 1979. *The Future of Cultural Minorities*. New York: St. Martin's Press.

Alexander, Alan. 1980. Scottish Nationalism: Agenda Building, Electoral Process, and Political Culture. *Canadian Review of Studies in Nationalism* 7:372-385.

Anderson, Alan B., and James S. Frideres, eds 1981. *Ethnicity in Canada: Theoretical Perspectives*. Toronto: Butterworths.

d'Anglejan, Alison. 1984. "Language Planning In Quebec: An Historical Overview and Future Trends. In Richard Y. Bourhis, ed., *Conflict and Language Planning in Quebec*. Clevedon, England: Multilingual Matters.

The Answer Is Likely to be Fuzzy. May 17, 1980. *The Economist*.

Après le discours de Gand. February 22, 1986. *Le Soir* (Brussels).

Assemblée Nationale. Première session de 1983–1984. (M.R. Pesce) Rapport "culture," 89–94.

Assemblée Nationale. Deuxième session ordinaire de 1983–1984. Proposition de loi sur la promotion des langues et cultures de la France. No. 2157.

Assemblée Nationale. Deuxième session ordinaire de 1984–1985. Proposition de loi relative au statut et à la promotion des langues et cultures régionales. No. 2711.

Aubert, Jean-François. 1978. "Switzerland." In David Butler and Austin Ranney, eds., *Referendums*. Washington: American Enterprise Institute for Public Policy Research.

Ayestarán, J.A., 1979. *Euskadi v el estatuto de autonomína*. San Sebastian: Erein.

Bac, Pierre. 1967. *La langue occitane*. Paris: Presses Universitaires de France.

Balsom, Denis, and Ian McAllister. 1979. The Scottish and Welsh Devolution Referenda of 1979: Constitutional Change and Popular Choice. *Parliamentary Affairs* 32:394–409.

Banting, Keith G., and Richard Simeon, eds. 1985. *Redesigning the State*. Toronto: Toronto Press.

Bassand, Michel. 1975. The Jura Problem. *Journal of Peace Research* 20:139–150.

Bassand, Michel. 1976. Le séparatisme jurassien: Un conflict de classes et/ou conflict ethnique. *Cahier International de Sociologie* 66: 221–246.

Bedarida, Catherine. August 8, 1985. Jack Lang crée le conseil des tribus françaises. *Libération*.

Beer, William R. 1977. "The Social Class of Ethnic Activists in Contemporary France." In Milton J. Esman, ed., *Ethnic Conflict in the Western World*. Ithaca: Cornell University Press.

Beer, William R. 1980. *The Unexpected Rebellion: Ethnic Activism in Contemporary France*. New York: New York University Press.

Behiels, Michael D. 1985. *Prelude to Quebec's Quiet Revolution: Liberalism Versus Neo-Nationalism, 1945–1960*. Montreal: McGill-Queen's Press.

Belgian Roulette. October 18, 1980. *The Economist*.

Belgian Voters Go to the Polls with the Economy on Their Minds. October 10, 1985. *Christian Science Monitor*.

Bell, Wendell, and Walter E. Freeman, eds. 1974. *Ethnicity and Nation-Building*. Beverly Hills: Sage Publications.

Benton, Ivor, and Gavin Drewry. 1980. Public Legislation: A Survey of the Sessions 1977/78 and 1978/79. *Parliamentary Affairs* 33:174–186.

Berger, Suzanne. 1972. *Peasants Against Politics: Rural Organization in Brittany, 1911–1967*. Cambridge: Harvard University Press.

Berger, Suzanne. 1977. "Bretons and Jacobins: Reflections on French Regional Ethnicity." In Milton J. Esman, ed., *Ethnic Conflict in the Western World*. Ithaca: Cornell University Press.

Bernard, Paul. 1983. *L'état et la décentralisation. Notes et études documentaires*. Paris: Documentation Française, 4711–14712.

Bernard, Philippe. November 14–15, 1985. Dites "13e" en mandarin. *Le Monde Aujourd'hui*.

Birch, Anthony. 1977. *Political Integration and Disintegration in the British Isles*. London: George Allen & Unwin.

Birch, Anthony. 1978. Minority Nationalist Movements and Theories of Political Integration. *World Politics* 30:325–344.

Bochel, John, David Denver, and Allan Macartney, eds. 1981. *The Referendum Experience: Scotland 1979*. Aberdeen: Aberdeen University Press.

Boeynaems, Maurice. 1973. Les années 1970 et 1971 sur le plan communautaire et linguistiquue. *Res Publica* 15:881–914.

Bogdanor, Vernon. 1979. *Devolution*. Oxford: Oxford University Press.

Bogdanor, Vernon. 1980. The 40 Percent Rule. *Parliamentary Affairs* 33:249–363.

Bogdanor, Vernon. 1981. *The People and the Party System*. Cambridge: Cambridge University Press.

Bordegarai, Kepa, and Robert Pastor. 1979. *Estatuto vasco*. San Sebastian: Ediciones Vascas.

Bourhis, Richard Y., ed. *Conflict and Language Planning in Quebec*. Clevedon, England: Multilingual Matters.

Brand, Jack. 1978. *The National Movement in Scotland*. London: Routledge & Kegan Paul.

Brand, Jack. 1986. Political Parties and the Referendum on National Sovereignty: The 1979 Scottish Referendum on Devolution. *Canadian Review of Studies in Nationalism* 13:31–48.

Brassine, J. and Yves Kreins. 1984. La réforme d'état et la communaté germanophone. Couurrier hebdomadaire du centre de recherche et d'information socio-politique (Ch du CRISP), nos. 1028–1029.

Brogan, Patrick. May 20, 1980. Confusion Abounds over Real Aims as Quebec Votes Today to Determine Relations with Ottawa. *The Times* (London).

Brogan, Patrick. May 22, 1980. Separatists Accept Resounding Quebec Defeat but Given Promise of Rewritten Constitution. *The Times* (London).

Brooks, Roger Allan. 1973. Scottish Nationalism: Relative Deprivation and Social Mobility. Unpublished Ph.D. Dissertation, University of Michigan.

Brown, Tim. October 25, 1979. Basques Expect Resounding "Yes" to Home Rule. *The Times* (London).

Brunet, Michel. 1958. "Trois dominantes de la pensée canadienne-française: L'agriculturalism, l'anti-étatisme et le messianisme." In Michel Brunet, *La présence anglaise et les Canadiens*. Montreal: Beauchemin.

Bulpitt, J. 1983. *Territory and Power in the United Kingdom*. Manchester: Manchester University Press.

Burdeau, François. May–June 1984. L'état jacobin et la culture politique française. *Projet* 185–186:635–648.

Burgess, Michael. ed. 1986. *Federalism and Federation in Western Europe*. London: Croom Helm.

Butler, David. 1978. "United Kingdom." In David Butler and Austin Ranney, eds., *Referendums*. Washington: American Enterprise Institute for Public Policy Research.

Butler, David, and Uwe Kitzinger, eds. 1976. *The 1975 Referendum*. New York: St. Martin's Press.

Butler, David, and Austin Ranney, ed. 1978. *Referendums: A Comparative Study of Practice and Theory*. Washington, D.C.: American Enterprise Institute for Public Policy Research.

Butler, David, and Dennis Kavanagh. 1988. *The British General Election of 1987*. London: Macmillan.

Callaghan, James. 1987. *Time and Chance*. London: Collins.

Cameron, David R. 1974. *Nationalism, Self-Determination, and the Quebec Question*. Toronto: Macmillan.

Campbell, David B. 1982. "Nationalism, Religion and the Social Bases of Conflict in the Swiss Jura." In Stein Rokkan and Derek W. Urwin, eds., *The Politics of Territorial Identity*. London: Sage Publications.

del Campo, Salustiano, Manuel Navarro, and J. Felix Tezanos. 1977. *La cuestión regional española*. Madrid: EDICUSA.

Canada, April 1985. *Keesing's Contemporary Archives*, 33524–33525.

Canada, Parliament. 1987. *The 1987 Constitutional Accord, The Report of the*

Special Joint Committee of the Senate and House of Commons. Ottawa: Queens' Printer.

Canada, Royal Commission on Bilingualism and Biculturalism. 1965. *Preliminary Report.* Ottawa: Queen's Printer.

Carr, Raymond, and Juan Pablo Fusi. 1981. *Spain: Dictatorship to Democracy.* London: George Allen & Unwin.

Carrington, David. 1980. *La Corse.* Paris: Arthaud.

Charlton, Sue Ellen. 1978. Nationalism and Regionalism in France's *Occitanie.* Presented at the European Studies Conference, Omaha.

Charlton, Sue Ellen M. 1979. Comparing Ethnic Movements in France. Presented at the annual meeting of the Southwestern Social Science Association, Ft. Worth.

Chikoff, Irinade. February 13, 1985. Sous la loi des indépendantistes. *Figaro.*

Clark, Robert. 1980a. *The Basques: The Franco Years and Beyond.* Reno: University of Nevada Press.

Clark, Robert. 1980b. Basque Socialism at the Polls: An Analysis of Four Post-Franco Elections. Presented at the Conference of Europeanists, Washington, D.C.

Clark, Robert. 1980c. "Euzkadi: Basque Nationalism in Spain Since the Civil War." In Charles Foster, ed., *Nations Without a State: Ethnic Minorities in Western Europe.* New York: Praeger.

Clark, Robert. 1981. Patterns of Insurgent Violence in Spain's Basque Provinces. Presented at the annual meeting of the Southwestern Political Science Association, Dallas.

Clark, Robert. March 1985. Spain's Autonomous Communities: A Case Study in Ethnic Power Sharing. *The European Studies Journal* 2:1–16.

Clark, Robert. 1987. 'Rejectionist' Voting as an Indicator of Ethnic Nationalism: The Case of Spain's Basque Provinces, 1976–1986. *Ethnic and Racial Studies* 10:427–447.

Clark, Robert, and Michael Haltzel, eds. 1987. *Spain in the 1980's: The Democratic Transition and a New International Role.* Cambridge, Massachusetts: Ballinger.

Clift, Dominique. 1982. *Quebec Nationalism in Crisis.* Montreal: McGill-Queen's Press.

Le Club de l'Horloge. 1985. *L'identité de la France.* Paris: Albin Michel.

Coleman, William D. 1984. *The Independence Movement in Quebec 1945–1980.* Toronto: University of Toronto Press.

Connor, Walker. 1973. The Politics of Ethnonationalism. *The Journal of International Affairs* 27:1–21.

Connor, Walker. 1977. "Ethnonationalism in the First World: The Present in Historical Perspective." In Milton J. Esman, ed., *Ethnic Conflict in the Western World.* Ithaca: Cornell University Press.

Connor, Walker. 1978. A Nation Is a Nation, Is a State, Is an Ethnic Group, Is a. . . . *Ethnic and Racial Studies* 50:377–400.

Connor, Walker. 1987. "Ethnonationalism." In Myron Weiner and Samuel P. Huntington, eds., *Understanding Political Development.* Boston: Little, Brown.

Cook, Ramsay. ed. 1969. *French Canadian Nationalism: An Anthology.* Toronto: Macmillan.

Corbett, Edward M. 1976. *Quebec Confronts Canada.* Baltimore: The Johns Hopkins University Press.

Corrado, Raymond. 1975. Nationalism and Communalism in Wales. *Ethnicity* 2:368–381.

La Corse à la dérive. May 25, 1987. *Le Point.*

Covell, Maureen. 1982. Agreeing to Disagree: Elite Bargaining and the Revision of the Belgian Constitution. *Canadian Journal of Political Science* 15:451–469.

Covell, Maureen. 1986. Regionalization and Economic Crisis in Belgium: The Variable Origins of Centrifugal and Centripetal Forces. *Canadian Journal of Political Science* 19:261–269.

Coulon, Christian. 1979. Idéologie jacobine, Etat, et ethnocide. *Pluriel* 17:3–20.

Coupland, Reginald. 1954. *Welsh and Scottish Nationalism: A Study.* London: Collins.

Coverdale, John F. 1979. *The Political Transformation of Spain After Franco.* New York: Praeger.

Dalyell, T. 1977. *Devolution: The End of Britain?* London: Jonathan Cape.

Da Silva, Milton. 1975. Modernization and Ethnic Conflict: The Case of the Basques. *Comparative Politics* 7:227–252.

Debelius, Harry. January 16, 1980. Andalusia Adds Its Voice to the Growing Clamor for Autonomy. *The Times* (London).

Debt Ridden Belgian City Pays Workers With IOU. April 4, 1983. *The Wall Street Journal.*

Delannoi, Gil. 1986. La politique culturelle, l'héritage et l'innovation. Presented at the colloquium of the Association Française de Science Politique, Aix-en-Provence.

Dias, Manuel. May–June 1986. La vie culturelle et associative des immigrés. *Projet* 199:61–66.

Dion, Léon. January 1964. The Origin and Character of the Nationalism of Growth. *Canadian Forum*: 229–33.

Dion, Léon. Quebec. 1976. *The Unfinished Revolution.* Montreal: McGill-Queen's Press.

Douglass, William A., and Milton da Silva. 1971. "Basque Nationalism." In Oriol Pi-Sunyer, ed., *The Limits of Integration: Ethnicity and Nationalism in Modern Europe.* Amherst: University of Massachusetts.

Dreyfus, François. 1986. La culture alsacienne entre la France et la R.F.A. depuis 1945. Presented at the colloquium of the Association Française de Science Politique, Aix-en-Provence.

Drucker, H.M. 1979. Crying Wolfe: Recent Divisions in the SNP. *Political Quarterly* 50:503–508.

Drucker, H.M., and Gordon Brown, 1980. *The Politics of Nationalism and Devolution.* New York: Longman.

Dubet, François. 1981. Défendre son identité: Approche du discours identitaire. *Esprit.*

Duchacek, Ivo D. 1977. *Federalism and Ethnicity. Publius* 4,4 (special issue).

Duchacek, Ivo D., ed. 1988. Bicommunal Societies and Polities. *Publius* 182 (special issue).

Dunn, James A. 1970. Consociational Democracy and Language Conflict: A Comparison of the Belgian and Swiss Experience. *Comparative Political Studies* 5:3–40.

Dunn, James A. 1974. The Revision of the Constitution in Belgium: A Study in the Institutionalization of Ethnic Conflict. *Western Political Quarterly* 27:143–164.

Du Toit, Pierre. 1987. Consociational Democracy and Bargaining Power. *Comparative Politics* 19:419–430.

Economics Is New Basis of Belgian Divisions. October 16, 1985. *Wall Street Journal*.

Edwards, Rob. July 17, 1987. Beware the Tories, Promising Devolution. *New Statesman*.

Eisenstadt, S.N., and Stein Rokkan, eds. 1973. *Building States and Nations*. Beverly Hills: Sage Publications.

Elegoët, Fanch. 1980. L'identité bretonne: Notes sur la production de l'identité négative. *Pluriel* 24:43–67.

Elorriaga, Gabriel. 1983. *La batalla de las autonomías*. Madrid: Editorial Azara.

Enloe, Cynthia. 1973. *Ethnic Conflict and Political Development*. Boston: Little, Brown.

Esman, Milton J. 1973. The Management of Communal Conflict. *Public Policy* 21:49–78.

Esman, Milton J., ed. 1977a. *Ethnic Conflict in the Western World*. Ithaca: Cornell University Press.

Esman, Milton J. 1977b. "Perspectives on Ethnic Conflict in Industrialized Societies." In Milton J. Esman, ed., *Ethnic Conflict in the Western World*. Ithaca: Cornell University Press.

Esman, Milton J. 1977c. "Scottish Nationalism, North Sea Oil, and the British Response." In Milton J. Esman, ed., *Ethnic Conflict in the Western World*. Ithaca: Cornell University Press.

Esman, Milton. 1978. Public Administration and the Struggle for Shares in Ethnically and Racially Plural Societies. Presented at the annual meeting of the American Political Science Association, New York.

Esman, Milton J. 1982. The Politics of Official Bilingualism in Canada. *Political Science Quarterly* 97:233–253.

Esman, Milton. 1987. Ethnic Politics and Economic Power. *Comparative Politics* 19:395–418.

Fenwick, Rudy. 1981. Social Change and Ethnic Nationalism: An Historical Analysis of the Separatist Movement in Quebec. *Comparative Studies in Society and History* 23:196–216.

Fitzmaurice, John. 1984. Belgium: Reluctant Federalism *Parliamentary Affairs* 37:418–433.

Flickinger, R.S. 1981. Ethnonationalism and Government Response in Post-Franco Spain. Presented at the annual meeting of the Midwest Political Science Association, Cincinnati.

Foon, Chew Sock. 1986. On the Incompatibility of Ethnic and National Loyalities: Reframing the Issue. *Canadian Review of Studies in Nationalism* 13:1–12.

Foster, Charles, ed. *Nations Without a State: Ethnic Minorities in Western Europe.* New York: Praeger.

Foulkes, David, J. Barry Jones, and R.A. Wilford, eds. 1983. *The Welsh Veto: The Wales Act 1978 and the Referendum.* Cardiff: University of Wales Press.

Frognier, André P., Michel Quevit, and Marie Stenbock. 1982. "Regional Imbalances and Centre-Periphery Relationship in Belgium." In Stein Rokkan and Derek W. Urwin, eds., *The Politics of Territorial Identity: Studies in European Regionalism.* Beverly Hills: Sage Publications.

Gagnon, Alain G., ed. 1984. *Quebec: State and Society.* Toronto: Methuen.

Gil, Jose. 1984. *La Corse entre la liberté et la terreur.* Paris: Editions de la Différence.

Gingras, F.P., and N. Nevitte. 1981. Religion, Values, and Politics in Contemporary Quebec. Presented at the annual meeting of the American Political Science Association, New York.

Ginizer, Henry. March 9, 1980. Divisions in Quebec Growing as Vote on Status Nears. *New York Times.*

Ginizer, Henry. May 11, 1980. Quebecers Wooing the Undecided Vote. *New York Times.*

Giordan, Henri. 1982. *Démocratie culturelle et droit à différence: Rapport au ministre de la culture.* Paris: Documentation Française.

Giordan, Henri, ed. 1984. *Par les langues de France.* CNRS, Laboratorie de Recherches Interculturelles. Paris: Centre Pompidou.

Glass, H.E. 1977. Ethnic Diversity, Elite Accommodation, and Federalism in Switzerland. *Publius* 7:31–49.

Gourevitch, Peter Alexis. 1979. The Reemergence of "Peripheral Nationalism": Some Comparative Speculations on the Spatial Distribution of Political Leadership and Economic Growth. *Comparative Study of Society and History* 21:303–322.

Grand, L., and P. Mayol. 1980. *L'invention du quotidien.* 2 vols. Paris: U.G.E.

Grant, Douglas, ed. 1960. *Quebec Today.* Toronto: University of Toronto Press.

Grau, Richard. 1985. *Les langues et les cultures minoritaires en France.* Quebec: Conseil de la Langue Française.

Green, Leslie. 1982. Rational Nationalists. *Political Studies* 30:236–246.

Greenwood, Davydd J. 1977. "Continuity in Change: Spanish Basque Ethnicity as a Historical Process." In Milton J. Esman, ed., *Ethnic Conflict in the Western World.* Ithaca: Cornell University Press.

Gunther, Richard. 1985. "Constitutional Change in Contemporary Spain." In Keith G. Banting and Richard Simeon, eds., *Redesigning the State: The Politics of Constitutional Change.* Toronto: University of Toronto Press.

Gunther, Richard, Giacomo Sani, and Goldie Shabad. eds. 1986. *Spain After Franco: The Making of a Competitive Party System.* Berkeley: University of California Press.

Hagy, James William. 1970. Le Parti Québécois in the 1970 Elections. *Queen's Quarterly* 77:261–273.

Hall, Raymond L., ed. 1979. *Ethnic Autonomy—Comparative Dynamics.* New York: Pergamon Press.

Hamilton, Richard, and Maurice Pinard. 1976. The Bases of Parti Québécois Support in Recent Quebec Elections. *Canadian Journal of Political Science* 9:3–26.

Hanham, H.J. 1969. *Scottish Nationalism.* Cambridge: Harvard University Press.

Hannoun, Michel. 1986. *L'autre cohabitation: Français et immigrés.* Paris: Editions L. Harmattan.

Hayward, Jack. 1976. Institutionalized Inequality Within an Indivisible Republic: Brittany and France. Presented at the International Political Science Association Congress, Edinburgh.

Heald, D. 1980. *Financing Devolution Within the United Kingdom: A Study of the Lessons from Failure.* Canberra: Centre for Research on Federal Financial Relations, Australian National University.

Heald, D. 1983. *Public Expenditure.* Oxford: Martin Robertson.

Hechter, Michael. 1975. *Internal Colonialism.* Berkeley: University of California Press.

Hechter, Michael, and Margaret Levi. 1979. The Comparative Analysis of Ethnoregional Movements. *Ethnic and Racial Studies* 2:260–274.

Heiberg, Marianne. 1975. Insiders/Outsiders: Basque Nationalism. *Archives de Europeane Sociologique* 16:169–193.

Heiberg, Marianne. 1979. "External and Internal Nationalism: The Case of the Spanish Basques." In Raymond L. Hall, ed., *Ethnic Autonomy-Comparative Dynamics,* New York: Pergamon Press.

Heiberg, Marianne. 1982. "Urban Politics and Rural Culture: Basque Nationalism." In Stein Rokkan and Derek W. Urwin eds., *The Politics of Territorial Identity: Studies in European Regionalism.* Beverly Hills: Sage Publications.

Heisler, Martin O. 1974. "Institutionalizing Societal Cleavages in a Cooptive Polity: The growing Importance of the Output Side in Belgium" In Martin O. Heisler, ed., *Politics in Europe: Structures and Process in Some Post-Industrial Democracies.* New York: David McKay Company, Inc.

Hinge, Patrick. 1983. Régions: Les conventions de dévelopment culturel. *Regards sur l'Actualité* 89:31–32.

Hollyman, John L. 1976. "Basque Revolutionary Separatism: ETA." In P. Preston, ed., *Spain in Crisis.* London: Harvester Press.

Horowitz, Donald. 1981. Patterns of Ethnic Separatism, *Comparative Studies in Society and History* 23:165–195.

Hudon, Raymond. 1977. The 1976 Quebec Election. *Queens Quarterly* 84:18–30.

Les immigrés: Enjeu electoral. November 24–25, 1985. *Le Monde Aujourd'hui.*

Inglehart, Ronald and Jacque-René Rabier. 1985. If You're Unhappy, This Must Be Belgium: Well-Being Around the World. *Public Opinion* :10–15.

Jacob, James. 1980. Ethnic Mobilization and the Pursuit of Post-Industrial Values. *The Tocqueville Review* 2:52–85.

Jacob, James E., and David C. Gordon. 1985. "Language Policy in France." In W.R. Beer and J.E. Jacob, eds., *Language Policy and National Unity.* Totowa, N.J.: Rowman & Allanheld.

Jones, Barry, and Rick Wilford. 1982. Further Considerations on the Referendum: The Evidence of the Welsh Vote on Devolution. *Political Studies* 30:16–27.

Jones, J.B., and D. Balsom. 1984. "The Faces of Wales." In I. McAllister and R. Rose, eds., *The Nationwide Competition for Votes.* London: Frances Pinter.

Jones, J.B., and M. Keating. 1982. The Resolution of Internal Conflicts and External Pressures: The Labour Party's Devolution Policy. *Government and Opposition* 17:279–292.

Jones, J.B. and M. Keating. 1985. *Labour and the British State.* Oxford: Oxford University Press.

Jones, Norman L. 1976. "The Catalan Question Since the Civil War." In P. Preston, ed., *Spain in Crisis.* London: Harvester Press.

Joy, Richard J. 1972. *Languages in Conflict.* Toronto: McClelland & Stewart.

Kalback, Warren E., and Wayne W. McVey. 1971. *The Demographic Bases of Canadian Society.* Toronto: McGraw-Hill.

Kauppi, Mark V. 1979. The 1979 Scottish Referendum Results: Explanations, Rationalizations, and Protestations. Presented at the Rocky Mountain Conference on British Studies, Colorado Springs.

Kauppi, Mark V. 1982. The Decline of the Scottish National Party, 1977–81: Political and Organizational Factors." *Ethnic and Racial Studies* 5:326–348.

Keating, Michael. 1975. The Role of the Scottish MP. Ph.D. thesis. Council for National Academic Awards.

Keating, Michael. 1978. Parliamentary Behaviour as a Test of Scottish Integration in the United Kingdom. *Legislative Studies Quarterly* 111:409–430.

Keating, Michael. April 6, 1985. Bureaucracy Devolved. *Times Higher Education Supplement.*

Keating, Michael. 1988a. Regionalism, Peripheral Nationalism and the State: The United Kingdom, France, Italy and Spain. Presented at the annual meeting of the Southwestern Political Science Association, Houston.

Keating, Michael. 1988b. *State and Regional Nationalism: Territorial Politics and the European State.* Hemel, Hempstead: Harvester.

Keating, Michael, and David Bleiman. 1979. *Labour and Scottish Nationalism.* London: Macmillan.

Keating, Michael, and P. Lindley. 1981. Devolution: The Scotland and Wales Bills. *Public Administration Bulletin* 37–54.

Keating, Michael, and A. Midwinter. 1983. *The Government of Scotland.* Edinburgh: Mainstream.

Kellas, James. 1975. *The Scottish Political System.* Cambridge: Cambridge University Press.

Kellas, James. 1981. "On to an Assembly?" In John Bochel, David Denver, and Allan Macartney, eds., *The Referendum Experience*. Aberdeen: Aberdeen University Press.

King, Anthony. 1977. *Britain Says Yes: The 1975 Referendum on the Common Market*. Washington, D.C.: American Enterprise Institute for Public Policy Research.

Kofman, Eleonore. 1982. Differential Modernisation, Social Conflicts and Ethno-Regionalism in Corsica. *Ethnic and Racial Studies* 5:299–312.

Kolinsky, Martin, ed. 1978. *Divided Loyalties*. Manchester: Manchester University Press.

Krejci, Jaroslav, and Vitezslav Velimsky, 1981. *Ethnic and Political Nations in Europe*. New York: St. Martin's Press.

Kwavnick, David. ed. 1973. *The Tremblay Report*. [Abridgement of the] Report of the [Quebec] Royal Commission of Inquiry on Constitutional Problems. Toronto: McClelland & Stewart.

Lafont, Robert. 1967. *La révolution régionaliste*. Paris: Gallimard.

Lafont, Robert. 1971. *Décoloniser la France*. Paris: Gallimard.

Lafont, Robert. August–September 1973. Sur le problème national en France. *Temps Modernes*.

Lafont, Robert. 1985. *Le dénouement français*. Paris: Editions Suger.

Lancaster, Thomas, and Gary Prevost, eds. 1984. *Politics and Change in Spain*. New York: Praeger.

Lederman, William R. 1975. Unity and Diversity in Canadian Federalism: Ideals and Methods of Moderation. *Canadian Bar Review* 53:597–620.

Léger, Jean-Marc. 1960. "Aspects of French-Canadian Nationalism of Growth." In Douglas Grant, ed., *Quebec Today*. Toronto: University of Toronto Press.

Leslie, Peter. 1987a. *Canada: The State of the Federation 1986*. Kingston, Ontario: Institute of Intergovernmental Relations.

Leslie, Peter. 1987b. *Rebuilding the Relationship: Quebec and Its Confederation Partners, A Conference Report*. Kingston, Ont.: Institute of Intergovernmental Relations.

Leslie, Peter, and Richard Simeon. 1977. "The Battle of the Balance Sheets." In Richard Simeon, ed., *Must Canada Fail?* Montreal: McGill-Queen's Press.

Levi, Margaret, and Michael Hechter. 1985. "A Rational Choice Approach to the Rise and Decline of Ethnoregional Political Parties." In Edward A. Tiryakian and Ronald Rogowski, eds., *New Nationalisms of the Developed West*. Boston: Allen & Unwin.

Levy, Roger. 1982. The Non-Mobilization of a Thesis: A Reply to Mughan and McAllister. *Ethnic and Racial Studies* 5:366–377.

Lijphart, Arend. 1969. Consociational Democracy. *World Politics* 21:207–225.

Lijphart, Arend. 1977a. *Democracy in Plural Societies: A Comparative Exploration*. New Haven and London: Yale University Press.

Lijphart, Arend. 1977b. "Political Theories and the Explanation of Ethnic Conflict in the Western World: Falsified Predictions and Plausible Postdictions." In Milton J. Esman, ed., *Ethnic Conflict in the Western World*. Ithaca: Cornell University Press.

Linz, Juan. 1966. Within-Nation Differences and Comparisons: The Eight

Spains. In Richard L. Merritt and Stein Rokkan, eds., *Comparing Nations: The Uses of Quantitative Data in Cross-National Research*. New Haven: Yale University Press.

Linz, Juan. 1967. "The Party System of Spain: Past and Future." In Seymour M. Lipset and Stein Rokkan, eds., *Party Systems and Voter Alignments: Cross-National Perspectives*. New York: The Free Press.

Loh, Wallace D. 1975. Nationalist Attitudes in Quebec and Belgium. *Journal of Conflict Resolution* 19:217–249.

Lopez, Cesar Diaz. 1982. "The Politicization of Galician Cleavages." In Stein Rokkan and Derek W. Urwin eds., *The Politics of Territorial Identity*. London: Sage Publications.

Lopez, Cesar Diaz. 1985. "Centre-Periphery Structures in Spain: From Historical Conflict to Territorial-Consociational Accommodation?" In Yves Meny and Vincent Wright, eds., *Centre-Periphery Relations in Western Europe*. London: George Allen & Unwin.

Lorwin, Val. 1966. "Belgium: Religion, Class and Language in National Politics." In Robert Dahl, ed., *Political Opposition in Western Democracies*. New Haven: Yale University Press.

Lubin, Martin. 1979. Pro-Canada Elements in the Forthcoming Quebec Referendum. Presented at the Canadian Studies Program of the annual meeting of the Western Social Science Association, Lake Tahoe, Nevada.

Lubin, Martin. 1980. System Maintenance in Quebec: The Parti Québécois. Presented at the annual meeting of the Northeastern Political Science Association, New Haven, Connecticut.

Lustick, Ian. 1979. Stability in Deeply Divided Societies: Consociationalism Versus Control. *World Politics* 31:325–344.

McKay, James. 1982. An Exploratory Synthesis of Primoridal and Mobilizationist Approaches to Ethnic Phenomena. *Ethnic and Racial Studies* 5:395–420.

MacMullen, Andres. 1979. The Belgian Election of December 1978: The Limits of Language-Community Politics? *Parliamentary Affairs* 32:331–338.

McRae, Kenneth, ed. 1974. *Consociational Democracy: Political Accommodation in Segmented Societies*. Toronto: McClelland & Stewart.

McRoberts, Kenneth. 1979. Internal Colonialism: The case of Quebec. *Ethnic and Racial Studies* 2:293–318.

McRoberts, Kenneth. 1984. The Sources of Neo-Nationalism in Quebec. *Ethnic and Racial Studies* 7:55–85.

McRoberts, Kenneth, and Dale Postgate. 1980. *Quebec: Social Change and Political Crisis*. Revised Edition. Toronto: McClelland & Stewart.

McWhinney, Edward. 1982. *Canada and the Constitution 1979–1982*. Toronto: University of Toronto Press.

Madgwick, Peter, and Richard Rose, eds. 1982. *The Territorial Dimension in United Kingdom Politics*. London: Macmillan.

Malone, Marc. 1986. *Une place pour le Québec au Canada*. Montreal: Institute for Research in Public Policy.

Marangé, James, and André Lebon. 1982. *L'insertion des jeunes d'origine étrangère dans la société française*. Paris: Documentation Française.

Markham, James. March 21, 1980. Madrid's Leader's Party Makes a Poor Showing in Catalonia Election. *New York Times*.

Mayer, Kurt B. 1969. The Jura Problem: Ethnic Conflict in Switzerland. *Social Research* 35:707–741.

Mayol, Pierre. January–February 1983. Du côté de chez eux. *Projet* 171–172:61n.

M. Chevènement fair les comptes. May 3, 1985. *La Bretagne à Paris*.

Meny, Yves, and Vincent Wright, eds. 1985. *Centre-Periphery Relations in Western Europe*. London: George Allen & Unwin.

Mesnard, André-Hubert. 1986. Les problèmes administratifs de la mise en oeuvre d'une politique des cultures. Presented at the colloquium of the Association Française de Science Politique, Aix-en-Provence.

Michelet, Jules. 1949. *Tableau de la France*. Paris: Société des Belles Lettres.

de Miguel, Amando. 1977. *Recursos humanos, clases y regiones en España*. Madrid: EDICUSA.

Miller, W.L. 1980. What Was the Profit in Following the Crowd?: The Effectiveness of Party Strategies on Immigration and Devolution. *British Journal of Political Science* 10:15–38.

Miller, W.L., with B. Sarlvik, I. Crewe, and James Alt. 1977. The Connection Between SNP Voting and the Demand for Scottish Self-Government. *European Journal of Political Research* 5:83–102.

Mitterrand, François. 1981. *L'homme, les idées, le programme*. Paris: Flammarion.

Morgan, Kenneth O. 1970. *Wales in British Politics*. Cardiff: University of Wales Press.

Morin, Claude. 1976. *Quebec Versus Ottawa: The Struggle for Self-Government 1960–72*. Toronto: University of Toronto Press.

Moulin, Jean-Pierre. 1985. *Enquête sur la France multiraciale*. Paris: Calmann-Lévy.

Mughan, Anthony. 1979. Modernization and Ethnic Conflict in Belgium. *Political Studies* 27:21–37.

Mughan, Anthony. 1983. Accommodation or Defusion in the Management of Linguistic conflict in Belgium. *Political Studies* 31:434–451.

Mughan, Anthony. 1985. "Belgium: All Periphery and No Centre?" In Yves Meny and Vincent Wright, eds., *Centre-Periphery Relations in Western Europe*. London: George Allen & Unwin.

Mughan, Anthony, and Ian McAllister. 1981. The Mobilization of the Ethnic Vote: A Thesis with Some Scottish and Welsh Evidence. *Ethnic and Racial Studies* 4:189–204.

Murray, V. 1976. *Le Parti Québécois: De la fondation à la prise de pouvoir*. Montreal: Hurtubise, HMH.

Nairn, Tom. 1977. *The Break-Up of Britain*. London: NLB.

Nevitte, Neil, and Charles H. Kennedy. eds. 1986. *Ethnic Preference and Public Policy in Developing States*. Boulder, Colo.: Lynne Rienner Publishers.

Nielsen, François. 1980. The Flemish Movement in Belgium After World War II: A Dynamic Analysis. *American Sociological Review* 55:76–94.

Neuchterlein, D.E. 1981. The Demise of Canada's Confederation. *Political Science Quarterly* 96:225–240.

New Chapter for Trudeau. April 5, 1980. *The Economist.*

Nordlinger, Eric. 1972. *Conflict Regulation in Divided Societies.* Occasional Paper in International Affairs, No. 29. Cambridge: Center for International Affairs, Harvard University.

Osborn, Alan. 1984. Linguistic Divide Key to Belgian Nation. *Europe*, 34–35.

Osmond, John. 1977. *Creative Conflict: The Politics of Welsh Devolution.* London: Gomer Press and Routledge & Kegan Paul.

Parti socialiste. 1981. *La France au pluriel.* Paris: Editions Entente, Collection "Minorités."

Pâquet, L.-A. 1969. "A Sermon on the Vocation of the French Race in America." [1902]. In Ramsey Cook, ed., *French Canadian Nationalism: An Anthology.* Toronto: Macmillan.

Pastor, Robert. 1980. *Autonomía año cero.* Bilbao: Editorial Iparraguirre.

Payne, Stanley, 1975. *Basque Nationalism.* Reno: University of Nevada Press.

Peroncel-Hugoz, J.P. August 9, 1985. La politique des langues minoritaires. *Le Monde.*

Phillips, Alan B. 1975. *The Welsh Question.* Cardiff: University of Wales Press.

Pinchemel, Philippe. 1973. *France: A Geographic Survey.* New York: Praeger.

Pi-Sunyer, Oriol. 1971. "The Maintenance of Ethnic Identity in Catalonia." In Oriol Pi-Sunyer, ed., *The Limits of Integration: Ethnicity and Nationalism in Modern Europe.* Amherst: University of Massachusetts.

Pi-Sunyer, Oriol, ed. 1971. *The Limits of Integration: Ethnicity and Nationalism in Modern Europe.* Amherst: University of Massachusetts.

Pi-Sunyer, Oriol. 1974. Elite and Noncorporate Groups in the European Mediterranean: A Reconsideration of the Catalan Case. *Comparative Studies in Society and History* 16:117–131.

La politique culturelle. August 6, 1985. *Le Monde.*

Preston, P., ed. 1976. *Spain in Crisis.* London: Harvester Press.

Profound Change in Quebec. December 16, 1985. *Newsweek.*

Projet socialiste. 1980. Paris: Club Socialiste du Livre, 56:252–258.

Que deviendrait Bruxelles si l'on fusionnait les exécutifs communautaire et wallon. January 1, 1986. *Le Soir* (Brussels).

Quéré, Louis. 1981. Le "pays" breton comme territorie minoritarie. *Pluriel* 25:37–39.

Queyranne, Jean-Jack. 1982. *Les régions et la décentralisation: Rapport au ministre de la culture.* Paris: Documentation Française.

Rabushka, Alvin, and Kenneth A. Shepsle. 1972. *Politics in Plural Societies.* Columbus, Ohio: Charles E. Merrill.

Ragin, Charles E. 1979. Ethnic Political Mobilization: The Welsh Case. *American Sociological Review* 44:619–635.

Ranney, Austin, ed. 1981. *The Referendum Device.* Washington, D.C.: American Enterprise Institute for Public Policy Research.

Rawkins, Philip. 1978. Outsiders as Insiders: The Implications of Minority Nationalism in Scotland and Wales. *Comparative Politics* 10:519–534.

Rawkins, P.M. 1979. An Approach to the Political Sociology of the Welsh Nationalist Movement. *Political Studies* 27:440–457.

Raynauld, André. 1973. "The Quebec Economy: A General Assessment." In Dale C. Thomson, ed., *Quebec Society and Politics: Views from the Inside*. Toronto: McClelland & Stewart, 1973.

Rayside, David M. 1978. The Impact of the Linguistic Cleavage on the "Governing" Parties of Belgium and Canada. *Canadian Journal of Political Science* 11:61–97.

Report of the Commission of Inquiry on the Position of the French Language and on Language Rights in Quebec. 1972. Vol. 3. Quebec: Editeur officiel.

Rhodes, R.A.W. 1985. "Intergovernmental Relations in the United Kingdom." In Yves Meny and Vincent Wright, eds., *Centre-Periphery Relations in Western Europe*. London: George Allen & Unwin.

Richez, Jean-Claude. 1983. Référent national et mouvement gréviste. *Pluriel* 36:52–80.

Richmond, Anthony H., ed. 1981. *After the Referenda: The Future of Ethnic Nationalism in Britain and Canada*. York University, Ontario: Institute for Behavioral Research.

Riggs, Fred. W. 1986. What is Ethnic? What is National? Let's Turn the Tables. *Canadian Review of Studies in Nationalism* 13:111–123.

Rogowski, Ronald. 1985. "Causes and Varieties of Nationalism." In Edward A. Tiryakian and Ronald Rogowski, eds., *New Nationalisms of the Developed West*. Boston: Allen & Unwin.

Rokkan, Stein, and Derek W. Urwin, eds. 1982. *The Politics of Territorial Identity: Studies in European Regionalism*. London: Sage Publications.

Rose, Richard. 1970. *The United Kingdom as a Multinational State*, Survey Research Centre Occasional Paper, No. 6. Glasgow: University of Strathclyde.

Rose, Richard. 1982. "Scotland: British with a Difference." In I. McAllister and R. Rose, eds. *The Nationwide Competition for Votes*. London: Frances Pinter.

Ross, Jeffrey A., and Ann Baker Cottrell, with Robert St. Cyr and Philip Rawkins, eds. 1980 *The Mobilization of Collective Identity: Comparative Perspectives*. Lanham, Md: University Press of America.

Rothchild, Joseph. 1981. *Ethnopolitics*. New York: Columbia University Press.

Rousseau, Mark O., and Raphael Zariski. eds. 1987. *Regionalism and Regional Devolution in Comparative Perspective*. New York: Praeger.

Rudolph, Joseph R. 1977a. Ethnic Sub-States and the Emergent Politics of Tri-level Interaction in Western Europe. *Western Political Quarterly* 3:537–557.

Rudolph, Joseph R. 1977b. Ethnonational Parties and Political Change: The Belgian and British Experience. *Polity* 9:401–426.

Rudolph, Joseph R. 1981. Ethno-regionalism in Contemporary Western Europe: The Politics of Accommodation. *Canadian Review of Studies in Nationalism* 8:323–341.

Rudolph, Joseph R. 1982. "Belgium: Controlling Separatist Tendencies in a Multinational State." In Colin Williams, ed., *National Separatism*. Cardiff: University Press.

Rudolph, Joseph R., and Robert J. Thompson. 1985. Ethnoterritorial Movements and the Policy Process: Accommodating Nationalist Demands in the Developed World. *Comparative Politics* 17:219–311.

Safran, William. 1984. The French Left and Ethnic Pluralism. *Ethnic and Racial Studies* 7:447–461.

Safran, William. 1985. The Mitterrand Regime and Its Policies of Ethnocultural Accommodation. *Comparative Politics* 18:41–63.

Safran, William. 1986. Islamization in Western Europe: Political Consequences and Historical Parallels. *Annals of the American Academy of Political and Social Science* 485:98–112.

Savard, Jean-Guy, and Richard Vigneault, eds. 1975. *Les états multilingues: Problèms et solutions/Multilingual Political Systems: Problems and Solutions*. Quebec: Les Presses de l'Université Laval.

Savigear, P. 1975. Corsica 1975: Politics and Violence. *World Today* 31: 462–468.

Saywell, John. 1977. *The Rise of the Parti Québécois 1967–1976*. Toronto: University of Toronto Press.

Schwarz, John E. 1970. The Scottish National Party: Nonviolent Separatism and Theories of Violence. *World Politics* 22:496–517.

Shabad, G., and R. Gunther. 1973. Language, Nationalism and Political Conflict in Spain. Presented at the Conference of Europeanists, Washington D.C.

Sheppard, Robert, and Michael Valpy. 1982. *The National Deal: The Fight for a Canadian Constitution*. Toronto: Fleet Books.

Shiels, Frederick L. 1984. *Ethnic Separatism And World Politics*. Lanham, Md.: University Press of America.

Simeon, Richard, ed. 1977. *Must Canada Fail?* Montreal: McGill-Queens Press.

Smiley, Donald V. 1977. "French-English Relations in Canada and Consociational Democracy." In Milton J. Esman, ed., *Ethnic Conflict in the Western World*. Ithaca: Cornell University Press.

Smiley, Donald V. 1980. *Canada in Question: Federalism in the Eighties*. Toronto: McGraw-Hill Ryerson.

Smith, Anthony D. 1979. Towards a Theory of Ethnic Separatism. *Ethnic and Racial Studies* 2:21–37.

Smith, Anthony D. 1981. *The Ethnic Revival*. Cambridge: Cambridge University Press, 1981.

Smith, Gordon. 1975. The Referendum and Political Change. *Government and Opposition* 10:294–305.

Smith, Gordon. 1976. The Functional Properties of the Referendum. *European Journal of Political Research* 4:1–23.

Soldatos, Panyotis. 1979. *Souveraineté-association: L'urgence de Réfléchir*. Montreal: Editions France-Amérique.

Spanish Basques Vote to Restore Home Rule. October 28, 1979. *New York Times*.

Stasi, Bernard. 1979. *La vie associative et la démocratie nouvelle.* Paris: presses Universitaires de France.

Stasi, Bernard. 1984. *L'immigration: Une chance pour la France.* Paris: Robert Laffont.

Supplement au no. 82. June 1979. *Le Poing et la Rose.* 44.

Steiner, Jurg. 1980. From Regionalism to Statehood: The Formation of the Jura Canton. Presented at the Second Conference of Europeanists, Washington, D.C.

Steiner, Jurg, and Jeffrey Obler. 1977. "Does the Consociational Theory Really Hold for Switzerland?" In Milton J. Esman, ed., *Ethnic Conflict in the Western World.* Ithaca: Cornell University Press.

Studlar, Donley T. 1977a. Ethnicity and the Policymaking Process in Western Democratic Countries. Presented at the annual meeting of the International Studies Association, St. Louis.

Studlar, Donley T. 1977b. Ethnicity and the Polity Process in Western Europe. Presented at the annual meeting of the Southern Political Science Association, New Orleans.

Studlar, Donley T., and Ian McAllister. 1988. Nationalism in Scotland and Wales: A post-industrial phenomenon? *Ethnic and Racial Studies* 11:48–62.

Switzerland. July 1984. *Keesing's Contemporary Archives* 30:33001.

Switzerland. February 1985. *Keesing's Contemporary Archives* 31:33423.

Taylor, Philip B., Jr. 1980. The Costs of Autonomy: Catalan Emergence from a Centralized State. Presented at the Segon Cololoqui d'Estudis Catalans a Nord-America, New Haven, Connecticut.

Taylor, Philip B. 1981. Autonomy and Public Policy in Catalunya. Is Spanish Centralism Really Weakening? Presented at the annual meeting of the Southwestern Political Science Association, Dallas.

Thomas, Keith. 1978. "The United Kingdom." In Raymond Grew, ed., *Crises of Political Development in Europe and the United States.* Princeton: Princeton University Press.

Thompson, Dennis L, and Dov Ronen, eds. 1986. *Ethnicity, Politics, and Development.* Boulder, Colo.: Lynne Rienner Publishers.

Thompson, Robert J. 1978. The Scottish National Party: A Study of Its Bases of Support, 1949–1978. *Historicus* 1:44–81.

Thompson, Robert J., and Joseph R. Rudolph. 1986. "Ethnic Politics and Public Policy in Western Societies: A Framework for Comparative Analysis." In Dennis L Thompson and Dov Ronen, eds., *Ethnicity, Politics, and Development.* Boulder, Colo.: Lynne Rienner Publishers.

Tierno Galván, Enrique, and Antoni Rovira. 1985. *La España autonómica.* Barcelona: Bruguera.

Tiryakian, Edward A., and Ronald Rogowski, eds. 1985. *New Nationalisms of the Developed West.* Boston: Allen & Unwin.

Titus, Dina. 1980. Recent Decentralization in Spain: A Look at the Andalucian Autonomy Movement. Presented at the annual meeting of the Southwestern Political Science Association, Dallas.

Tozzi, Michel. 1984. *Apprendre sa langue.* Paris: Syros.

Trudeau, Pierre Elliott. 1968a. *Federalism and the French Canadians.* Toronto: Macmillan
Trudeau, Pierre Elliott. 1968b. "New Treason of the Intellectuals." In Pierre Elliott Trudeau, *Federalism and the French Canadians.* Toronto: Macmillan.
Tschaeni, Hanspeter. 1982. Constitutional Change in Swiss Cantons: An Assessment of a Recent Phenomenon. *Publius* 12:113–130.
Urwin, Derek W. 1985. "The Price of a Kingdom, Identity and the Centre-Periphery Dimension in Western Europe." In Yves Meny and Vincent Wright, eds., *Centre-Periphery Relations in Western Europe.* London: George Allen & Unwin.
Vote As You Care. October 27, 1979. *The Economist.*
Webb, Keith. 1977. *The Growth of Nationalism in Scotland.* Glasgow: The Moledinar Press.
Weiner, Myron. 1983. The Political Consequences of Preferential Politics: A Comparative Perspective. *Comparative Politics* 16:35–52.
Weiner, Myron, and Samuel P. Huntington. eds. 1987. *Understanding Political Development.* Boston: Little, Brown.
Weinstein, Brian. 1979. Language Strategists: Redefining Political Frontiers on the Basis of Linguistic Choices. *World Politics* 31:345–364.
Williams, Colin. 1976. Cultural Nationalism in Wales. *Canadian Review of Studies in Nationalism* 4:15–37.
Williams, Colin. 1981 *National Separatism.* Cardiff: University Press.
Williams, Colin. 1982. Social Mobilization and Nationalism in Multicultural Societies. *Ethnic and Racial Studies* 5:349–365.
Wilson, Frank. 1967. French-Canadian Separatism. *The Western Political Quarterly* 20:116–131.
Wolf, Ken. 1986. Ethnic Nationalism: An Analysis and a Defense. *Canadian Review of Studies in Nationalism* 13:99–110.
Young, Crawford. 1976. *The Politics of Cultural Pluralism.* Madison: The University of Wisconsin Press.
Zariski, Raphael. Forthcoming 1989. Ethnic Extremism Among Ethnoterritorial Minorities in Western Europe: Dimensions, Causes, and Institutional Responses. *Comparative Politics* 21.
Zolberg, Aristides. 1974. The Making of Flemings and Walloons: Belgium, 1830–1914. *Journal of Interdisciplinary History* 5:179–235.
Zolberg, Aristides R. 1975. "Transformation of Linguistic Ideologies: The Belgian Case." In Jean-Guy and Richard Vigneault, eds., *Multilingual Political Systems: Problems and Solutions.* Quebec: Les Presses de l'Universite Laval.
Zolberg, Aristides. 1976. Culture, Territory, Class: Ethnicity Demystified. Presented at the International Political Science Association Congress, Edinburgh.
Zolberg, Aristides. 1977. "Splitting the Difference: Federalization Without Federalism in Belgium." In Milton J. Esman, ed., *Ethnic Conflict in the Western World.* Ithaca: Cornell University Press.

INDEX